A History of Architectural Mo(in Britain

Architectural modelmakers have long carried out their work hidden behind the scenes of architectural design, and in presenting a history of architectural modelmaking in Britain for the first time, this book casts a new light on their remarkable skills and achievements.

By telling the story of the modelmakers who make architectural models rather than architects who commission and use them, this book seeks to celebrate their often-overlooked contribution to the success and endurance of the architectural model in Britain over the past one hundred and forty years. Drawing from extensive archival research and interviews with practicing and retired modelmakers, this book traces the complete history of architectural modelmaking in Britain from its initial emergence as a specialist occupation at the end of the nineteenth century through to the present day. It reveals the legacy of John Thorp, the first professional architectural modelmaker in Britain, who opened his business in London in 1883, and charts the lives and careers of the innovative and creative modelmakers who followed him. It examines the continually evolving materials, tools, and processes of architectural modelmaking and outlines the profound ideological, economic, and technological influences that have shaped the profession's development.

Illustrated with over one hundred photographs of architectural models from previously undocumented archives, this book will be of great interest to architectural modelmakers, academics, and historians, as well as anyone with an interest in architectural history and modelmaking.

David Lund is Senior Lecturer on the BA (Hons) Modelmaking and BA (Hons) Design courses at Arts University Bournemouth, UK.

A History of Architectural Modelmaking in Britain

The Unseen Masters of Scale and Vision

David Lund

 Routledge
Taylor & Francis Group

LONDON AND NEW YORK

Designed cover image: Courtesy Thorp Archive, AUB.

First published 2023
by Routledge
4 Park Square, Milton Park, Abingdon, Oxon OX14 4RN

and by Routledge
605 Third Avenue, New York, NY 10158

Routledge is an imprint of the Taylor & Francis Group, an informa business

British Library Cataloguing-in-Publication Data
A catalogue record for this book is available from the British Library

Library of Congress Cataloging-in-Publication Data
Names: Lund, David, 1980– author.
Title: A history of architectural modelmaking in Britain: the unseen masters of scale and vision / David Lund.
Description: New York: Routledge, 2022. | Includes bibliographical references and index.
Identifiers: LCCN 2022029154 | ISBN 9781032286822 (hardback) | ISBN 9781032286785 (paperback) | ISBN 9781003298007 (ebook)
Subjects: LCSH: Architectural models—Great Britain.
Classification: LCC NA2790 .L86 2022 | DDC 720.220941—dc23/eng/20220719
LC record available at https://lccn.loc.gov/2022029154

ISBN: 978-1-032-28682-2 (hbk)
ISBN: 978-1-032-28678-5 (pbk)
ISBN: 978-1-003-29800-7 (ebk)

DOI: 10.4324/9781003298007

Typeset in Sabon
by Apex CoVantage, LLC

Contents

Acknowledgments

The idea for writing this book developed as I uncovered the full extent of the private archive of Thorp Modelmakers during the writing of my doctoral thesis in 2017. In 2019 I was able to secure the archive's acquisition for public preservation, and I am especially grateful to both Alec Saunders at Thorp and Tim O'Reilly Bennett, Head of Library and Special Collections at Arts University Bournemouth, for making this happen. Much of the research that this book draws from was also undertaken as part of my PhD studies, and so my sincere appreciation is offered to Susan Lambert, Christian McLening, Willem de Bruijn, Michael Biggs, Penny Sparke, and Phil Jones for their guidance and feedback during that time.

Thanks must be extended to everyone who contributed to my research, either through taking part in interviews or providing documents or images: Artemis Antonopoulou, Richard Armiger, Lee Atkins, Clare Baxter, John Blythe, Shajay Bhooshan, Adam Burdett, Robert Danton-Rees, Matthew Driscoll, Alan East, Mike Fairbrass, Tim Feron, Stephen Fooks, Bruno Gordon, Simon Hamnell, Joseph Henry, Roger Hillier, George Rome Innes, Ken Houghton, Kamran Kiani, Helmet Kinzler, Robert Kirkman, John Leatherdale, George Lee, David MacKay, Patrick McKeogh, Daniel McWilliam, Neil Merryweather, Paul Miles, Tina Miller, Dan Oppenheimer, Emily Oppenheimer, Andrew Putler, Duncan Robertson, Alec Saunders, Christian Spencer-Davies, Will Strange, Neil Vandersteen, and Paul Wood. At the Medmenham Association, thanks are due to Jean Churchwood, Tim Fryer, Michael Mockford, Andrew Scott, and Paul Stewart. Thanks also go to Gemma Blake at Lucite International and Katy Whitaker at Historic England.

At Arts University Bournemouth, I would also like to thank the following: Phil Anderson, Gideon Bohanan, Claire Holman, Jonathan Hoyle, Paul Johnson, Valerie Lodge, Will Strange, and Graham Wood. The purchase of image licences from Alamy, the Imperial War Museum Archives, Leodis, the National Trust, Northamptonshire County Archives, the RIBA, the John Soane Museum, and the V&A was kindly supported by the AUB Small Grants Scheme. At Routledge, thanks must be extended to Fran Ford and the editorial and production teams, and finally, enormous thanks are due to my family and friends, and especially to Edward, for reasons too numerous to put down in print.

Figures

Introduction

On March 25, 1930, a highly anticipated architectural model was unveiled at County Hall in London. Throughout much of the following week the model was showcased in large photographic features by all the daily newspapers as the eighty-square-foot model of the proposed Charing Cross road bridge, made by the architectural modelmaker John Thorp, had become something of a national celebrity during the preceding months by virtue of its absence. Commissioned by the London County Council (LCC) to better illustrate its plan to replace the existing railway bridge with a new road crossing that would involve the demolition of many buildings on both sides of the Thames, it had been hoped that the model would help overcome the seemingly insurmountable opposition to the fifteen-million-pound project. Upon submitting an ambitious bill to Parliament in the Autumn of 1929, the proposal faced an immediate wave of criticism. In his inaugural address that November, Sir Bannister Fletcher, the incoming president of the Royal Institution of British Architects, firmly condemned the plans, but in noting the difficulties the public faced in understanding architectural drawings, remarked that he was 'strongly of the opinion that, before anything further is done, a scale model of the whole scheme, showing the approaches on both sides of the river, should be made, and that a full discussion take place.'[1]

From this point on, the public debate regarding the bridge proposal gripped the nation, and a model was eagerly expected; *The Times* newspaper published articles and letters almost daily for the next three months commenting on the lively Parliamentary discussions taking place as the bill made its way through the Commons. Seemingly startled by the barrage of criticism from the RIBA, the Royal Academy, the Architectural Association, the Thames Bridges Conference, and the Town Planning Institute, it was announced that the Ministry of Transport and the LCC had already jointly commissioned a model of the scheme, denying that the move was in response to Fletcher's suggestion. For the next three months, one question was constantly asked in both Parliament and the press: when would the model be ready? In January the Government was pressed in the House of Commons as to when the model would be available for inspection, with Sir Percy Simmons, Chair of the LCC's Improvements Committee, responding that he could not give an exact date, but 'it was hoped, however, that the model would be completed within the next few weeks.'[2] Two weeks later, *The Times* argued that 'Members of Parliament would be in a better position to judge the scheme of the Bill for themselves if the large-scale model which is being prepared had been ready for their inspection.'[3] During the

DOI: 10.4324/9781003298007-1

second reading of the bill, the absence of the model was raised again, with the MP Sir William Davidson complaining that the reading of the bill should have been postponed until the model was ready.[4] Herbert Morrison, Minister of Transport, replied with exasperation that the 'model is not yet ready. The model is taking its normal course.'[5] While frustration over the much-anticipated model continued to grow, several impatient newspapers even paid a visit to see the model under construction, printing photographs of John Thorp and his team of modelmakers working on the half-completed baseboard (Figure 0.1). The model was still unfinished when Parliament was called to vote on the bill, with the proposal being reluctantly carried and referred to a Commons Select Committee for further debate, where on March 25, they were finally presented with the completed model for inspection (Figure 0.2).

Thorp's model was an astonishing achievement, one of the most complicated, detailed, and accurate architectural models ever made in Britain at the time. With the new bridge at the centre, the model included huge swathes of London on both sides of the river, with hundreds of individual buildings meticulously recreated in miniature (Figure 0.3). For three months, John Thorp, his son Leslie, and eighteen

Figure 0.1 John Thorp overseeing the making of the 1930 Charing Cross model.

Source: Image courtesy Thorp Archive, AUB.

Figure 0.2 Model of the Charing Cross bridge proposal, made by John Thorp, 1930.

Source: Image courtesy Thorp Archive, AUB.

Figure 0.3 Model of the Charing Cross bridge proposal, made by John Thorp, 1930.

Source: Image courtesy Thorp Archive, AUB.

other modelmakers worked tirelessly in his workshop at 98 Gray's Inn Road in London, the team putting in an average of over two hundred hours overtime each week just to get it finished. To make the model as accurate as possible, Thorp not only commissioned aerial photography of the area taken from an Aerofilms biplane but carried out a detailed street level and rooftop survey of the whole of Charing Cross and Waterloo, photographing the profiles and roof lines of hundreds of individual buildings to supplement the two-dimensional information they could extract from Ordnance Survey maps and the LCC's plans. Building shapes were then cut from timber blocks and dressed with card façades that were carefully inked by hand to represent all the surface textures and windows. Columns, balustrades, finials, turrets, and chimneys were added, with miniature boats, vehicles, and trees completing the illusion of being suspended over an unbuilt vision of the city's future (Figure 0.4).

All this work, the exhaustive research and planning, the testing and prototyping, and the painstaking construction, prepared for a Select Committee meeting that lasted just under an hour, came too late to change public opinion, however, and despite having been approved by Parliament, the Select Committee held grave reservations and delayed its final decision, the whole proposal eventually being quietly dropped the following year. After thousands of hours of work put into making the model, in less than sixty minutes its task was complete, and public interest (and Thorp's modelmakers) moved on.

Figure 0.4 Model of the Charing Cross bridge proposal, made by John Thorp, 1930.

Source: Image courtesy Thorp Archive, AUB.

The Unseen Modelmaker

The publicity given to the making of the Charing Cross model in 1930 was highly unusual even by today's standards, and the volume of information relating to its construction that survives is equally notable considering how little of the history of architectural modelmaking has been properly recorded. Modelmakers have long carried out their work hidden behind the scenes of architectural design, taking even the sketchiest ideas and turning them into physical models that communicate an architect's intentions to a client, a competition panel, or the public, and it is rare that the names of the individuals who make architectural models ever accompany them. That photographs of John Thorp in the process of making the Charing Cross model were so widely circulated demonstrates the exceptional clamour for its completion; it is almost unheard of even today for images of modelmakers and their uncompleted work to be shared with the public in that manner. More commonly the work of the modelmaker tends to remain 'hidden behind the reputations of the architectural practices who commission them,'[6] with models too often credited as somehow being the work of the architects whose buildings they represent; even modelmakers' nameplates have been known to be prised off models by architects moments before they go on display.[7] As early as 1452 the Renaissance architect and philosopher Leon Batista Alberti had warned that architectural models should 'demonstrate the ingenuity of him who conceived the idea, and not the skill of the one who fabricated the model,'[8] and throughout their history the makers of architectural models and their practices have been shrouded in requisite anonymity.

Telling the story of these modelmakers is not then an easy task. As architectural historian Karen Moon has noted, 'despite the limelight bestowed on their creations, these makers remain shadowy figures,'[9] and of the countless modelmakers featured in this book, too many exist merely as names and an occasional photograph of their work, the full details of their lives and careers long forgotten. It is only during the past twenty years that the historiography of the architectural model has begun to gather pace, and even today the total volume of literature remains comparatively small. With historians of architecture having understandably gravitated towards the use of models within architectural practice rather than their making, it is also only fleetingly that the role of the modelmaker has been acknowledged.[10] Consequently, as Oliver Elser and Peter Schmal have admitted, 'we know too little about modelmakers themselves,'[11] while the architectural writer Thomas Fisher has observed that modelmakers 'have not always been treated with the greatest respect or given the proper credit,' and that 'we need to see them and their work anew.'[12]

While architectural models in one form or another have been made and used by different cultures for millennia, architectural modelmaking as a professional practice, as a dedicated occupation with its own identity, is a much more recent development. Today, architectural modelmakers can be found across Europe, North America, China, India, Australia, and the Middle East; however, it was in Britain that the modern template for the profession was first established at the end of the nineteenth century. In aiming to cast a new light on the modelmaker's achievements, this book is therefore focused on where the modern profession began and presents a history of architectural modelmaking in Britain.

Today, in twenty-first century Britain, architectural modelmaking is a thriving profession with over forty commercial architectural modelmaking companies and around thirty of the largest architectural practices employing dedicated professional modelmakers, but it has not always been so. John Thorp, the maker of the Charing Cross model, was the first professional architectural modelmaker in the modern sense (Figure 0.5). Before Thorp established his company in London in 1883, architectural models had largely been made by craftsmen from within the building trades as asides to their principal full-scale architectural work. Very few individuals before Thorp were able to dedicate themselves to the making of architectural models full time, and yet by the time of the Charing Cross model Thorp was employing a team of twenty modelmakers, with at least three other major competitors also having set up business in Britain.

In pulling back the curtain to reveal the history of architectural modelmaking in Britain for the first time, this book charts how the making of architectural models emerged as a specialist occupation during the late-nineteenth century and how John Thorp's remarkable career established the template for everything that followed. It examines the profession's rapid expansion during the inter-war years and outlines the unexpected circumstances of a top-secret military application of architectural modelmaking during the Second World War and its consequences for the post-war modelmaking boom that followed. It charts the radical shifts in architectural modelmaking that took place in Britain during the 1950s as a result of the adoption of

Figure 0.5 John Thorp, circa 1925.

Source: Image courtesy Thorp Archive, AUB.

plastics to help better represent modernist architecture, addresses how the turbulent architectural changes of the 1960s and 1970s severely impacted the professional modelmaker's standing, and reveals the backlash against realism in architectural models that followed. It examines the dramatic expansion of the creative potential of architectural modelmaking that took place in the 1980s and outlines the consequences of the digital revolution that has affected the making of architectural models from the 1990s through to the present day.

This book, and the history that it tells, is the result of six years spent examining thousands of documents and photographs held in public and private collections, tracking down historic journals and publications, interviewing over forty practicing and retired architectural modelmakers, and – perhaps most significantly – combing through the contents of the Thorp Archive, which (thanks to the foresight of John Thorp, his son Leslie, and the owners and directors of Thorp's company that followed them) has preserved an incredibly rich record of their work over the course of more than a century. Thorp's company still trades today under the ownership of Atom, and its archive, containing fifteen thousand photographs of architectural models made by the firm alongside countless documents charting the company's long and influential history, is the largest known collection relating to architectural modelmaking anywhere in the world.

By telling the story of John Thorp, the profession he built, the modelmakers who followed him, and the changing materials, tools, and processes of architectural modelmaking in Britain during the twentieth and twenty-first centuries, this book seeks to celebrate the skills and talents of the architectural modelmaker, and in outlining John Thorp's significance in establishing the template that all other architectural modelmakers followed, recognises Thorp as the single most influential figure in the history of the profession. As each chapter makes clear, however, this book is not merely a history of a single modelmaker or a single company. The history of architectural modelmaking in Britain is a complex weave of the people, processes, materials, and ideas that have combined to shape it into what it is today, and this book aims to reveal the myriad influences that have been central to its development. With so little of modelmaking's history having been explored, however, it is inevitable that there will be many other stories of individuals, companies, and events that remain to be told, although this book endeavours to be as comprehensive as it can.

The historical narrative that this study puts forward also makes a deliberate effort to counter the anonymity of the modelmaker and the hidden nature of their work that has long shrouded their achievements. In the broadest of terms, modelmaking – whether for architecture, design, heritage, education, or media – can be defined as the communication of messages through the creation of material culture. An earlier age would have described the modelmaker's practice as a craft, and the greatest modelmakers as master craftsmen, but these are labels that today fail to encompass the full extent of the skills they employ. Even the term *modelmaker* gives little indication of the complexity of their role, nor the 'breadth and expertise of knowledge that is possessed by a practitioner.'[13] It is therefore too simplistic to describe modelmaking as a craft, but the most successful architectural modelmakers are certainly masters of their discipline. Their mastery of the practical skills and intellectual processes of taking an often-incomplete vision of the future and turning it into a scaled tangible representation does not come easy, nor quickly, and requires the same dedication and focus as would have elevated the greatest medieval craftsmen to the top of their trades. Throughout this book I have therefore attempted to highlight the evolution of the skills of the professional modelmaker and describe how they adapted to the ever-changing demands placed upon them as both modelmaking and architecture have developed over the past one hundred and forty years.

In learning the skills and abilities of architectural modelmaking, as with any creative pursuit, an individual modelmaker learns the basics of their tools and materials and the technicalities of how to use them first, before then turning their imagination to what they could do with those skills. In the chronology of architectural modelmaking in Britain the same broad progression can be seen, with the mastery of the practicalities of making models developing first and the full appreciation of the communicative and creative potential of the practice coming later. There is no clear delineation between these two elements, however, as changes in materials and technology have continually served to influence the expression of an architect's vision, while the need to communicate radically different ideas has in turn influenced the development of innovative ways of making and the adoption of new materials and technologies. To master the practice of architectural modelmaking, then, is to wield both the practicalities of making at scale and the conceptual requirements of communicating an architect's vision together, creating a physical object that stands as a miniaturised realisation of a proposed, fictional, or alternate reality that we are drawn into through a process of 'imaginative occupation.'[14]

To celebrate the skills of the architectural modelmaker and their contribution to the success and endurance of the architectural model in Britain, this book aims to tell their story for the first time. It is a story of modelmakers rather than architects, of making and materials, of the lives of the men and women who built a thriving profession that remains to this day curiously unseen. It is a story of a pioneering Victorian who created the basis for an entirely new occupation, of grand utopian visions expressed in miniature, of secret wartime endeavours, of profound ideological, material, and technological revolutions, and of creativity, adaptability, and perseverance. This is the hidden story of how architectural modelmakers in Britain became the masters of their miniature domain.

Notes

1 Bannister Fletcher, 'The Inaugural Address,' *The Architectural Journal*, November 9, 1929, 10.
2 'Charing Cross Bridge,' *The Times*, January 29, 1930, 11.
3 'Charing Cross,' *The Times*, February 17, 1930, 15.
4 Hansard. HC Deb, February 19, 1930, vol 234, col 1482.
5 Ibid, col 1536.
6 Tom Porter and John Neale, *Architectural Supermodels* (London: Architectural Press, 2000), vi.
7 Richard Armiger, interview with author, December 17, 2018.
8 Leon Batista Alberti, *On the Art of Building in Ten Books*, trans. J. Leach and R. Tavenor (Cambridge: MIT Press, 1988), 34.
9 Karen Moon, *Modelling Messages* (New York: Monacelli Press, 2005), 137.
10 Examples of the erasure of the modelmaker from the historical narrative can be found in Matthew Mindrup, *The Architectural Model: Histories of the Miniature and the Prototype* (Cambridge: MIT Press, 2019), 173; A. Lange, 'This Year's Model,' *Journal of Design History* vol 19, no 2 (2006), 233–245; Mark Morris, *Models: Architecture and the Miniature* (Chichester: Wiley-Academy, 2006).

11 Oliver Elser and Peter Schmal, eds. *The Architectural Model: Tool, Fetish, Small Utopia* (Frankfurt: DAM, 2012), 8.

12 Thomas Fisher, *Communicating Ideas Artfully* (New York: Steelcase Partnership, 1990), 23.

13 Helen Lansdown, *Digital Modelmaking* (Marlborough: Crowood Press, 2019), 2.

14 Christian Hubert, 'The Ruins of Representation,' in *Idea as Model*, ed. Kenneth Frampton and Silvia Kolbowski (New York: Rizolli, 1981), 18.

Chapter 1

A Secondary Craft

Three hundred years before John Thorp's model of Charing Cross became the focus of so much debate in Parliament and the London press, another architectural model made a much more modest but equally important entry into the historical record. On December 10, 1567, a note was made in the accounts of the Longleat estate in Wiltshire that Adrian Gaunt, a French joiner, was paid an initial instalment of £4 15s for a model of the proposed new house for Longleat's owner, Sir John Thynne.[1] Gaunt had already been employed to construct a series of elaborate wooden screens for the house's interior, and so given his background it can be assumed that Gaunt's model was made from timber; but beyond this the model's size and general appearance remain unknown.[2] What is certain, however, is that the record of Gaunt's payment is the earliest known reference to an architectural model in Britain.

That Gaunt was a joiner and not a modelmaker is typical of early British architectural models, as the architectural model as an object is far older than architectural modelmaking as an occupation. Until the late-nineteenth century most architectural models in Britain were made by craftsmen from the building trades – initially carpenters or joiners such as Gaunt, but later also stonemasons and architectural sculptors – who were applying their skills to a secondary purpose. Being associated with building construction meant that these trades were the obvious choices for architects and patrons seeking skilled craftsmen to produce models of their proposed buildings; they were familiar with the architectural styles of the day, were confident with the materials of their respective trades, and were able to work at a reduced scale having been used to making samples during their apprenticeships and for clients in order to demonstrate their skills.

In the history of architectural modelmaking the road from Adrian Gaunt to John Thorp is a long and surprisingly slow one. From the initial introduction of architectural models in Britain to there being a dedicated profession of specialist architectural modelmakers took over three hundred years, and for much of their early history the employment of joiners and carpenters such as Gaunt remained the standard means of commissioning a model (Figure 1.1). While it may seem unusual that such an important and specialist class of objects lacked a trade dedicated to their making for so long, the growth in demand for architectural models in Britain was a gradual process, and it was not until the nineteenth century that the circumstances emerged in which the role of the specialist architectural modelmaker became both possible and required.

DOI: 10.4324/9781003298007-2

Figure 1.1 Model of Easton Neston, modelmaker unknown, 1690.
Source: Image courtesy RIBA Collections.

Early Building-Trade Modelmakers

The practice of making and using architectural models arrived on British shores during the late-sixteenth century as part of the gradual tide of Italian architectural techniques that had been slowly spreading across Europe since the Renaissance. Demonstrating an inseparability from architectural practice that would maintain the model's standing for the next five hundred years, just as the notion of the architect as a distinct role within building construction began to take hold in Britain, so too the use of architectural models started to be recorded alongside.

The writing of Roman architects such as Vitruvius indicate that architectural models were in common use during the ancient world in much the same way they are today;[3] however, their re-emergence in modern Europe as a significant tool for the communication of architectural designs is generally traced to the planning and construction of Florence Cathedral in the fourteenth and early-fifteenth centuries. The administration of this enormous project was initially carried out by the city authority using public money rather than church funds, which led to a greater importance being placed on keeping the public and their representatives informed, and models quickly proved to be the ideal means of doing so.[4] The competition for designing the cathedral's dome held in 1418 saw countless models submitted by carpenters, masons, and cabinet makers, including Filippo Brunelleschi's enormous twelve-feet-high brick model, made with the assistance of four masons over a period of three months.[5]

With such complex and large-scale projects taking place during the Renaissance, the position of the architect began to emerge as a separate role within building construction, a division of labour that separated the medieval master stonemason's role of designer, procurer, and supervisor into distinct tasks.[6] As the design and supervisory role of the architect became an increasingly intellectual position distanced from the manual toil of building work, architectural models proved to be a highly effective means of communication that could transmit complex design information to the masons actually carrying out the construction, allowing the principle designer to work away from the building site. Consequently, by the middle of the fifteenth century, the practice of using models to both test and communicate ideas within the architectural design process had begun to percolate across Europe. Italian architect and philosopher Leon Battista Alberti wrote enthusiastically about the use of architectural models in his 1452 treatise *On the Art of Building in Ten Books*, noting that:

> I will always commend the time-honoured custom, practiced by the best builders, of preparing not only drawings and sketches but also models of wood or any other material. . . . These will enable us to weigh up repeatedly and examine, with the advice of experts, the work as a whole and the individual dimensions of the parts.[7]

The Italian influence, and the accompanying use of models, had evidently trickled through to British architectural practice by the time of Gaunt's 1567 model of Longleat, and by the early-seventeenth century the use of architectural models had gradually become more routine. Under the auspices of architects such as Sir Christopher Wren and Nicholas Hawksmoor, and aided by a trend for wealthy landowners to rebuild their medieval or Tudor homes to better match newly fashionable and more elaborate neoclassical architectural styles, the use of architectural models in Britain underwent a steady increase, in part due to the need to explain these new architectural styles to everyone involved.[8]

With the use of architectural models in Britain pre-dating the existence of a profession dedicated to their making by several centuries, the growing demand for models that followed during the seventeenth century continued to be met by carpenters and joiners associated with the building trades, as had been the case with Gaunt's sixteenth-century model of Longleat House. Consequently, most British architectural models during this period were made using timbers such as pine or oak. Surviving models such as those for Sudbury Hall and Melton Constable Hall, both dating to the 1660s, evidence a broad range of construction styles in use, with the Sudbury Hall model merely a solid block model (Figure 1.2), while the much larger model for Melton Constable Hall was built to include a full interior, with painted representations of brick and stone detailing on the exterior.

Beyond being able to identify the trades that the makers of these early models belonged to, almost everything else about their identities remains lost in time, although it is likely that the model of Melton Constable Hall was the work of the estate's own carpenter rather than having been contracted to an external party.[9] Only very occasionally do surviving documentary accounts provide more than fleeting glimpses of the lives of the craftsmen making architectural models in Britain during the sixteenth and seventeenth centuries. The archive of Sir Christopher Wren, a prolific user of architectural models, includes a record of a mahogany model made by an anonymous craftsman during the construction of Pembroke College in 1663, while an entry from 1676 notes that 'Mr Bancks and a Mr Grove' were paid £31 13s 4d for their models

Figure 1.2 Model of Sudbury Hall, modelmaker unknown, circa 1660.

Source: Image copyright SBS Eclectic Images/Alamy.

of Wren's designs for Trinity College.[10] For Wren's 1675 *Great Model* of his design for St. Paul's Cathedral (Figure 1.3), one of over seventy made during the project, it is recorded that the bulk of the work was carried out by the joiner brothers William and Richard Cleere at a cost of over £500. Made from oak, pear, and plaster of Paris, their model contained over nine hundred separate detailing items and was originally painted to represent stone and lead.[11]

Both the *Great Model* and a model of Wren's 1699 design for the Royal Naval Hospital in Greenwich made by the carpenter John Smallwell still survive today (Figure 1.4), but beyond being able to place their makers' names against the models, the lives and careers of these early modelmakers remain tantalisingly hidden, with little insight given as to the balance of their activities between making models and their more regular employment completing full-scale architectural work. William and Richard Cleere, given the size and complexity of the St. Paul's *Great Model*, appear likely to have been employed full-time on model construction for at least a year, while John Smallwell was later commissioned by Nicholas Hawksmoor to make several models in 1717, some eighteen years after he worked for Wren, implying that Smallwell – or possibly his son, as it has been suggested[12] – continued to make architectural models for at least several decades.

Prior to the seventeenth century, the role of the building-trade carpenter also included work that later became more associated with that of the joiner. Until this period carpenters had traditionally been tasked with making all the fixed timber elements of a building, while joiners had been employed making portable furniture such as cabinets, chairs, and screens, as had been the case with Adrian Gaunt.[13] As fashions began to demand that the permanent fixtures within a house such as doors, staircases,

Figure 1.3 The *Great Model* of St. Paul's Cathedral, made by William and Richard Cleere, 1675.

Source: Image copyright James Davidson/Alamy.

Figure 1.4 Model of the Royal Naval Hospital Greenwich, made by John Smallwell, 1699.

Source: Image copyright National Maritime Museum, Greenwich, London, Greenwich Hospital Collection.

and wall panelling became ever more elaborate with complex carvings and details, joiners – considered to be the more highly skilled of the two trades – began to take on more of this work in place of the carpenter. As this distinction grew, the carpenter's work became more focused on the structural elements of a building – roof trusses, floors, beams, and walls. The carpenter's role was then further reduced following the Great Fire of London in 1666, after which regulations were imposed to ensure buildings were mostly constructed from brick, limiting the carpenter's input to the construction of roof frames and joists, and so the demand for timber architectural models during the late-seventeenth century would likely have been a welcome, if infrequent, alternative source of income.

Apprentice carpenters generally started at a later age than many other trades, with the physical demands of lifting heavy timbers ruling out anyone below the age of eighteen. During their apprenticeship a young carpenter worked for their master in exchange for food, lodging, clothing, and training, and they were forbidden from marrying, gambling, or drinking. When working on a building site, a carpenter typically worked from sunrise to sunset in the winter and from 5 a.m. to 8 p.m. in the summer, with a twenty minute break allowed for breakfast, an hour for lunch, and five minutes for a drink in the late afternoon.[14] Wages varied by location and were largely set by the local guilds, although rural carpenters tended not to be members and as such often earned much lower wages than those in towns and cities. Due to the nature of their work, carpenters also moved between building sites, so (given the need for an indoor workshop space to make an architectural model) it is likely that the early modelmakers referred to as 'carpenters' were actually those who would later be termed 'joiners,' occupying their own workspaces in which they made furniture and fittings to be sent to a building site when required.

By the early eighteenth century the practice of building-trade carpenters and joiners making architectural models as a side business to their main work had become a regular practice, with the architectural model having been firmly established as a highly successful tool for architects to employ. The 1734 edition of *The Builder's Dictionary* includes an entry for architectural models that notes they are 'particularly used in Building for an artificial Pattern made in Wood, Stone, Plaister [sic], or other Matter, with all its Parts and Proportions, in order for the better conducting and executing some great Work, and to give an Idea of the Effect it will have in large.'[15] The same dictionary further advises that it is best to use a three-dimensional model rather than relying on 'a bare Design or Draught' when planning a large building.

Despite the growing demand for architectural models during this period there is nevertheless little evidence of any timber-based craftsmen dedicating themselves to their making on a permanent basis, and it was instead through the introduction of other materials that the first instances of specialist architectural modelmakers began to emerge in Britain. As had been the case with the initial importation of the architectural model from Europe during the sixteenth century, it was again an exposure to European culture that brought new approaches to architectural modelmaking – and, crucially, new materials – into the country during the late-eighteenth and early-nineteenth centuries, driven by a trend for young British gentry to undertake the rite of passage of the Grand Tour through Europe to immerse themselves in the culture of the Italian Renaissance. Initially, the desire to obtain mementoes of the architecture they encountered during their travels generated a brief craze for collecting souvenirs in the form of cork models of the classical architecture of Italy, which provided intermittent work for several British craftsmen including Joseph Parkins, who made several cork models for Sir John Soane.[16] Richard Du Bourg, who learned the then novel technique of making cork architectural models while living in Italy during the 1760s as part of his own Grand Tour, produced on his return to England more than forty models over the next fifty years (Figure 1.5), displaying the complete collection in several dedicated exhibitions in London between 1775 and 1819.[17] Both Parkins' and Du Bourg's models were firmly intended as souvenirs of existing buildings rather than as architectural models of proposed designs, and cork remained a somewhat niche modelmaking material outside of the souvenir trade.

The desire for models of the classical works of architecture encountered during the Grand Tour did, however, have a much more lasting influence on the making of architectural models in Britain through the work of the Parisian father-and-son modelmakers Jean-Pierre and Francois Fouquet, who started to gain fame during the 1780s.

Figure 1.5 Cork souvenir model, made by Richard Du Bourg, 1765.

Source: Image courtesy RIBA Collections.

Rather than working in timber or cork, the Fouquets were using plaster of Paris, initially making a range of miniatures depicting ancient classical architecture before extending their work to contemporary architectural commissions. John Nash was so taken by their quality that he ordered from them a set of fifteen models of Greek and Roman buildings for £1000,[18] while both Sir John Soane and the South Kensington Museum added several to their respective collections.[19]

Primarily, the Fouquets' models were gifts for collectors, with commissions for models of proposed buildings appearing only occasionally – their largest, and most famous, being a model of the design for the Capitol building in Richmond, Virginia, made for Thomas Jefferson.[20] As the Fouquets' models began to appear in Britain it quickly became evident that they were achieving a quality that far outstripped anything being produced in timber (Figure 1.6). Impressed by their quality, and with the classical revival sweeping change through European architecture, architects such as John Nash and John Soane began to favour plaster models over timber ones, as although the timber models being produced at this time were of admirable quality, timber – which nevertheless remained the dominant material used in architectural modelmaking throughout the eighteenth century – was a challenging material in which to reproduce the intricately detailed forms and the material likeness of stone that neoclassical architecture demanded. Consequently, plaster models increasingly began to appear alongside timber models in Britain during the early-nineteenth century, adding stonemasons and sculptors to the list of those involved in architectural modelmaking. As with carpenters such as Smallwell and Gaunt, such modelmaking

Figure 1.6 Model of the Temple of Vesta, made by Jean-Pierre and Francois Fouquet, 1800.
Source: Image courtesy RIBA Collections.

was rarely more than an adjunct to their main businesses, however. The architectural sculptor R. N. Hanwell was noted as having produced several plaster models in 1860,[21] while in 1866, the sculpting firm of Farmer and Brindley produced the model for the proposed Albert Memorial in London.[22] C. H. Mabey, who produced architectural details for the Houses of Parliament, also made several scale models,[23] as did the architectural sculptor William Grinsell Nichol.[24] The same trend of occasional modelmaking as part of a larger business dedicated to full-scale architectural work also continued for timber models through the early-nineteenth century; the models for John Soane's design for the Westminster Law Courts (Figure 1.7), for example, were produced by the Greenwich timber merchants and carpenter brothers Thomas and George Martyr in 1827.[25]

While surviving plaster models from this period demonstrate very high levels of skill and artistry, the Fouquets' full-time dedication to modelmaking clearly gave their work a significant edge over the work of their British counterparts. Although plaster was indeed suited to better represent the neoclassical architectural styles of the period, the Fouquets' models evidence that it was a change in focus rather than a change in

Figure 1.7 Model of the Westminster Law Courts, made by Thomas and George Martyr, 1827.

Source: Image copyright Sir John Soane's Museum, London.

material that was behind their impressive work. An important difference between the Fouquets and the building-trade craftsmen making architectural models in Britain during the late-eighteenth century was that the Fouquets were making models full-time. Having established a thriving business selling their plaster miniatures, Jean-Pierre and his son Francois were able to direct their focus onto mastering their craft, not as a secondary off-shoot from full-scale architectural work, but as modelmakers first and foremost. This was the opposite of the approach dominating Britain, where specialists working in timber or plaster were commissioned to make architectural models purely because they were adept at working with their materials at full size.

The first British craftsman known to have followed in the Fouquets' footsteps was the mason Richard Day, who (while not yet a professional modelmaker in the modern sense) succeeded in dedicating what proved to be almost his entire working life to making plaster architectural models. While the 1851 census lists him as a 'modeller,' which implies he was a full-scale architectural sculptor, Day appears to have almost exclusively worked as a modelmaker from a very young age. The son of a mason, Day was born in Camberwell in 1816 and by the age of twelve had already completed a period of employment as a stonemason for John Nash. It was at this point that Day built a highly regarded plaster model of the proposed Royal Academy in London. His talent was already sufficient at this age to have been immediately engaged by King George IV to make a model of his plans for the renovation of Windsor Castle.[26] By the mid-1830s, Day appears to have established himself as a prolific maker of architectural models, including one of the then under construction National Gallery in Trafalgar Square. The catalogue for the 1836 exhibition held by the Society for the Illustration and Encouragement of Practical Science lists fourteen of his models on display, with major competition models following in the 1840s.[27] Although Day is still recorded as a modeller in the 1860 London Post Office directory, he appears to have fallen on desperately hard times in the late-1840s. A notice in *The Builder* on October 7, 1848, reports that while 'there are few architects who are not acquainted with the admirable models made by Mr Day,' he had for several years been struggling to make a living as a modelmaker and 'must either seek some other occupation or starve.'[28] By this point Day was only thirty-two years old, and given his later 1860 listing, he seems to have enjoyed a resurgence in his fortunes, appearing in the 1891 census as a 'retired modeller living by his own means' in Maidstone.

In being able to devote over thirty years of his career to making architectural models Richard Day was highly unusual. Despite a steady increase in demand for architectural models throughout the first half of the nineteenth century there was still no dedicated trade or profession devoted to their making. It appears likely that there was still more work – or perhaps more profitable work – available in the building trades their makers were primarily working in, leading to few individuals solely pursuing modelmaking rather than full-scale architectural work as Day had attempted. The making of architectural models was more often advertised as a service alongside architectural work by architectural sculptors, carpenters, and plasterers such as Farmer and Brindley, Jackson and Sons, the Maybey brothers, and Thomas and George Martyr. These firms were evidently producing high-quality timber and plaster models, however their modelmaking work continued the tradition of the past three hundred years in not drawing on either materials or processes from beyond their established trades nor dedicating themselves solely to the making of architectural models. Day too, while specialising in making models for most of his adult career, was effectively still working as an architectural sculptor, albeit producing items at a reduced scale, working purely in the single material he had honed his skills on during his earlier career as a mason.

Throughout much of the nineteenth century the continued dominance of craftsmen from the building trades as the makers of architectural models meant that whoever an architect commissioned a model from had a profound influence on the appearance of the model that was produced. The properties of the materials used led to radically different visual styles, and so choosing between craftsmen who worked in specific materials determined the type of model the architect was ordering. Plaster of Paris continued to be used alongside timber in model construction throughout the whole of the nineteenth century, but while able to capture intricate detail, plaster was too fragile for regular handling, as well as extremely heavy when used in large-scale models.[29] As a consequence, timbers such as oak, pine, mahogany, and lime remained the principle modelmaking materials. Other than the use of small plaster details on timber models such as William and Richard Cleere's seventeenth-century model of St. Paul's, the two materials were largely not found together. This reflected the continued practice of craftsmen such as Richard Day working solely in the materials of their primary trade.

Before the professionalisation of architectural modelmaking in Britain during the late-nineteenth century, the makers of architectural models rarely, if ever, strayed beyond the boundaries of their principal trades. Carpenters and joiners made models from timber, while masons and sculptors used plaster. The strict divisions that separated architectural models by material were an over-lasting legacy of the medieval guild system that had imposed an effective monopoly on craft production. The intended purpose of the guilds was to maintain standards of craft skill and to protect craftsmen from both exploitation and competition.[30] This was achieved by regulating a firm division of the crafts, confining practitioners to a single trade and preventing one craftsman's market from being encroached upon by another. The strict differentiation of trades that the guild system established therefore prohibited members of one guild from carrying out the work of another, which undoubtedly restricted the choice available to the architects and patrons commissioning architectural models. If a joiner was already engaged on a building site, their services would likely be used, and the model made from timber. If a mason were called upon, however, the model would be cast in gypsum plaster. Pre-professional architectural modelmaking therefore largely involved starting with a set material and process and then applying that trade's skills at a reduced scale.

By the end of the eighteenth century the peak influence of the guilds had already passed, however, and the labour structures of craft production had undergone a period of radical change because of industrialisation, whereby the increasing complexity of manufactured goods had generated a need for coordination across multiple trades. This led to the role of the master in any given trade increasingly becoming that of a merchant-craftsman, liaising between the different trades while also acting as a bridge between the craftsmen and the customer.[31] Rather than craftsmen and artisans banding together for mutual protection while selling directly from an individual trader to an individual customer, industry began to be organised around the concept of multiple employees working for capitalist employers, who then sold their combined outputs. This contributed to a substantial change in social structures as workers began to choose the protection and security offered by employers rather than the guilds.[32] The main consequence of this change was an erosion of the vertical divisions that separated the different trades from one another, replacing them with a common horizontal division between worker and employer.[33] While in principle this meant that workers could then utilise materials and processes from across multiple trades, workers' roles instead became increasingly specialised as the demand for standardised products for mass consumption required complex manufacturing processes that necessitated a division of labour that would ensure high standards across a virtually identical batch of goods.[34] Individual craftsmen were then no longer responsible for the complete manufacturing process of a single item, and the design of the item itself was further removed from their control and developed into a separate role.

Significantly, however, the changes to labour structures that took place during industrialisation entirely bypassed the construction of architectural models, principally due to there being no dedicated trade for them to affect. Architectural models were being made by individuals who were primarily involved in the construction of full-size buildings, and the division of labour within building construction had already taken place during the Renaissance through the separation of the role of the architect from that of the mason. This meant that the carpenters, masons, and plasterers making architectural models in Britain were being doubly affected by the vertical division of trades inherited from the guild system and by the horizontal division of labour that separated the design of a building from its construction. Building construction labour structures largely resisted the consequences of industrialisation due to the bespoke nature of the work and because of the continued need to specialise in single trades such as masonry and carpentry, effectively extending guild-based trade distinctions right through to the nineteenth century. While craftsmen could in theory specialise in making architectural models full-time if demand were sufficient, as had been the case with Richard Day, there was still an unquestioned tradition that these would be made using only the materials and processes belonging to one specific trade. Models would remain either timber or plaster, the choice simply coming down to the background of the maker.

Into the Drawing Office

During the nineteenth century the long-standing dominance of the carpenter and mason modelmakers of the pre-professional era eventually began to decline as the making of architectural models shifted away from the craftsman's workshop and into the drawing offices of the newly formed architectural practices. Liberated from the siloed building trades, architectural modelmaking began to distinguish itself as a pursuit in its own right, and it was through the adoption of another new material – card – that the emergence of architectural modelmaking as a specialist occupation began to take place.

By the middle of the century the demand for architectural models for public presentation, architectural competitions, and general everyday use by architects had dramatically expanded. The architect Sir John Soane had already become well-known for his use of models as educational aids during the lectures he presented in his role as Professor of Architecture at the Royal Academy in London, emphasising that he saw the making of architectural models as being of vital importance to architectural practice as they could help avoid making potentially costly mistakes.[35] As well as commissioning models of his own work, Soane's interest in cork and plaster Grand Tour models from craftsmen such as Joseph Parkins and the Fouquets resulted in a private collection of over one hundred architectural models and miniature souvenirs. The collection, when opened to the public according to Soane's wishes after his death in 1837, quickly became a popular attraction, as public interest in viewing and even making architectural models had grown significantly throughout the first half of the century. An exhibition held by the Society for the Illustration and Encouragement of Practical Sciences in 1836 displayed over three hundred engineering, patent, and architectural models, while in 1839 seventy models alone were submitted for the competition to design Nelson's Column in Trafalgar Square.[36] A year later a £400 timber model was displayed for the competition to design the Royal Exchange Building in London,[37] and in 1851 an entire temporary structure had to be built to show the models of the proposed Smithfield Market, while the Great Exhibition of the same year included a model of Liverpool Docks that occupied ninety-six square feet and cost £750 to construct.[38] A notice in the architectural journal *The Builder* in 1870 called for submissions for a major exhibition to be held the following year dedicated to architectural models of schools and colleges,[39] and by 1876 the South Kensington Museum had over one hundred and fifty architectural models on display, many of which had been presentation models for competition committees.[40] Repeated calls were also made within *The Builder* for the establishment of an entire museum dedicated to architectural models.[41]

One of the major factors driving the demand for architectural models during the middle of the nineteenth century was the increased professionalisation of architectural practice itself. Eighteenth-century architects had largely conformed to the image of the gentleman architect, classically educated and drawn to Italian styles as a result of their experiences on the Grand Tour.[42] Though highly skilled, there remained an air of the amateur about most British architects at the time; even Sir Christopher Wren side-stepped into greatness having been foremost an astronomer during his early life. Architecture, as understood from the work of Vitruvius, Alberti, and Palladio, was based on harmony and proportion, and, certainly for Wren, was viewed almost as an extension of mathematics. Learned gentlemen could therefore move into the field – often with spectacular success – without any specific training. This changed during the nineteenth century as the architectural profession became much more formally organised with the founding in 1834 of the Institute of British Architects (later gaining its Royal charter in 1866). The Institute set out to promote high standards of architectural practice, and by introducing regulations that its members had to adhere to, formalised the ways in which architects worked.[43] By the 1890s degrees in architecture were being regulated by the then Royal Institute, and as its hold over the profession continued to grow, the distinction between recognised architects (the RIBA's members) and builders began to be much more rigorously defined, ultimately leading to the 1936 Registration Act that closed the profession and made membership of the organisation a requirement to be able to use the term *architect* at all.

At the same time that architecture was becoming more professionalised, however, the intensive demand for housing during the population boom of the first half of the nineteenth century had led to a gradual deskilling among the building trades as the contracting of general labourers became the only way to meet demand.[44] This was compounded by the 1813 repealing of the 1562 Statue of Artificers, which had given powers to the guilds to regulate the pay of skilled workers, opening up the building trades by removing any requirement for an apprenticeship and enabling a shift towards a system of competitive tendering for building work whereby interested contractors submitted competing bids, inevitably leading to a lowering of prices that further encouraged the use of less-skilled labour in order to reduce wage costs.[45] The role of the master craftsman within the building trades was gradually coming to an end, and a consequence of this was that architects had to increasingly provide very clear specifications and detailed drawings as instructions for less-skilled labourers to follow, further bolstering the desire for architectural practice to become more regulated and standardised in order to compensate for the decline in construction skills. As a result, the availability of skilled craftsmen in the building trades who could make architectural models was therefore dropping just at the time when the demand for architectural models was rapidly growing. An 1843 article in *The Builder* noted that 'of late the models of houses and other structures and their grounds have been used by our intelligent architects and civil engineers to convey to themselves and others the appearance of the real or proposed originals,'[46] and by the 1870s the benefits of models over drawings were being more confidently expressed: 'Few clients can understand plans and sections, and perspective drawings are made so deceptive as to mislead the client so that they become dissatisfied.'[47] The same article further repeated Sir John Soane's earlier observation that it was cheaper to make mistakes in a model than in the real building, and that 'a well-executed model, instead of being an additional cost, proves in the end to be a considerable saving.'[48]

With a dramatic leap in demand for architectural models coinciding with a sudden decrease in the number of skilled craftsmen able to make them, and a growing trend for architects to use experimental models as part of their design process, architectural models increasingly began to be made within architectural drawing offices rather than the workshops of carpenters and sculptors, with young architectural assistants regularly assigned the task. T. Richardson's 1859 book on architectural modelmaking specifically addressed 'a large and increasing body, the architectural assistants, [to whom] it is hoped that this little hand-book will prove to be acceptable,'[49] and by the 1870s it appears that the practice of architects – or their assistants – making 'sketch' models in their offices had become routine. At the same time, architectural modelmaking was also becoming a popular hobby for the growing middle classes. As early as 1827 a publication describing the construction of architectural models noted that it was aimed at both architects and amateurs,[50] while an 1843 article suggested architectural modelmaking was an ideal hobby for women.[51] The same journal also published letters from amateurs seeking advice on the hobby,[52] suggesting a much wider public awareness of architectural models evolving by the 1840s.

The shift to making architectural models in drawing offices rather than workshops during the middle of the nineteenth century was further aided by the adoption of much cleaner and more readily accessible materials. Rather than offices and private studies being filled with woodworking tools and bags of gypsum plaster, card and paper quickly became the materials of choice for architects and their junior assistants. The use of paper in architectural modelmaking dates back until at least 1521 in France when a papier-mâché model of a church in Rouen was recorded, with further evidence of cardboard models dating to 1601.[53] In Britain, a pasteboard model of University College Oxford was made in the 1630s,[54] while in 1806 a large card model of James Wyatt's design for Fonthill Abbey was constructed.[55] Pasteboard, an early type of cardboard made from laminations of paper and glue, was still being promoted as a common and suitable material for the construction of architectural models during the 1820s.[56]

The change to using card and paper rather than timber or plaster marked an important shift in the fundamental properties of the materials used in model construction, as being sheet materials they required a significantly different approach to not only making a model but also in planning its assembly. Solid materials such as timber and plaster needed to be considered three-dimensionally from the start; timber could be cut and shaped to the required size of the overall mass of the required model, and then either be further cut into or extended and detailed with additional pieces. Using sheet materials changed this completely, forcing a conceptual shift to consider a model as a series of elevations. This may suggest why card was so enthusiastically adopted by architects. Not only did the relatively clean construction methods of working with card allow the making of models to move out of the workshop and into the drawing office, but their reliance on flat elevations was also much more familiar to architects used to working with drawings. Card models, using either pasteboard or Bristol board to construct the basic walls, could also be easily painted to create much more realistic representations of brick, tile, or stone. Warm sepia was suggested for stone, with Indian red ink for brick, while cork or softwoods could also be used to create more three-dimensional details such as columns.[57]

Demonstrating the impact that card had on architectural modelmaking, in 1859 the architect T. Richardson published *The Art of Architectural Modelling in Paper*, which the author described as 'the first ever published practical dissertation upon the Art of Architectural Modelling.'[58] Noting that students and others in the architectural profession had been demanding such a book for some time, Richardson's book takes the reader through the construction of models in remarkable detail. Observing that paper and card could be easily procured, Richardson suggested that the beauty of a model was not in 'the material employed, but in the skill displayed in the working.'[59] This marked an important move away from the materials-focused approach of modelmakers working in timber or plaster. Because of its ready availability, and the lack of specialist knowledge necessary to work with card and paper, the use of paper products acted as a democratising influence on the architectural model. Anyone could obtain card, and anyone could use it. It did not require specialist equipment or a workshop, and so paper and card further moved the making of models out of the effective control of the building trades, additionally contributing to their declining position within the making of architectural models as the century progressed.

For architectural modelmaking, Richardson recommended the use of Whatman's double-elephant drawing paper, which was sold under the name of Crayon paper.[60] Its suitability was highlighted due to its natural colour being reminiscent of Bath stone, its relative flexibility, and the fact that it did not absorb the paste that was used to stick sheets together. Richardson also included a recipe for making a suitable adhesive paste using sugar, flour, corrosive sublimate, and lavender oil or peppermint to reduce odour; the mixture to be boiled and stirred into a paste.[61] A modelling press was then used to make cardboard to the correct thicknesses required by pressing layers of paper and paste together (Figure 1.8). Ivory obtained from comb manufacturers was suggested as an ideal material from which to carve moulds for pressing textures into the surface of the card, while windows could be carefully cut out and clear sheets of mica placed behind to represent glazing – either left clear to see internal spaces or backed with a piece of blue paper.[62]

As well as reducing the mess associated with the making of models, bringing their construction into offices and homes, card and paper also provided a range of alternative materials that allowed for more choice in the appearance of architectural models. By the 1870s, card was becoming recognised as the more superior material – timber being heavy, cork being unsuitable for accurate detail, and plaster not offering realistic representations of anything other than stone. Cardboard models, on the other hand, could be coloured to imitate different materials with an 'excellent level of detail obtained.'[63] As a result of card's introduction as a modelmaking material, references to building trade craftsmen making architectural models begin to be replaced by references to artists during the latter decades of the century. Stephen Salter is recorded as having made many card architectural models during the 1860s and 1870s, and alongside Thomas Dighton was credited as having 'first brought cardboard modelling

Figure 1.8 Drawing of a cardboard modelling press, 1859.

Source: Thomas Richardson, The Art of Architectural Modelling in Paper (London: John Weale, 1859), 27.

Figure 1.9 Card model of Scotney Castle, made by Thomas Dighton, 1844.

Source: Image copyright National Trust/Charles Thomas.

to very high perfection.'[64] While almost nothing is known about Salter's work, Dighton's exquisite 1844 model of Scotney Castle in Kent survives to this day (Figure 1.9). An artist by training, Dighton's model demonstrates the combination of the fineness of detail and realistic colouring that card offered over both timber and plaster, and it stands in stark contrast to the simpler timber models illustrated earlier in this chapter. Dighton's work was evidently very highly regarded, it being noted in a description of one particular model in 1848 that his models were 'well known to the profession, and have given him a reputation which will be further increased by the work to which we are alluding.'[65] Such models were extremely expensive due to the time and skill required to make them, and at £100 each it was observed at the time that few people were willing to pay for them.[66]

How much of Dighton's time was dedicated to making models is unknown, though it appears that as with almost all his contemporaries his model commissions were only a part of his regular income, reflecting the great expense that modelmaking entailed during the nineteenth century. An editorial in 1877 questioned why models were not more widely used, given their obvious benefits, and – noting a lack of modelmakers – concluded that 'those who have given to it a lifelong study have been so inadequately rewarded that they have thrown it up in disgust.'[67] The author continued with a more hopeful note that 'there is no reason why architectural modelling should not assume its place among the art-industries of the country. Few pursuits afford a finer scope for the exercise of the inventive faculties.'[68]

The use of card as a modelmaking material continued to expand during the 1860s and 1870s, with an increasing number of individuals working almost exclusively on model construction for at least parts of their careers, both on a commercial basis and within architects' offices. Alongside Stephen Salter and Thomas Dighton, C.N. Thwaite appears to have sustained a career dedicated to making card architectural models for over twenty years. Thwaite's work was first reported in 1862, when he was producing models for architects in Manchester before moving to Peckham in London sometime before 1867.[69] Thwaite's models were noted as being 'executed in cardboard in a painstaking and careful manner,'[70] and in 1872 he made a model of the proposed chapel at Tyntsfield house (Figure 1.10), continuing to work until the 1880s.[71] During the same period, the architect George Devey employed an assistant as a full-time in-house modelmaker making cardboard architectural models that were presented to clients in custom briefcases. While the identity of Devey's modelmaker remains unknown, contemporary accounts report that he was in constant work.[72]

By the end of the nineteenth century the making of architectural models within architectural practices had become the norm, with a sizeable number of architectural assistants effectively working as modelmakers as the role became a major part of their daily duties. The architect Robert Kerr advised the profession to favour architectural models over drawings as the latter were 'useless. They speak a language which is only understood by architects.'[73] The trade journal *The Builder* further noted how 'you can walk round a model, examine the contour, the details, the relative proportion that the various parts of a building bear to each other and the whole . . . and thus realise a far better impression of them.'[74]

Card had by this time become the material of choice for office-based architectural modelmaking, used either on its own or to clad simple timber shapes; the card being coloured with ink to provide the illusion of surface detail without any depth. A surviving cut-through model of a proposed building in Whitehall made in 1869 by the assistants to the architect Lieutenant-General Sir Andrew Clarke (Figure 1.11) demonstrates how significantly the construction of architectural models had shifted during the nineteenth century. Using a combination of timber, card, and glass for the building itself, and with plaster used for the base, the model employs almost all the materials

Figure 1.10 Card model of Tyntsfield House Chapel, made by C. N. Thwaite, 1872.

Source: Author's Image.

Figure 1.11 Mixed media model made by the office of Lieutenant-General Sir Andrew Clarke, 1869.

Source: Image copyright Victoria and Albert Museum, London.

then suited to architectural modelmaking. Such a mixed-media approach stands in dramatic contrast to the separate timber or plaster models that had by this point been the typical approach to modelmaking in Britain for some three hundred years, with the construction methods and choice of materials clearly having been selected for their suitability for meeting the demands of the model rather than being dictated by its maker's familiarity or expertise. While this model was not yet one constructed by a dedicated professional, the specific activity of architectural modelmaking within some architectural offices had clearly by this point become an identifiable task that was able to take an overall view of the needs of the model and that was no longer restricted to individual materials. By moving the making of models out of the rigid, materials-based silos of the mason, sculptor, and carpenter and into the drawing offices of the architect, different materials could be brought together and a broader range of making processes employed. Whereas architectural models had previously been made by individual craft disciplines, each utilising different materials and processes in pursuit of the same outcome, by the end of the nineteenth century the making of architectural models had become a much more consolidated activity. With artists and the newly professionalised architectural assistants demonstrating how effective card could be as a modelmaking material, the making of architectural models, no longer relegated to being secondary off-shoots of the building trades, was ready to follow the architect and emerge as a dedicated profession.

Notes

1 Mark Girouard, *Robert Smythson and the Architecture of the Elizabethan Era* (Chicago: University of Michigan, 1966), 57.
2 John Wilton-Ely, 'The Architectural Model 1: English Baroque,' *Apollo Magazine*, October 1968, 250–251.
3 Milena Stavric, Predrag Sidanin and Bojan Tepavcevic, *Architectural Scale Models in the Digital Age* (Vienna: Springer, 2013), 25.
4 Matthew Mindrup, *The Architectural Model: Histories of the Miniature and the Prototype* (Cambridge: MIT Press, 2019), 82; Simona Valeriani, 'Three-Dimensional Models as "In-Between Objects" – the Creation of Knowledge in Early Modern Architectural Practice,' *History of Technology*, vol 31 (2012), 26–46; Leopold Ettlinger, 'The Emergence of the Italian Architect during the Fifteenth Century,' in *The Architect: Chapters in the History of the Profession*, ed. S. Kostof (New York: OUP, 1977), 108.
5 Martin Briggs, 'Architectural Models II,' *The Burlington Magazine for Connoisseurs*, April 1929; Ross King, *Brunelleschi's Dome* (London: Vintage, 2008), 40 and 45.
6 Bradley Starkey, 'Models, Architecture, Levitation: Design-Based Research into Post-Secular Architecture,' *The Journal of Architecture*, vol 11, no 3 (2006), 324.
7 Leon Batista Alberti, *On the Art of Building in Ten Books*, trans. J. Leach and R Tavenor (Cambridge: MIT Press, 1988), 33–34.
8 Wilton-Ely, 'The Architectural Model 1,' 250–251; John Wilton-Ely, 'The Architectural Models of Sir John Soane: A Catalogue,' *Architectural History*, vol 12 (October 1969), 6.
9 Wilton-Ely, 'The Architectural Model 1,' 252.
10 Briggs, 'Architectural Models II,' 246.
11 Wilton-Ely, 'The Architectural Model 1,' 253.
12 Ibid.
13 Martin Briggs, *A Short History of the Building Crafts* (Oxford: OUP, 1925), 137.
14 Ibid.
15 'Model,' *The Builder's Dictionary Vol II* (London: Bettesworth and Hitch and Austen, 1734).

16 Richard Gillespie, 'The Rise and Fall of Cork Models Collections in Britain,' *Architectural History*, 60 (2017), 117–118.

17 Ibid, 126.

18 Fiona Leslie, 'Inside Out: Changing Attitudes Towards Architectural Models in the Museums at South Kensington,' *Architectural History*, 47 (2004), 163.

19 Ibid, 169.

20 Karen Moon, *Modelling Messages* (New York: Monacelli Press, 2005), 143; Leslie, 'Inside Out,' 196.

21 'The Architectural Exhibition,' *The Builder*, April 28, 1860, 262.

22 Leslie, 'Inside Out,' 198.

23 John Physick and Michael Darby, *Marble Halls* (London: V&A, 1973), 15.

24 Matthew Wells, 'Relations and Reflections to the Eye and Understanding: Architectural Models and the Rebuilding of the Royal Exchange, 1839–44,' *Architectural History*, 60 (2017), 8.

25 'Notice,' *The London Gazette*, April 13, 1827, 848; Malcolm Baker, 'Representing Invention, Viewing Models,' in *Models: The Third Dimension of Science*, eds. Soraya de Chadarevian and Nick Hopward (Stanford: Stanford University Press, 2004), 198.

26 'New Building for the Royal Academy,' *Mechanics Magazine*, April 12, 1828, 191.

27 Wells, 'Relations.'

28 'Day, The Architectural Modelmaker,' *The Builder*, October 7, 1848, 490.

29 H. Liddell, 'Letter to the Editor,' *The Builder*, May 27, 1843, 198.

30 Edward Lucie-Smith, *The Story of Craft* (Oxford: Phaidon, 1981), 126.

31 Raizman, *History of Modern Design*, 21–22.

32 Lucie-Smith, *The Story of Craft*, 128–9.

33 F. Cope, 'The Rise and Decline of the English Guilds,' *The Churchman*, vol 54, issue 3 (1939), 142.

34 Adrian Forty, *Objects of Desire* (London: Thames and Hudson, 1995), 34.

35 John Wilton-Ely, *The Architect's Vision* (Nottingham: University of Nottingham, 1965), 7; Baker, 'Representing Invention, Viewing Models,' 26.

36 Physick and Darby, *Marble Halls*, 13.

37 Wells, 'Relations,' 7.

38 'Models,' *The Builder*, July 20, 1850, 345.

39 'Buildings for Educational Purposes and the International Exhibition,' *The Builder*, August 27, 1870, 692.

40 Physick and Darby, *Marble Halls*, 13; Leslie, 'Inside Out,' 170.

41 H. Benson, 'Museum of Architectural Models,' *The Builder*, February 5, 1848, 67; 'Architectural Modelling,' 1146.

42 *The Architect: Chapters in the History of the Profession*, ed. S. Kostof (New York: OUP, 1977), 183.

43 Ibid, 192–3.

44 Ibid, 194.

45 J. Bowyer, *History of Building* (London: Crosby Lockwood Staples, 1973), 240.

46 'On the Proper Display of Models,' *The Builder*, August 5, 1843, 317.

47 'Architectural Modelling,' 1145.

48 Ibid.

49 Thomas Richardson, *The Art of Architectural Modelling in Paper* (London: John Weale, 1859), 16.

50 D. Boileau, *The Art of Working in Pasteboard upon Scientific Principles* (London: Boosey and Sons, 1827).

51 'Architectural Modelling,' *The Builder*, May 27, 1843, 189.

52 H. Liddell, 'Letter to the Editor,' *The Builder*, May 27, 1843, 198; Benson, 'Museum of Architectural Models,' 67.

53 Mindrup, *The Architectural Model*, 33 and 130.

54 Ibid, 133.

55 John Wilton-Ely, 'The Genesis and Evolution of Fonthill Abbey,' *Architectural History*, 23 (1980), 50.

56 Boileau, *The Art of Working in Pasteboard*, 93–106.

57 H. Benson, 'Card-Board Models,' *The Builder*, March 25, 1849, 141; C.L.O, 'On the Construction of Skew Arches,' *The Civil Engineer and Architect's Journal*, 11 (August 1838), 314.

58 Richardson, *The Art of Architectural Modelling in Paper*, iii.

59 Ibid, 19.

60 Ibid, 20.

61 Ibid, 22–22.

62 Ibid, 76.

63 'Architectural Modelling,' 1145.

64 Ibid, 1146.

65 'Architectural Models,' *The Builder*, May 6, 1848, 225.

66 Ibid.

67 'Architectural Modelling,' 1145.

68 Ibid.

69 'Chips,' *The Building News*, July 18, 1862, 57; 'Chips,' *The Building News*, August 1, 1862, 95; 'Model of Proposed New Dock Approaches,' *The Builder*, May 18, 1867, 353.

70 'The Photographs at the Architectural Exhibition,' *The Building News*, May 21, 1869, 452.

71 Physick and Darby, *Marble Halls*, 15.

72 Jill Allibone, *George Devey, Architect, 1820–1886* (Cambridge: Lutterworth Press, 1991), 118.

73 Robert Kerr, *The Consulting Architect* (London: John Murray, 1886), 95.

74 'Architectural Modelling,' 1145.

Chapter 2

98 Gray's Inn Road

The term *modelmaker*, or *model maker* as it was more commonly written at the time, began to be used in earnest to describe a specific occupation during the second half of the nineteenth century. The accelerating process of industrialisation had established a need for countless models of the products of modernity – engines, machines, and so forth – to either promote their existence or to explain their operation. In response to this demand, dedicated industrial modelmakers began to set up shop in the manufacturing and engineering centres of Britain such as Glasgow, Liverpool, Birmingham, Sheffield, and London. Many of these modelmakers had begun their careers as industrial pattern makers, having been employed to produce the original masters for engineering components before they were cast, most commonly out of timber. With their skills and employment within manufacturing firms making them ideally suited to the task, pattern makers began to be called upon to make scale models of what their companies were making, initiating a gradual transition whereby a growing number of pattern makers began to specialise purely in making models rather than actual masters, and by the beginning of the twentieth century the notion that industrial modelmaking was a specialist trade in its own right had become widely accepted.

The transition from pattern maker to industrial modelmaker was nevertheless a slow process, as according to the 1911 census while there were over twelve thousand pattern makers working in Britain at the time, there were just three hundred modelmakers. Confusingly, seventy of those listed as modelmakers were working as 'terra cotta model makers' and were actually still pattern makers – the term referring to the production of 'models' or masters for the mass production of pottery, ceramics, and ornamental bricks and tiles. This role had originally been referred to as a 'modeller,' but ostensibly they were producing originals to be copied in the same manner that industrial pattern makers were making originals of engineering components. Of the two hundred and forty other modelmakers recorded in the census, sixty-six were employed making ship models; sixty-one referred to themselves as engineer's modelmakers; and one hundred and eleven were described as either 'model makers' or 'pattern and model makers', demonstrating the increasingly blurred distinction between the two occupations. Only two were recorded as architectural modelmakers, however.

Despite the growth in industrial modelmaking during the late-nineteenth century and its recognition as a distinct trade, architectural modelmaking as an occupation remained curiously under-developed. The key difference between the two forms of modelmaking at the time was that the role of the pattern maker itself had been a recent and highly specialised product of industrialisation, and so the shift from pattern

DOI: 10.4324/9781003298007-3

maker to modelmaker had followed swiftly and logically as the demand for models grew. The making of architectural models on the other hand was just one small aspect of the work undertaken by craftsmen working within the building trades, and so to make the jump from carpenter to modelmaker meant giving up most of your business to focus purely on making models. With industrial models being made by individuals who were increasingly recognised as modelmakers, architectural modelmaking itself remained spread over a number of disparate occupations: Richard Day and C.N. Thwaite had both been able to sustain intermittent but dedicated careers making architectural models in specific materials over the course of several decades; architectural assistants were busy producing card and timber models on a regular basis in drawing offices; and building-trade companies such as Farmer and Brindley and Jacksons and Sons continued to produce detailed plaster models alongside their full-scale architectural work.

An obvious gap remained, however, in that as the nineteenth century drew to a close, architectural modelmaking still lacked the specialist attention that industrial modelmaking was beginning to benefit from. If a model of an engine, a ship, a clock, or a mechanism was called for, the services of a specialist industrial modelmaker could be employed. If a model of a building was needed, however, it was either made by an architect's assistants or commissioned from the dwindling number of skilled carpenters, joiners, or masons who were still offering to make models. The opportunity for a dedicated architectural modelmaker to apply the same specialist attention to the task as had become the norm for industrial models was apparent, and when twenty-one-year-old John Thorp opened his architectural drawing office in London in 1883, that opportunity was finally seized and the making of architectural models in Britain was irrevocably changed.

John Thorp and the Birth of the Profession

John Brown Thorp (Figure 2.1) was born in Brighton in 1862, and by the time he had completed his schooling at Christ's Hospital School in Horsham, Thorp had already developed both a keenness for modelmaking and a commercial streak that would characterise his entire career, on one occasion charging his school friends the price of a sewing pin each to view a model stage set he had designed and presented in a cardboard theatre.[1] With a clear interest in theatrical design and display, Thorp went on to study at the Royal Academy in London before working for the architect Frederick Nesbitt Kemp in Chancery Lane. Quickly becoming known for his skill as a draughtsman, Thorp soon set out on his own, finding his drawing work in much demand by the local architectural firms clustered around Bloomsbury. Opening the London Drawing and Tracing Office in Telegraph Street in 1883, Thorp then moved to two different premises on Cheapside before settling into offices at 98 Gray's Inn Road in Holborn in 1887, where his company was to remain for over a century.

Despite his initial focus on producing architectural drawings, within just a few years of opening his business Thorp had added the preparation of models to his list of services.[2] Thorp's offices on Gray's Inn Road were in close proximity to one of the four Inns of Court, and he began to receive commissions for architectural models to be used in legal cases, particularly lawsuits relating to party wall disputes and 'light and air cases'[3] (Figure 2.2). These models, as Thorp himself described, were

Figure 2.1 John Thorp in his workshop, circa 1915.

Source: Image courtesy Thorp Archive, AUB.

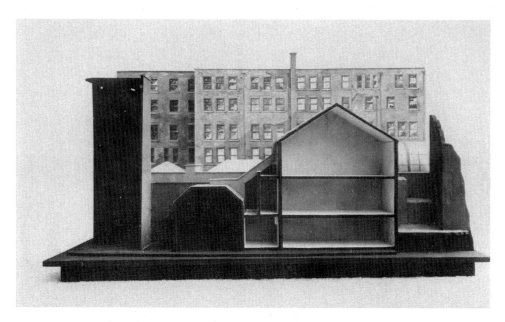

Figure 2.2 Sectional legal model, made by John Thorp, circa 1900.
Source: Image courtesy Thorp Archive, AUB.

'indispensable for enabling Counsel to grasp fundamental facts of a case, and are of primary service to him when describing to the court the principle points in question.'[4] As they were to be presented in court, these legal models had to be highly detailed and accurate, and Thorp made them as realistic as possible using a combination of card, timber, paper, and plaster to recreate the required scenes. Thorp's legal models were explanatory, designed to communicate what were often complex structural issues to people who had little or no technical knowledge, and quite rapidly Thorp found the demand for such models outstripping calls for architectural drawings. Until the outbreak of the First World War a substantial part of Thorp's business was given over to making these legal models, but by the mid-1890s the architects he had previously been providing drawings for had begun to order models from him as well; early commissions included a model of the Savoy hotel in 1898 and one of the proposed Jubilee Market at Covent Garden in 1899 (Figure 2.3). Thorp's income soared, and in 1902 he purchased the freehold of number 98 for £2600, moving his family into the flat above the offices. Models quickly became such a significant proportion of his business that sometime between 1906 and 1910, as evidenced by Thorp's stationery items and newspaper advertisements, although still registered as a business as the London Drawing and Tracing Office, Thorp began trading as John B. Thorp and exclusively marketed his work as an architectural modelmaker.

Thorp's models were radically different from most of the architectural models that the remaining building-trade carpenters and masons were producing at the time. His architectural training, while having only lasted a few years, had evidently equipped Thorp with an understanding of the principles of architectural design as opposed to

Figure 2.3 Model of Covent Garden Market, made by John Thorp, 1899.

Source: Image courtesy Thorp Archive, AUB.

the knowledge of architectural construction that earlier makers such as Richard Day had accumulated through their primary trades. Combined with the precision and accuracy he was required to achieve for his legal models, Thorp's architectural models demonstrated a strong appreciation of the ability of models to communicate and the vital role of context. Visually this translated into a greater sense of realism, with much greater attention being paid to fine detail and the inclusion of a portion of the existing landscape in which the proposed building was intended to be located. In 1900 Thorp was commissioned to make two hospital models for the World Exposition in Paris, and both included roads, paths, grassland, and trees, as well as boundary walls and other landscape features that had rarely ever been included in architectural models before. Both models were six feet square and made from a combination of timber and card, with billiard table felt used for grass and stained sponges for trees.[5] Combined, the two models cost £400, approximately £50,000 today, and took nine months to complete.[6] Thorp's model of an improvement scheme for Derby dating to around 1910 showed the proposed buildings in an even larger context, with minute details such as telegraph poles and railings being carefully represented, while a model of Angmering village demonstrated his impressive and realistic landscaping skills (Figure 2.4).

Effectively teaching himself the skills of architectural modelmaking while drawing from his art studies at the Royal Academy, Thorp employed an imaginative approach to materials that allowed for working in whichever medium provided the best solution for the model in question. Where previously craftsmen working in the material silos of their respective trades had found their materials and processes limiting the

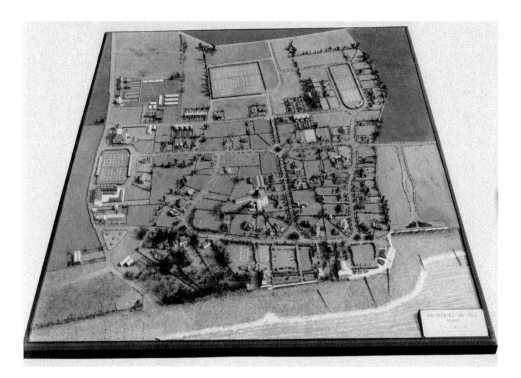

Figure 2.4 Model of Angmering-on-Sea, made by John Thorp, circa 1910.
Source: Image courtesy Thorp Archive, AUB.

scope for the design of a model, Thorp was able to conceive the finished model first and then select from the variety of materials and processes that would best realise it. For Thorp, modelmaking was as much a process of exploration as it was a craft; he was able to make decisions about the style, function, and cost of a model before determining the materials he was going to use (Figure 2.5).

In not being restricted to the use of a single material, as the earlier building-trade makers of architectural models had been, the models that Thorp produced varied quite significantly in terms of appearance, level of detail, and construction methods, depending on the needs and budgets of his clients. Thorp typically began his models with the construction of the baseboards, drawing a plan of the building in the centre. For legal models, compo-board – an early form of plasterboard – tended to be used, with Thorp noting that for presentation models for architects 'a more elaborate base, made from some choice timber, with moulded and polished edges, is required.'[7] For the buildings themselves Thorp used a variety of approaches and materials depending on what the model required and the client could afford. In 1906 he received a commission for a large and highly complex model of a proposed brewery in Wandsworth (Figure 2.6), and the model needed to separate into layers so that each floor could be removed and individually viewed.[8] With strength and repeated use being important considerations for the design of the model, Thorp used an all-timber construction; had card façades been applied, they would have been easily damaged through regular

Figure 2.5 John Thorp painting a timber and card architectural model, circa 1920.

Source: Image courtesy Thorp Archive, AUB.

Figure 2.6 Model of Wandsworth Brewery, made by John Thorp, 1907.

Source: Image courtesy Thorp Archive, AUB.

handling. For a 1905 riding school model Thorp used both timber and Bristol board, a combination of materials necessary to achieve a hollow dome; had the model not been a cut-through, a solid block of timber might have instead been turned on a lathe.

Around 1915, Thorp produced a set of sample models of the external façade of 98 Gray's Inn Road that could be shown to clients to illustrate three levels of detailing and the corresponding costs that came with them (Figure 2.7). The simplest, and cheapest, approach on offer was to cut thin sheets of timber and then clad them with cartridge paper, upon which the elevations were carefully drawn and coloured – the same approach that had become favoured within architectural practices during the end of the previous century. The intermediate level followed the same basic construction method but applied more detail in relief, such as columns, balustrades, and roof tiles. The most expensive option was for the entire model to be rendered in full relief, and for this sample model Thorp included window apertures backed with either celluloid sheet or gelatine, and if the model was to be internally lit, less flammable mica.[9] For smaller-scale buildings solid timber blocks were shaped and then clad. This combination of timber cores and card façades provided a reliable mix of strength and stability with a fineness of surface detail and realistic colouring (Figure 2.8). The use of

Figure 2.7 Sample model made by John Thorp, circa 1915.

Source: Image courtesy Thorp Archive, AUB.

Figure 2.8 Timber and card model made by John Thorp, 1917.

Source: Image courtesy Thorp Archive, AUB.

card also allowed Thorp to produce models at a lower cost than wholly timber ones,[10] and without as many specialist tools during the early days of his career. In 1901 Thorp wrote of cardboard models that 'the elevations should be drawn and then inked in [and] the whole then carefully cut up, care taken to bevel the corners so not to show a square joint.'[11] The drawing of two-dimensional elevations in card modelmaking was a natural fit for Thorp given his initial work as a draughtsman, though it is clear that from a very early stage he was making extensive use of timber and plaster where these materials were appropriate for a particular model.

Having been privately educated and tutored at the Royal Academy, John Thorp was quite literally of a different social class than the craft-based modelmakers who had preceded him, and his background could not have been more removed from that of Richard Day, who was largely uneducated, having begun working as a mason around the age of eight or nine. Where Day had been a skilled working-class tradesman, Thorp was very much a middle-class gentleman – of a typically Victorian entrepreneurial kind – who embraced the possibilities of business and marketing as well as his creative interests. An active member of his local masonic lodge, Thorp's connections undoubtedly aided his growing business, and having realised the uniqueness of what he was offering – the first dedicated commercial architectural modelmaker in the country, and quite possibly in the world – Thorp aggressively promoted his services and centred his marketing efforts on extolling the benefits that architectural models had to offer (Figure 2.9). A focus on efficiency and cost is clear in all of his publicity, outlining at

Figure 2.9 John Thorp's promotional stand, circa 1915.

Source: Image courtesy Thorp Archive, AUB.

first the problem that architects faced – convincing potential clients who had difficulty reading architectural drawings of the merit of particular designs – and then how he, as a modelmaker, could solve it: 'How frequently has an architect experienced a difficulty in getting a client to understand his working drawings, and had to prepare a perspective, sometimes more or less "faked", to bring out a certain feature.'[12] Noting that with a perspective, only one view can be obtained, Thorp highlighted that the cost of a model, 'which compares favourably with say two perspectives,' gave the client unlimited views for the price of two drawings.[13]

Thorp clearly took pride in his work and put a great deal of effort into both presenting his business and recording the publicity his efforts achieved. Investing in free gifts that he sent to potential clients, placing expensive adverts, and encouraging favourable editorials in the major architectural journals, Thorp employed modern business techniques to establish himself and generate future commissions. In 1900, he produced a complementary wall calendar promoting his work, while in both 1906 and 1913 he issued editions of a 'handy little booklet on models,'[14] sending copies to every architect in London. The booklet was illustrated with photographs of some of the many architectural models he had made for clients over the past decade, the accompanying text extolling the benefits of commissioning them. Suggesting that when an architect needed a model, they 'communicate with one, who from long experience and knowledge, could undertake to turn the work out in an efficient way,'[15] Thorp's innovative marketing efforts were well-received by the architectural press, one journal noting that 'as the use of models is now becoming so common we have no doubt readers will be glad to know where they can get them prepared.'[16]

With a strong reputation for high-quality work and a shrewd eye for marketing and publicity, John Thorp quickly established himself as a well-known architectural modelmaker in the capital, and for quite some time Thorp was also the only architectural modelmaker in London. Making good use of this monopoly, Thorp's marketing efforts led to a rapid growth in the business, and by 1906 he was employing an average of fifteen other modelmakers at any one time. Additional workshop space had been created using the flat at number 98, with Thorp having moved his family to a house in Chiswick. The make-up of Thorp's workforce would be very familiar to any modelmaker today: a core of long-serving, experienced staff supplemented by regular contract workers called upon whenever demand required and short-term help employed to work on specific projects. Frederick George Adcock, a trained architect, completed a single week's work for Thorp in 1908, and returned for short periods in 1911, 1913, 1919, and 1921, a pattern of repeat employment that many others followed. Having a pool of reliable contract workers to call upon meant Thorp was rarely forced to turn a job away, and their presence eased the pressure on Thorp's permanent team.

As the first specialist architectural modelmaker in the modern sense, Thorp was in the unique position whereby there were no other existing architectural modelmakers to employ, which meant that his staff came from understandably diverse backgrounds, hiring draughtsmen, industrial modelmakers, architect's clerks, and pattern makers, all based purely on the artistic and creative skills they had to offer. Many of these newly converted architectural modelmakers continued to work for Thorp for many years, if not decades. William Noyce spent nine years on contract working forty-five-hour weeks before joining the permanent roster for a further decade in 1919; Henry Pullinger worked for Thorp for at least fifteen years; and Percy Walker spent nearly thirty years with the company. By 1910, Thorp's core team of eight held a combined sixty years' experience as architectural modelmakers, and by the 1930s the figure had risen to one hundred and eighty years' experience.

In 1908, the growing company received a significant financial boost when Thorp put his long-standing interests in theatre and performance to profitable use and produced a series of large-scale historical models of the City of London as it was before the Great Fire of 1666, under the collective title 'Old London'[17] (Figure 2.10). Displayed at the Franco-British Exhibition at Shepherds Bush that year, the entrance fee of sixpence to view the models generated £7000 over the five months they were on display. A statement from the exhibition shows Thorp received a quarter share of the income, bringing him just under £2000 – around £150,000 today.[18] Over the next decade Thorp continued to offer the models for hire, before eventually becoming part of the Museum of London's collection, where several can still be seen today. The success of the models allowed Thorp to expand his premises by building a new workshop behind the offices at number 98 that he fitted out with the latest equipment,[19] while the popularity of the Old London models generated further demand for his company's work. By 1910, the workshop at Gray's Inn Road was described as having 'hundreds of models stored there,'[20] and in 1912 a section of the *Ideal Homes Exhibition* in

Figure 2.10 Model of Old London Bridge, made by John Thorp, 1908.
Source: Image courtesy Thorp Archive, AUB.

London was given over to a large display of models of houses Thorp had been commissioned to make especially for the event.

By the outbreak of the First World War, Thorp's business had grown into a major success, his financial reserves no doubt helping him to weather the steady decline in trade that followed during the conflict. Initially, business continued as normal, but as Thorp's payroll records show, his team quickly began to contract as more and more of his modelmakers either volunteered or were conscripted into the Army. A handful of long-serving modelmakers returned after the war, but many became casualties never to return. George Goodwin, who began working for Thorp aged fourteen, was drafted into the Army in 1915 and presumed killed later that same year. The anguish John Thorp must have felt when even his son Leslie, who had just begun to work alongside his father, was called up in 1917 can only be imagined.

Thorp was viewed by those who worked for him as kind and generous, and his open offer for departing soldiers to return to their old jobs after the war was likely greatly received. In 1917 Thorp offered employment to a disabled solider who had lost an eye, but after a week Thorp made a note in his records that the solider could not cope with the work and was released. Thorp also rewarded good work, securing talented modelmakers by increasing their wages after their first few weeks if they showed promise. One incident in particular demonstrates not only Thorp's generosity towards his staff but also something of the loyalty his team felt to the company. One of Thorp's earliest and longest-serving employees was Florence North, who began working for the company in 1909 as the company secretary. In September 1914, North was reported as absent for several weeks, and as staff were not routinely paid for sickness or other absences from work, on her return, John Thorp forwent his own salary of £4 a week and gave it to her. Mrs North then remained with the company for the rest of her life, eventually being bequeathed shares in the company alongside Leslie Thorp after John's death in 1939. It seems likely that North's husband had been killed in the war, with John's payment a typically kindly offer; however, no surviving records confirm precisely what happened.

The Profession Expands

After the war, Leslie Thorp returned from three years serving as an aircraft mechanic in the Royal Flying Corps and began working full-time alongside his father. After an unsettled few years during which new recruits came and went with quite a rapid turnover, Thorp's staffing numbers returned to their pre-war levels as business picked up once again. Major projects such as models of Industry House for ICI, the National Gallery, Cambridge University Library (Figure 2.11), the National Cash Register Company building (Figure 2.12), and the Royal Hospital School in Holbrook all added to the company's growing success – the latter model alone bringing in over £1000 in revenue.[21] Thorp's reputation was also growing, and the importance of his treatment of architectural modelmaking as a specialist business was beginning to be recognised. One trade journal wrote in 1924 that 'Few people have realised how much we owe to Mr John B. Thorp, who more than twenty years ago started making these most instructive and invaluable models,'[22] while another described an enormous model under construction in Thorp's workshop of an entire town with 'town hall, church,

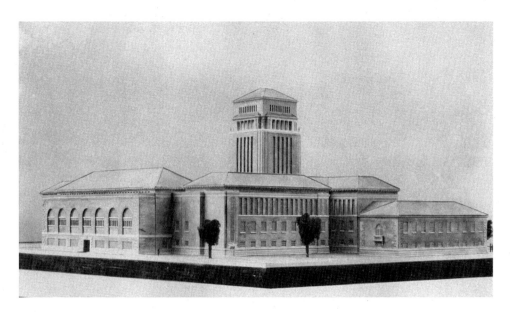

Figure 2.11 Model of Cambridge University Library, made by Thorp, 1931.
Source: Image courtesy Thorp Archive, AUB.

shops and other buildings, and also a park with a bandstand and a river, a large factory [and] a flower mill.'[23] It continued:

> This is a marvellous piece of work, and everything is correct even to the smallest details. There is a railway line which runs into the factory grounds, and model trains on the line, with miniature lorries and wagons all complete, and it gives the whole scheme a realistic appearance of industrial activity. Even a system of lighting has been efficiently installed, and a great variety of beautiful effects are obtained. The various buildings and even the trains are lighted in sections, as well as the small street lamps; and the lighting of the clock face in the town hall gives a charming finish to the whole model.[24]

The improvements that Thorp's dedicated approach had brought to the quality of architectural models did not go unnoticed by both the architectural profession and the public at large, generating a substantial increase in their demand during a period of extensive property-building during the inter-war years. After the First World War, however, Thorp's business was no longer the only commercial architectural model-making firm working in Britain, as having proved a company could thrive by tending to this niche industry, the inter-war years saw several competing architectural model-making companies being established. By 1925 J. W. Clarke and Cyril Sidney Ibbott were both advertising as architectural modelmakers in London, and Sidney Lloyd Young in the then brand-new town of Welwyn Garden City,[25] while by the early-1930s Cyril Mills had set up as an architectural modelmaker in Ruislip.[26] Alongside

Figure 2.12 Model of the National Cash Register Company Building, made by Thorp, 1935.
Source: Image courtesy Thorp Archive, AUB.

these, the inter-war years also saw the flourishing of two major competitors for Thorp – Twining Models and Partridge's Models. Ernest Twining had begun making models for Bassett-Lowke in Northampton in 1912, while Leslie Partridge established his business in London around 1920 after returning from service as an Army officer during the war. Partridge's were advertising as early as 1922 and continued trading after Leslie Partridge's death in 1947 until the late-1960s. The company became well known for a substantial model of the proposed new Bank of England made in 1925, which twenty-five years later was still proudly featured on its letterhead, the company advertising as 'Model Makers to H. M. Government – The Bank of England, etc.'[27] Work on models of the proposed Guildford Cathedral, the Quarry Hill Estate in Leeds, and a new library for Leeds City Council soon followed as Partridge's business grew (Figures 2.13 and 2.14).

Many of these new architectural modelmakers closely followed the template John Thorp had established, Leslie Partridge notably copying Thorp's success with models of historic London, which in their adverts appeared suspiciously similar to Thorp's own work. It is unlikely to be a coincidence that Thorp engaged the services of the legal company W. P. Thompson, a specialist in intellectual property infringements, in 1921, the same time that Partridge's began advertising. While Partridge's appears to

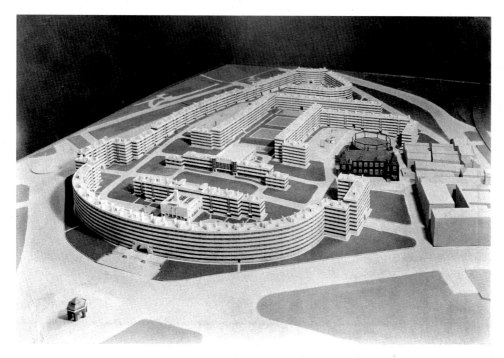

Figure 2.13 Model of Quarry Hill, Leeds, made by Partridge's Models, 1935.

Source: By kind permission of Leeds Libraries, www.leodis.net.

Figure 2.14 Model of Leeds Central Library, made by Partridge's Models, 1936.

Source: By kind permission of Leeds Libraries, www.leodis.net.

have sailed a little too close to the wind for John Thorp's liking, there was no denying that his approach of using multiple materials to achieve a high degree of realism was a worthwhile template to follow. Put simply, it was how architectural models were understood to be made during the inter-war years, it being noted in 1926 that 'there is no hard and fast rule for the use of a particular material, but the builder should utilise any which is appropriate for the purpose and will yield the desired result.'[28]

For Thorp and his growing number of new competitors there was plenty of work to go around due to an accelerated demand for architectural models because of the housing boom that followed the First World War. During the 1920s and 1930s, four million new homes were constructed in Britain, with many slums being cleared in a large-scale transition from high-density housing to suburban living that resulted in some twelve million people being re-housed.[29] Exhibitions such as *New Homes for Old* toured the country during the 1930s, using architectural models to demonstrate to the public the plans that were being proposed. From slum clearances in the major cities – Leeds seeing a quarter of its housing, some thirty thousand back-to-back terraces, being demolished – to the garden city experiments at Letchworth and Welwyn, models were frequently used to both educate and sell these new ways of living. Photographs of models were also in great demand to provide content for the boom in illustrated magazines during the same period. This was particularly the case for the *Architects' Journal*, which began to make heavy use of model photography to illustrate articles about the work of new modernist architects such as Le Corbusier and Lubetkin.[30]

At the same time, the inter-war years also saw an expansion of public interest in modelmaking itself, with many books and periodicals dedicated to both architectural and general modelmaking being published. The making, collecting, and even playing with models became a popular adult pastime during this period, with boats, railways, and houses being the principal subjects of interest. Central to this movement was the publisher and champion of model engineering, Percival Marshall. Marshall established a publishing house that produced a wide range of books and periodicals that both responded to, and fuelled, a boom in hobbyist modelmaking. Other publishers soon followed, with titles such as *Pictorial House Modelling*,[31] *Models of Buildings: How to Make and Use Them*,[32] *Model Maker's Workshop*,[33] and *The Craft of Model Making*[34] being just a selection of architecturally focussed titles within an enormous range of modelmaking topics that were covered. Marshall was well-connected in the hobbyist modelmaking and model engineering scenes, and he was an acquaintance of John Thorp, having delivered a paper in tribute of Thorp's achievements at the Institute of Junior Engineers in 1902.[35] His connections proved especially useful when in 1899 Wenman Bassett-Lowke approached him for his advice in setting up a mail-order model engineering supplies company. Marshall provided Bassett-Lowke with a list of contacts, and the company went on to become the country's largest supplier of railway and ship models, based in Northampton.

In 1908, Bassett-Lowke opened a showroom in Holborn in London, not far from Thorp's workshops at 98 Gray's Inn Road, recruiting the marine architect Edward W. Hobbs as the manager. Through Percival Marshall's publishing firm, Hobbs also authored many books on modelmaking, varying from ship building and model engineering to timber turning and architectural modelmaking. With Bassett-Lowke's increased presence in London, the firm soon began to receive commissions for architectural models, even though these were quite removed from their usual hobby-orientated models of steam locomotives and battleships. As many industrial modelmakers found during this period, the growing public interest in amateur modelmaking could be suc-cessfully married with supplying models for industry, and Bassett-Lowke rarely turned away any customer, whether the models were for home display or professional use.

In 1912, the firm began the construction of its first architectural model, a large diorama of Blackpool seafront; however, halfway through the project Bassett-Lowke's newly hired architectural modelmaker Berthold Audsley announced he was emigrating to the United States. Audsley had previously worked as an interior decorator and fur-niture maker for his architect father and began making cardboard models as a hobby.[36] After his brief employment as a professional modelmaker for just a few months with Bassett-Lowke, Audsley later became known as the 'foremost cardboard modeller in the world' – at least to American audiences – having pursued a successful career as one of the first dedicated architectural modelmakers in New Jersey, including a long period working for General Electric.[37] With Audsley's departure imminent, Bassett-Lowke invited Ernest Twining (Figure 2.15), a thirty-seven-year-old telephone cabling engineer and amateur model locomotive builder from Bristol whom he had known for several years, to complete the model.[38] Twining was likely introduced to Bassett-Lowke through Percival Marshall, who had already published numerous articles by Twining in his model engineering titles. Accepting the commission, Twining moved to Northampton to continue to work on further architectural models that Bassett-Lowke had been approached to make, including two large models of Port Sunlight in 1913 that contained fully glazed buildings that were internally lit from below[39] (Figure 2.16).

Figure 2.15 Ernest Twining at work, 1913.

Source: Image courtesy Northamptonshire County Archives.

Figure 2.16 Model of Port Sunlight, made by Ernest Twining, 1913.
Source: Image courtesy Northamptonshire County Archives.

For the next twenty-seven years Ernest Twining made every architectural model that left Bassett-Lowke's workshop, despite never actually working for the company. As with much of his business, Bassett-Lowke acted as a commissioning agent, sub-contracting all the architectural work to Twining, who set up his own company and eventually moved from Bassett-Lowke's facility and established his own workshop nearby in Dychurch Lane in Northampton. Bassett-Lowke encouraged Twining to take on his own commissions directly from other clients when his workload permitted, though in practice his company appears to have operated as a direct subordinate to Bassett-Lowke. All architectural models that have been credited to Bassett-Lowke were in fact made by Twining, putting his architectural output at around two hundred models during his career.[40] Business quickly boomed, and in 1914 Twining recruited Harry Clifton as a workshop foreman straight from school, the pair continuing to make models for Bassett-Lowke during the First World War, providing both ship recognition and landscape models.[41] As with Thorp, Twining quickly found enough work to warrant employing additional modelmakers, reaching a peak of around eight staff by the late-1930s, and from 1920 he was advertising solely as an architectural modelmaker.

Twining's models were often quite large and highly detailed in an attempt to be as realistic as possible, even going to the extremes of ensuring that the trees on his models were of the correct species for the location (Figure 2.17). For most of the models, timber and cardboard were the principal materials used, with timber for the internal structure and card used for the façades – just as Thorp had been using them. Bristol board and other forms of card were still popular materials during the inter-war years, with various timbers and cork continuing to be used alongside newer materials such as timber veneers and plasticine.[42] Shrubs and flock wallpapers could be purchased from the art supplier Sanders & Sons in London, who also stocked basic modelmaking materials.[43]

A major difference between Twining's models and those being produced by John Thorp was that most of Twining's models were of industrial buildings. Factories proved to be the main commissions Twining received, indicative of his location outside of London, away from most architectural offices and closer to the industrial heartlands of the midlands. Despite the differences in the types of models being made by the two companies, however, the same strive for realism was shared by both. In an advertising brochure not unlike Thorp's 1913 publication, Ernest Twining wrote that 'we pride ourselves on the fact that not only in the wealth of detail of an artificial nature . . . but also in the reproduction of landscapes, we have reached a point which we claim to be as near to perfection as possible.'[44] This desire for as realistic models as possible was boosted not only by the advancement of construction methods that Thorp and Twining were exploring but also through the improvement of their workshop facilities. Machine tools had progressed to the stage where the modern band saw, self-contained milling machine, precision lathes, and pillar drills had become available, and both Thorp and Twining frequently updated their equipment. In 1924, John Thorp's workshop was already benefiting from electric lighting and electrically

Figure 2.17 Model of Bourneville Works, made by Twining Models, 1920.

Source: Image courtesy Northamptonshire County Archives.

Figure 2.18 Thorp modelmaking workshop, 1924.

Source: Image courtesy Thorp Archive, AUB.

powered table saws, alongside a variety of hand tools (Figure 2.18); one observer noting that 'Mr Thorp's workshops are equipped in the most excellent fashion with all the most modern machinery.'[45]

By the end of the 1920s, Thorp's initial success in establishing architectural modelmaking as a dedicated commercial occupation had spread well beyond his own company at 98 Gray's Inn Road, and through Partridge's Models, Twining Models, and others, the skills of the professional architectural modelmaker had become highly admired. In the United States, the arrival of British modelmakers such as Berthold Audsley, William McCallum, and H. E. Woodsend had helped establish the first footings of the profession there during the 1910s and early-1920s, with an American article on the role of the modelmaker arguing that 'a model should be made by an artist and a craftsman. . . . The modelmaker should be familiar with the fundamental principles of architectural design so that he can interpret the architect's ideas with the minimum of effort and supervision.'[46]

In Britain, William Harvey wrote in 1927 that he was 'firmly convinced that modelmaking is a necessary part of architectural design'[47] and that 'professional model-makers can be trusted to make faithful representations to scale in minute detail.'[48] In America, despite no modelmakers as yet reaching the levels of success experienced by Thorp or Twining in Britain, it was deemed prudent by the end of the 1930s that, while architects were frequently making their own sketch models, 'it pays in this as in other important matters to go to a specialist, a professional modelmaker.'[49] That there were such established specialists in Britain advertising and promoting their services no doubt meant that architects found it much easier to commission models, having enough business to sustain a growing number of architectural modelmaking companies during the inter-war years and turning the fledgling profession into a small but recognised industry.

In just a few decades John Thorp had completed the transformation of architectural modelmaking from a side pursuit belonging to craftsmen within the building trades into a dedicated profession. Architectural modelmaking was now not just a possible career, as Richard Day and C. N. Thwaite had proved it could be, but a viable business with multiple employees. The architectural historian Sir John Summerson, in writing about the professionalisation of the architect, noted that it was not simply the architect's ability to draw that separated them from the craftsmen builders who had preceded them, but 'their state of mind.'[50] Summerson's observation equally applies to the professionalisation of architectural modelmaking, in that it was not Thorp's mastery of a particular material or medium that separated him from earlier makers of architectural models but his attention to the process of modelmaking itself. Models, as Thorp saw them, were beautiful objects but also practical ones. They had a job to fulfil and had to be completed on time and within a budget that was acceptable to the client, and with an appropriate profit margin to keep the business sustainable. Mixing materials was a large part of achieving this efficiency, as were attempts to move towards hollow-model construction, making them lighter and cheaper to build, but ultimately Thorp had identified a market and developed the architectural model into a product that could be successfully sold to that market (Figure 2.19). Having seized

Figure 2.19 Architectural model made by Thorp, circa 1930.

Source: Image courtesy Thorp Archive, AUB.

the opportunity presented by the gradual liberation of architectural modelmaking from within the building trades during the nineteenth century, John Thorp established a template for the profession that would remain until the present day.

As the success of Thorp and the others who followed his example both drove and responded to demand, however, the eagerness of the first generation of professional architectural modelmakers during the inter-war years began to push the architectural model to new levels of sophistication that, while demonstrating the extent to which the model had been transformed by the emergence of the profession dedicated to their making, raised serious questions over the suitability of the materials being used as architectural models ballooned in both size and complexity. A quest for alternative materials and methods of construction began that, while cut short by the outbreak of the Second World War, served to highlight the tantalising potential of plastics in revolutionising how architectural models could be made.

Notes

1 Thorp Modelmakers, 'A History of John B. Thorp,' 1983, 1, Thorp Modelmaking Archive.
2 'The London Drawing & Tracing Office,' *The Builder*, November 27, 1897, press cutting, Thorp Modelmaking Archive.
3 'Architectural Models,' *The Builder's Journal*, July 4, 1906, press cutting, Thorp Modelmaking Archive.
4 John Thorp, *Models of Buildings, Estates, Works, etc. for Exhibitions or Law Cases* (London: London Drawing & Tracing Office, 1913).
5 'Two Interesting Models,' *The Builder's Journal*, February 21, 1900, press cutting, Thorp Modelmaking Archive.
6 A. Soutar, 'Made in Court,' *The Strand Magazine*, May, 1910, 614.
7 John Thorp, quoted in P. Collins, 'Architectural Modelmaking,' *American Homes and Garden*, Vol. 12, No. 8 (1915), 262.
8 Thorp, *Models*, 17–21.
9 Collins, 'Architectural Modelmaking,' 263.
10 Karen Moon, *Modelling Messages* (New York: Monacelli Press, 2005), 146.
11 John Thorp, 'How to Make Models of Buildings,' *The Builder's Journal*, January 9, 1901, press cutting, Thorp Modelmaking Archive.
12 Thorp, *Models*, 13–16.
13 Ibid.
14 'Editorial,' *The Builder's Reporter*, September 18, 1906, press cutting, Thorp Modelmaking Archive.
15 Thorp, *Models*, 3–4.
16 'Architectural Models,' *The Builder's Journal*.
17 Soutar, 'Made in Court,' 613.
18 The receipts from the 1908 exhibition still survive as part of the Thorp Modelmaking archive.
19 Thorp Modelmakers, 'A History of John B. Thorp,' 4.
20 Soutar, 'Made in Court,' 614.
21 Thorp Modelmakers, 'A History of John B. Thorp,' 4.
22 'The Fascination of Models,' *The Building News*, March 28, 1924, specially reprinted copy of the original article made by John Thorp, Thorp Modelmaking Archive.
23 Adrian Gaunt, 'The Value of Models,' *The Illustrated Country Review*, November, 1924, specially reprinted copy of the original article made by John Thorp, Thorp Modelmaking Archive.
24 Ibid.
25 S. Lloyd Young to L. Bradley, June 17, 1925, letter, Imperial War Museum Archives.
26 Cyril Mills to L. Bradley, January 26, 1932, letter, Imperial War Museum Archives.

27 I. Partridge to L. Bradley, January 31, 1950, letter, Imperial War Museum Archives.
28 Edward Hobbs, *Pictorial House Modelling* (London: Crosby Lockwood and Son, 1926), 15.
29 Peter Scott, *The Making of the Modern British Home* (Oxford: OUP, 2013), 233.
30 Davide Deriu, 'The Architectural Model in the Age of its Mechanical Reproducibility,' in *Proceedings of the Second International Conference of the European Architectural History Network, Brussels, 2012* (Brussels: Contactforum, 2012), 166–170.
31 Edward Hobbs, *Pictorial House Modelling* (London: Crosby Lockwood and Son, 1926).
32 William Harvey, *Models of Buildings: How to Make and Use Them* (London: Architectural Press, 1927).
33 Edward Hobbs, *Model Maker's Workshop* (London: Percival Marshall, 1934).
34 Thomas Bayley, *The Craft of Model Making* (Leicester: Dryad Press, 1938).
35 Soutar, 'Made in Court,' 614.
36 H. Asbury, 'He Has Built Fame with Cardboard,' *Popular Science Monthly*, June, 1920, 54.
37 Ibid; Hobbs, *Pictorial House Modelling*, xi.
38 Stan Buck, *Ernest Twining: Model Maker Artist & Engineer* (Ashbourne: Landmark Press, 2004), 11.
39 Berthold Audsley, 'Miniatures and their Value in Architectural Practice,' *The Brick Builder*, September, 1914, 216.
40 Buck, *Ernest Twining*, 85.
41 Ibid, 82.
42 Hobbs, *Pictorial House Modelling*, 14; Harvey, *Models of Buildings*, 86; Bayley, *The Craft of Model Making*, 7.
43 Hobbs, *Pictorial House Modelling*, 118.
44 Ernest Twining, 'Models for Advertising,' circa 1936, 5, Northamptonshire County Archives.
45 'The Fascination of Models,' *The Building News*.
46 LeRoy Grumbine, 'The Use of Scale Models as an Aid to the Architect,' *The Western Architect*, June, 1925, 60–61.
47 Harvey, *Models of Buildings*, vii.
48 Ibid, 26.
49 Robert Murray, 'Models and Scotch,' *Pencil Points*, July, 1939, 429.
50 John Summerson, *Architecture in Britain 1530 to 1830* (London: Penguin, 1954), 62.

Chapter 3

Growth and Expansion

By the start of the 1930s, the newly formed profession of architectural modelmaking in Britain had begun to mature, with the success of Thorp, Partridge's Models, and Twining Models demonstrating the full potential of architectural models when made by specialist modelmakers. Despite the economic turmoil that followed the 1929 stock market crash, the demand for architectural models skyrocketed in the decade that followed due to an extensive house-building program and a general recognition of the value of architectural models by both architects and the public. This strong demand, combined with their improved quality in the hands of a growing number of dedicated professionals, was having a dramatic effect on the models that were being produced. Quite simply, they were getting larger, heavier, and more expensive. Even singular models of proposed buildings were becoming ever more sophisticated and costly, being made at larger scales than had previously been the norm (Figure 3.1). While clearly highlighting the significant advances that had taken place because of the professionalisation of architectural modelmaking, such models also demonstrated the rapidly increasing costs associated with making them, ultimately pushing the architectural model to the limits of what architects could afford.

The Inter-War Years Boom

The period between the two World Wars not only saw a significant growth in the size of architectural models but also in the size of the profession, and while Thorp was still by far the dominant player, there were at least seven other specialist architectural modelmaking companies operating in Britain by the start of the 1930s. After the unsettled years immediately following the First World War, staff turnover at Thorp had slowed during the 1920s, stabilising with a core of regular staff who mostly remained in place for the next fifteen years. By the early 1930s, Thorp was employing an average of eighteen modelmakers each week, growing to over twenty by 1937.

Despite modelmaking being a very male-dominated profession, especially with industrial modelmaking having evolved from the role of the pattern maker, during the early-twentieth century a small but not-insignificant number of women began to be recorded as working as modelmakers across several fields, including architectural modelmaking. Ten percent of the modelmakers listed in the 1911 census were female, producing wax models, figurative models, yacht and ship models, and even retail models for shop fitters. Annie Solman, Edith Coomber, Elizabeth Dean, Lena Friend, and around fifteen others were all recorded as working as modelmakers in London,

DOI: 10.4324/9781003298007-4

Figure 3.1 Model of Bush House, made by Thorp, 1929.
Source: Image courtesy Thorp Archive, AUB.

although it is notable that women were generally restricted to the 'softer' elements of the occupation – making fabric sails for boat models, for example. This was an attitude that persisted for quite some time, with a book on professional modelmaking written in 1952 noting in a chapter entitled 'A Career for Girls' that 'while some of the tasks require the knowledge of heavy trades such as metal-working and joinery, some of the work is eminently suitable for the deft touch of gentle fingers,' suggesting models of soft furnishings and landscapes as suitable tasks for women.[1]

It is difficult to ascertain precisely how many women were working for Thorp during the early-twentieth century as photographs of modelmakers at work during this period almost exclusively only show men (Figure 3.2). Additionally, the surnames and initials of the employees listed in Thorp's records do not always allow for their gender to be determined. Florence North, for example, who worked for the company for forty-seven years and was made a shareholder in the business alongside Leslie Thorp in John's will, is simply listed as F. North in the wages book, and her gender is only revealed in legal papers dating to the late-1930s. A Mrs Harris certainly worked for Thorp between 1906 and 1917, while a Miss Groebel briefly joined the company in 1939. Harris at least appears to have been a full-time modelmaker rather than a secretary or cleaner, as might have been more common roles for women at the time, and a photograph taken in Thorp's workshop for *American Homes and Gardens* in 1915

Figure 3.2 Thorp modelmakers at work, circa 1938.

Source: Image courtesy Thorp Archive, AUB.

clearly shows a woman standing behind an architectural model. Whether this was Mrs North, Mrs Harris, or possibly even John Thorp's wife, Annie, remains unknown.

Thorp was not alone in employing female modelmakers, with Edward Hobbs' 1926 book on architectural modelmaking including a note of thanks to a 'Miss Joyce Inall' for preparing all of the demonstration models used in the book, the photographs of her making them confirming that she was indeed a skilled architectural modelmaker. With Hobbs working for Bassett-Lowke, and Twining Models also thanked in the book for the inclusion of images of their work, it is likely that Inall may have worked for Ernest Twining in Northampton. William Harvey's 1927 book on architectural modelmaking also refers to a 'Miss Swift' making models[2] – although in both cases little information survives regarding their respective careers.

The overwhelming majority of the profession's workforce remained male, however, and the expansion of modelmaking as an occupation, and the shift of pattern makers becoming industrial modelmakers, meant there was a much wider pool of skilled workers for Thorp, Twining, and other architectural modelmaking firms to draw from. By the 1930s, former pattern making companies such as Braun and Company; Crawford and Sons; and Marshall, Stewart, and Sons were advertising as modelmakers first, pattern makers second. Having initially focused on purely mechanical engineering models, an increased demand for scenic models and dioramas for museum and exhibition display meant their skills began to overlap with those of the architectural modelmaker. The Models Manufacturing Company, which specialised in aircraft models, also advertised that it could take on architectural work during the 1920s,[3] and by the 1930s, the role of the industrial modelmaker had broadened into being a generalised modelmaker, producing whatever types of models were required, whether for industry, exhibition, or architecture. Due to the dominance of the specialist firms such as Thorp, Twining, and Partridge's, however, the architectural sides of these businesses remained quite small until well after the Second World War. Taking advantage of this expansion of modelmaking as an industry, however, John Thorp cannily opened the material stores at 98 Gray's Inn Road to sell to his competitors and the public, the ground floor shop becoming a major supplier of modelmaking supplies in London until its eventual establishment as a separate retail business, 4D Modelshop, in the 1990s.

A consequence of the growth of generalised modelmaking, and the presence of competing architectural modelmaking firms, was that by the mid-1930s Thorp was able to recruit existing modelmakers with prior experience for the first time. Alongside these established modelmakers other recruits included Francis Bull, a scenic artist, and Arthur Werrett, a registered architect and watercolourist, while a specialist electrician was even kept on the books for whenever models required lighting or movement. A growing community of architectural modelmakers had also begun to establish itself, with Thorp, Twining, and Bassett-Lowke all known to one another. In 1935, Edward Hobbs, the manager of Bassett-Lowke's London showroom, and by then a prolific author of books on modelmaking, began working part-time hours for Thorp whenever demand was high.

By the end of the 1930s, five of Thorp's staff each had over twenty years' experience, a further nine had over a decade, and over the course of the thirty years leading up to the Second World War, of the one hundred and forty people who worked for the company, half had stayed for at least a year. Thorp's modelmakers were also well-paid, his most senior regulars earning between £2 and £4 a week, considerably higher than the average salary for skilled manual work at the time. Professionals, whether at Thorp or elsewhere, were by this point the dominant force behind the making of architectural models in Britain. Whenever major new buildings or planning schemes were ready to be communicated to either clients or the public, professional modelmakers such as Thorp were hired. While architectural assistants continued to make sketch models, few architects considered making their own presentation models given the high quality of work that was on offer from Thorp, Twining, and others.

The option of employing the services of dedicated professional modelmakers was by this time no longer unique to Britain, but in both Europe and America it remained far more common for architects and their assistants to be making whatever architectural models were required. In France and Germany a number of individual modelmakers appear to have been working during the 1930s, although most continued to be sculptors and joiners taking on model commissions as asides to their full-scale work, while in the United States Theodore Conrad established his own modelmaking workshop in New York in 1931, having discovered the potential of commercial modelmaking while working for the architect and champion of the architectural model Harvey Wiley Corbet as a student.[4] Conrad's post-war career was to dominate American modelmaking for several decades, but during the 1930s, aside from Conrad and the California-based modelmaker LeRoy Grumbine, modelmaking was largely carried out within architectural practices by architects themselves, or by former architects who had lost their jobs after the 1929 stock market crash and who turned to making models as alternative employment.[5]

With the role of the professional architectural modelmaker firmly established in Britain, however, their rapidly accumulating experience was having a direct impact on the quality of the models that companies such as Thorp were able to offer. With each new model the scale seemingly became larger, the detail became crisper, the construction more seamless, and the surroundings more realistic. The popularity of highly detailed planning models, often for public exhibition, further pushed both the size and complexity of architectural models towards ever-increasing extremes, a trend that was inevitably accompanied by a commensurate increase in costs. In 1921, Ernest Twining produced a large model of Cardiff docks for the Great Western Railway that showed every building, railway line, and siding over several scale miles (Figure 3.3), while in 1924 Thorp produced a similar yet even larger model of Hull docks for display at the British Empire Exhibition in Wembley that was over forty feet long and seven feet wide (Figure 3.4). The model included every dock, warehouse, crane, bridge, hedge, and tree,[6] and it was only outdone at the exhibition by a similarly sized model of Liverpool docks that included moving ships.[7]

The same exhibition also contained many hundreds, if not thousands, of models of all types. Large and impressive models were the main attractions in many of the exhibits at Wembley, with the Port of London Authority's pavilion alone including an entire hall dedicated to them. Several architectural and engineering models for the exhibition were built by Ernest Twining, with countless more being supplied by other modelmakers whose identities have since been lost. Spotting an opportunity to provide such three-dimensional exhibits, John Thorp's younger son, Eric, having studied art at the City of London School before later becoming a noted marine artist, established Thorp Studios in 1936, specialising in making high-quality exhibition stands, models, and window displays. The company produced a number of high-profile exhibition displays for several British Government departments before ceasing to trade in 1940 due to the lack of business in wartime.[8]

Theatrics were fast becoming expected in exhibition models, and in 1924 Ernest Twining's company made a large and highly complex model for the American National

Figure 3.3 Model of Cardiff docks, made by Twining Models, 1921.

Source: Image courtesy Northamptonshire County Archives.

Figure 3.4 Model of Hull docks, made by Thorp, 1924.

Source: Image courtesy Thorp Archive, AUB.

Cash Register Works that was constructed almost entirely from sheet metal, with glass windows built in to give visibility to the fully electric internal lighting system that illuminated the model from ventilated troughs containing low-wattage light bulbs.[9] The use of such lighting in architectural models was becoming increasingly common in larger models made during the 1920s, with Thorp having built a 1:24 scale model of the London Coliseum that included a five-stage lighting system that used two hundred and fifty twenty-watt lamps and fifty dimmers to operate a choreographed lighting sequence.[10]

As the size and complexity of such models increased, so too did the cost of making them. A sectional model of a suburban house made by Thorp to demonstrate a hot water installation system cost the National Radiator Company £3,600,[11] while Thorp's most famous model, that of Edwin Lutyens' design for Liverpool Cathedral, occupied ten modelmakers for an entire year in 1934 at the cost of £5,000, over £200,000 today[12] (Figure 3.5). The all-timber Liverpool model was an enormous construction, with five modelmakers including Henry Bull, W. Shepherd, and Frank Dodsworth hired specifically to boost Thorp's team to allow them to continue with smaller projects so as not to paralyse the entire business while the Liverpool project rumbled on. The model's construction was further aided by the availability by the

Figure 3.5 Leslie Thorp with the Liverpool Cathedral model, 1934.

Source: Image courtesy Thorp Archive, AUB.

1930s of more advanced workshop machinery that contained integral electric motors, Thorp having invested in the very latest equipment to replace his older machines that were powered by belt drives drawing from a common transfer shaft. A catalogue of machine tools from the time lists two hundred and thirty-eight machines for sale, of which only eleven contain electric motors; the vast majority were still belt-driven as late as the 1930s,[13] indicating how forward-thinking Thorp was when it came to investing in equipment. With electric pistol-grip hand drills, radial arm table saws, and electric disk and belt sanders having been introduced during the 1920s, the availability of motor-driven machinery undoubtedly served to speed up the modelmaker's work. Further gigantic models, such as the Charing Cross scheme described in the introduction, were contriving to push the boundaries of architectural modelmaking to its limits.

Ernest Twining's largest and most dramatic project was a pair of dioramas of Bournemouth that was displayed in Waterloo Station in 1934 (Figure 3.6). Encompassing the entire town, the models included over four thousand individual buildings, each with an average of ten windows that allowed interior lighting to shine through. Two thousand vehicles were added to the models along with location-appropriate trees and shrubs. Twining cleverly designed the models to include an element of forced perspective – the scale shrinking from 1:550 at the front to a much smaller scale at the rear, where they merged with highly detailed painted backdrops. A timed lighting

Figure 3.6 Model of Bournemouth, made by Twining Models, 1934.

Source: Image courtesy Northamptonshire County Archives.

sequence lit both models with white for daylight, orange for mornings and evenings, and a blue hue for moonlight.[14]

Although the cost of the Bournemouth models is unknown, Twining's method of estimating his prices was based on a standard charge-out rate that included all overheads and expenses plus a small profit margin for each man hour the model required. To this was added the actual cost of materials, and for models sold through Bassett-Lowke an additional thirty-three percent was charged for their own costs and profits – which no doubt did much to contribute towards price inflation.[15] Clients were evidently accepting these costs, however, and a strong desire for elements of showmanship and spectacle appears to have been behind the increased commissioning of larger and more complex models. Just as Thorp's Old London models had shown before the First World War, the public were deeply attracted to large, well-presented models, and displaying one to promote a proposed scheme was a sure way to gain attention, as was the case with Twining's model of a concrete city of the future designed by Marcel Breuer for the 1936 *Ideal Homes Exhibition* (Figure 3.7).

Models such as these were, however, reaching the limits of affordability. Thorp's 1913 claim that a good model should cost no more than two perspective drawings had been continually repeated by others,[16] as was the idea that models ought to cost no

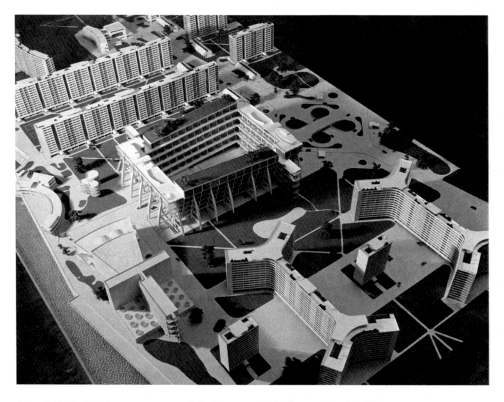

Figure 3.7 Model of a concrete city of the future, made by Twining Models, 1936.

Source: Image courtesy RIBA Collections.

more than one percent of the total cost of a building.[17] Nevertheless, a perception was developing that architectural models were both costly and difficult to make, with rising costs and high demand pushing up prices.[18] In a 1936 article, architectural modelmaker Kenneth McCutchon attempted to counter this opinion by stressing that 'models are not so costly as is generally supposed,' noting that the price of a model was ultimately determined by the requirements of the client in terms of quality and finish, before outlining a range of ways in which models could be specified that would allow them to be made at a lower cost.[19] As well as increasingly being viewed as expensive, the weight of models was also becoming a problem, and this was largely down to the use of timber – if not for the buildings themselves, but for the base, which had to be strong enough to support the model and survive transport, which could sometimes include travel abroad. A large timber model was therefore extremely heavy, time consuming, and expensive to build and deliver, while card, despite being cheaper, lighter, and quicker to work with, was much more susceptible to the effects of wear and humidity and not sufficiently rigid to be used without internal timber supports. Consequently, throughout the inter-war years there was a growing awareness that the standard materials of architectural modelmaking were potentially no longer the most suitable choices as models began to grow to such extremes of size and complexity (Figure 3.8).

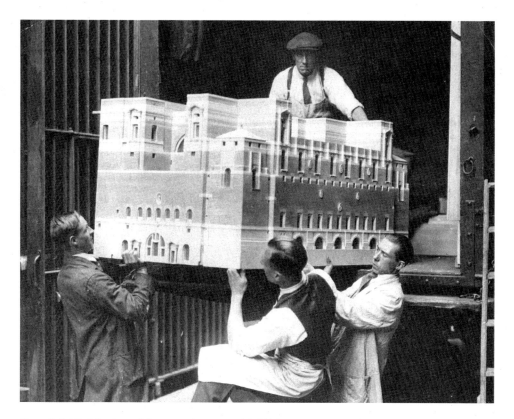

Figure 3.8 Modelmakers delivering a heavy model, 1934.

Source: Image courtesy Thorp Archive, AUB.

With these problems in mind, throughout the 1920s and 1930s, modelmakers began to keenly explore potential alternatives to the traditional materials of timber and card. In 1926 Edward Hobbs described the 'considerable skill and manipulative dexterity coupled with originality of thought [that] is required in the construction of these elaborate models,' adding that 'many different materials are pressed into service and in some cases in a most unlikely manner, yet with pleasing and satisfactory results.'[20] One American commentator at the time also wrote that 'The practitioners of the art of model making are almost invariably good resourceful craftsmen and the ingenuity which they show in finding and adapting accessory materials for various details is amazing,'[21] with another deftly summarising the modelmaker's attitude towards materials, noting:

> Modelmaking, it appears, is essentially the adaptation of numerous tools and materials to purposes for which they were not originally intended. Thus, the success of a modelmaker often depends upon his imaginative use and ingenious adaptation of available tools and materials to meet his own particular requirements. It is this quest for new methods, tools and materials that makes modelmaking [an] interesting occupation.[22]

Given the pressures they were facing, architectural modelmakers at the time were constantly open to exploring the potential of new substances, especially if they were lighter or cheaper. This exploration of new materials is particularly evidenced by the publication of Edward Hobbs' 1932 book *Modern Handicraft Materials and Methods*, which acknowledged that 'one of the most interesting developments of chemical science during recent years has been the production of many new materials adapted to the requirements of the amateur worker, the craftsman and the creative artist.'[23] The focus of the book was on 'synthetic materials,' with the aim of explaining the characteristics of these new materials and the best ways of working with them. These materials were the early plastics, and Hobbs described the properties and potential applications of, among others, Nacrolaque, an artificial timber inlay; Cristalux and Celastoid, translucent acetate sheets; and Bakelite (phenol formaldehyde), the first fully synthetic plastic. Lactoid (casein) had also become available in both sheet and rod form, making it suitable for carving into small details such as model furniture,[24] but none of these materials presented themselves as viable alternatives to card and timber for the bulk of architectural model construction. While these new materials failed to offer much promise to architectural modelmakers, the fact that Hobbs' book was published suggests there was a growing sense that the ongoing development of new plastics might potentially be of use to them, particularly as lightweight replacements for heavy glass, which was still often being used in models that featured internal lighting. Celluloid had been used as a glazing material by Thorp as early as 1905, although its rapid discolouration rendered it unsuitable for permanent use.[25] Its high flammability also ruled out its use where models were to be lit.

In 1938, however, just two years after its commercial introduction, Thomas Bayley commented in his book *The Craft of Model Making* on the suitability of a brand new transparent material, Perspex, for use in models as a lightweight glazing material.[26] Listing Perspex alongside both clay and plaster as 'plastics' – the broadest use of the term in reference to their general plasticity – Bayley hinted that the 'new materials also known as plastics [might be] very useful to the model maker.'[27] Quite how revolutionary Perspex was going to be to the professional modelmaker would not be realised until after the Second World War, and while its benefits as a glazing material were immediately recognised, it is unclear how widely acknowledged it was at the time that plastics might offer a potential solution to the growing problem of weight and cost that the success of the professional modelmaker had effectively created.

Modelmaking in the Plastics Age

Initially developed as the result of a demand for a laminated interlayer for safety glass that could replace the badly yellowing cellulose nitrate, Perspex was first developed by the British chemicals company ICI in 1931,[28] while at almost precisely the same time identical materials were also being developed quite independently by Rohm and Hass in Germany, who named their material 'Plexiglass,' and 'Lucite,' which was formulated by the American firm DuPont. Commercial production of Perspex began at ICI in 1936 by pouring what was effectively a thick syrup between two sheets of glass before heating it and fixing it into shape. As a transparent thermoplastic, Perspex could be cast, extruded, or injection moulded into a variety of forms, and it was made available in sheets of varying thicknesses. Almost immediately after its development Perspex's potential use within the aircraft industry was identified, as being less than half the weight of the comparable amount of glass and being shatterproof, it was ideally suited for use in cockpit canopies. By 1937, ICI had opened a dedicated casting plant in Birmingham with much of its output going to the production of aircraft.[29]

As Edward Hobbs' 1932 book *Modern Handicraft Materials and Methods* indicates, the development of new plastics was of great interest to modelmakers, and it was virtually impossible to be unaware of the potentially revolutionary offerings being created by the plastics industry as a combination of aggressive marketing and extensive press coverage greeted each new material with excitement. During the inter-war years plastics were seen as wonder materials and miracles of the modern age[30] and quickly became associated with utopian visions of a transformed society where the conditions of everyday human life would be dramatically improved.[31] This optimistic view of the promise of plastics was especially strong in the United States, where plastics began to absorb the moral overtones of the modern movement.[32] Even in Britain the development of plastics such as Perspex seemed set to help realise a new prosperous future that was a welcome contrast to the economic depression that had followed the 1929 financial crash.[33] The expectant reverence in which plastics were held during the 1930s meant that modelmakers such as Hobbs were likely acutely aware of their development, although as his 1932 book makes clear, their interest in plastics was much more mundane than bringing about a plastics age utopia. For modelmakers, the physical properties of plastics were immediately attractive as lightweight alternatives to glass.

In 1938, the same year that Thomas Bayley first wrote about the potential of Perspex as a glazing material for architectural models, the twenty-eight-year-old architectural modelmaker Kenneth McCutchon made a pair of models that were quite possibly the first to be entirely constructed from the brand-new material. McCutchon, like John Thorp, had begun his career training under an architect but by 1935 had established himself as a freelance architectural modelmaker, even working for Thorp for several months before starting his own business. McCutchon's models had been made to illustrate the winning entries of a *News Chronicle* competition for new designs of schools, one for an urban location designed by Denis Clarke Hall, and one for a rural location designed by the firm of Durell, Penn, and Walter. The designs themselves were not especially remarkable, but McCutchon made both models using thin sheets of Perspex with paint applied directly to their surfaces around masked-off areas left clear to represent the windows (Figure 3.9).

Whether McCutchon chose what was then an entirely novel material to meet the requirements of the models or whether the properties of the material dictated the models' designs remains unknown; however, McCutchon had evidently realised that Perspex's transparency and its ease of working could allow for a very different approach to making architectural models. The extensive amount of glazing in both the designs would have been particularly difficult to achieve on such a small scale using existing materials, as with the lack of a suitable alternative to glass most architectural models at the time were either solid constructions or hollow façades with opaque representations of windows. Where glazing was included on a model, this was usually to allow internal lighting to shine through rather than to give visibility to their interiors, internal floors and wall divisions normally being omitted unless specifically called-for in a sectional or cut-through model. The crispness of the construction of McCutchon's

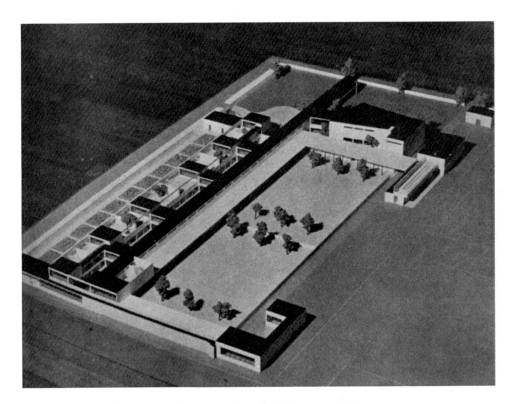

Figure 3.9 Roofless Perspex model, made by Kenneth McCutchon, 1938.

Source: *Architects' Journal,* January 13, 1938, 87.

roofless model would have been almost impossible to achieve using the standard methods and materials of the day. Using sheets of card or thin strips of timber for the walls, window apertures would have needed to have been cut out, with squares of either mica or celluloid inserted into the corresponding gaps. Given the small scale of the model, and the lack of anywhere to hide any joints between overlapping surfaces when viewed from above, this would have been an extremely challenging exercise.

McCutchon's apparent realisation was that he could make entire models from the same material – sheets of transparent Perspex – and then paint on the wall surfaces where appropriate, leaving the windows clear, a much cleaner and more effective way of representing such a large expanse of glazing. This approach was a considerable shift from how models had previously been constructed, enabled by the physical properties of this new synthetic material, and McCutchon's models were a tantalising hint of what was to come – both in terms of model construction and the style of architecture that models would have to represent in the post-war era.

What McCutchon's experiments with Perspex showed was that its use as a material in architectural models could be applied to far more than just glazing as Thomas Bailey had initially suggested. What plastics offered architectural modelmakers was a single material group that could convincingly imitate almost any other, being 'a material that lends itself so readily to transformation.'[34] Architectural models had always been made with the intention of using one material to represent another – timber, plaster, or card in a model standing in for brick, stone, slate, or even glass, with pigments and paints being used where possible to render the deception less obvious and the overall effect more realistic. The development of Perspex provided architectural modelmakers with a material that was lighter than glass and most timbers, stronger than mica and card, and with a smoother surface than both timber and card it could be marked and painted much more effectively, making Perspex an ideal replacement for not just one but all these materials.

The potential of Perspex as a material for architectural models would have to wait, however, as less than eighteen months after McCutchon so convincingly demonstrated its use, Perspex was no longer available as the start of the Second World War saw the diversion of all Perspex production to military applications. Just as an ideal material solution to the problem of spectacular growth in both the size and cost of architectural models during the inter-war years was identified, the issue itself was rendered moot as the outbreak of war and the ensuing period of austerity put an end to the demand for such grand and expensive models until well into the 1960s.

The End of an Era

On June 26, 1939, at the age of seventy-seven and still making models, John Thorp died. He had just begun to oversee a major extension of his premises at 98 Gray's Inn Road, adding an additional floor of workshop space that was finally completed after the Second World War.[35] John's son Leslie, who had been working alongside his father for twenty years, took over the business, and the company continued with both Leslie and Florence North serving as joint directors and shareholders (Figure 3.10). The transition was not an easy one, with various legal and financial complications having to be resolved, particularly regarding the future of the firm's long-term tenancy at 98 Gray's Inn Road, the freehold of which had been sold to raise money to fund the firm's

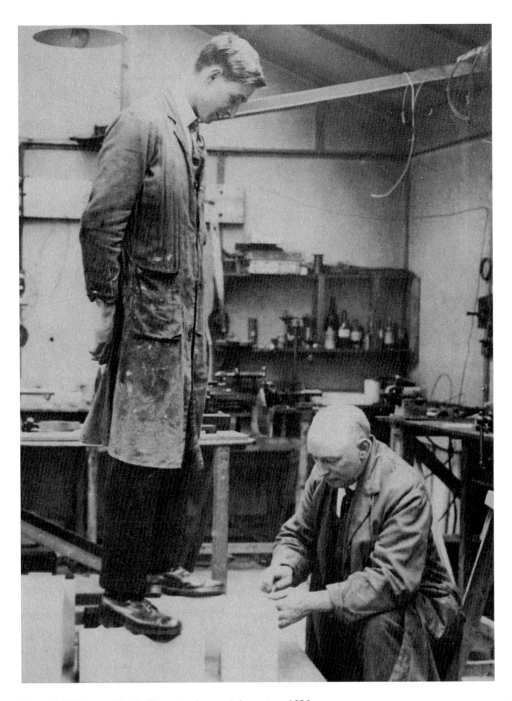

Figure 3.10 John and Leslie Thorp in the workshop, circa 1930.

Source: Image courtesy Thorp Archive, AUB.

expansion. By the time of John's death many of the company's longest-serving model-makers had also retired – William Noyce had passed away in 1930 after twenty-seven years' service, Percy Walker left in 1933 aged sixty after twenty-nine years' employment, while Edward Limmer retired in 1936 after thirty years. As wartime loomed, many of the company's younger modelmakers were also lost to the armed forces, with Leslie Thorp inheriting a staff of less than half that of just two years before.

A few months after John Thorp's death, Ernest Twining sold his interest in Twining Models to Harry Clifton, retiring to focus on his passion of making working miniature steam locomotives. The end of the company's relationship with Bassett-Lowke had reduced the scale of the business during the early-1930s, and while Clifton carried on making architectural models under the Twining brand until 1967, the firm continued as a much smaller operation. Partridge's Models and Kenneth McCutchon's career also continued, but with the loss of both John Thorp and Ernest Twining from the industry, the first generation of professional modelmakers had effectively handed control over to the next.

By the outbreak of the Second World War, the profession of architectural model-making was barely fifty years old, and yet its emergence had already substantially altered what an architectural model could be. Models were now vastly more sophisticated, realistic, and, as their greatly increased use suggests, more successful in communicating architectural designs to clients and the public. Gone were the material silos of the previous centuries, and in their place was a specialist role that through adopting a much broader, open, and adaptable approach to the choice of materials was now tightly focused on the needs of the model without being restricted by the choice of materials available to any one specific pre-existing trade. By bringing together previously separate processes and materials into one defined activity, architectural model-making had become specialised in terms of its output but generalised in its approach to making them. Architect Price Nunn remarked in 1942 that 'it is now possible to select for any kind of model the right material with the most appropriate finish,' commenting on the benefits of the wide variety of materials then available for mod-elmaking.[36] That selection of materials now included Perspex, and with modelmakers having explored the limits of what the existing materials and process of the time could achieve, the possibilities afforded by plastics were eagerly anticipated.

Their potential, and the ongoing consequences of the professionalisation of architectural modelmaking that had already manifested themselves by the end of the 1930s continued to unfold during the post-war era, when an unprecedented demand for models during the rebuilding and modernisation of Britain generated an almost overwhelming modelmaking boom. To get there, however, the profession, and Britain, had to survive another war, and it was one in which architectural modelmaking was to play an unexpectedly vital role, with the precision and accuracy that modelmakers were able to achieve becoming quite literally a matter of life and death.

Notes

1 Thomas Hendrick, *Model Making as a Career* (London: Percival Marshall, 1952), 68.
2 William Harvey, *Models of Buildings: How to Make and Use Them* (London: Architectural Press, 1927), 86.

3   Models Manufacturing Company to L. Bradley, November 28, 1928, letter, Imperial War Museum Archives.

4   Teresa Fankhanel, *The Architectural Models of Theodore Conrad* (London: Bloomsbury, 2021), 19.

5   Ibid, 22.

6   'The Fascination of Models,' *The Building News*, March 28, 1924, specially reprinted copy of the original article made by John Thorp, Thorp Modelmaking Archive.

7   L. Weaver, *Exhibitions and the Arts of Display* (London: Country Life, 1925), 81.

8   Eric Thorp to Leslie Thorp, January 6, 1940, letter, Thorp Modelmaking Archive.

9   Stan Buck, *Ernest Twining: Model Maker Artist & Engineer* (Ashbourne: Landmark Press, 2004), 108.

10 Thorp Modelmakers, 'A History of John B. Thorp,' 1983, 4, Thorp Modelmaking Archive.

11 Edward Hobbs, *Pictorial House Modelling* (London: Crosby Lockwood and Son, 1926), 109.

12 Thorp Modelmakers, 'A History of John B. Thorp,' 5.

13 Lee & Hunt Ltd, *Reliable Machine Tools by the Best Makers* (Nottingham: Lee & Hunt Ltd, 1934).

14 Buck, *Ernest Twining*, 108–109.

15 Ibid, 103.

16 LeRoy Grumbine, 'The Use of Scale Models as an Aid to the Architect,' *The Western Architect*, June, 1925, 61; Kenneth McCutchon, 'Architectural Models,' *Architects' Journal* 84 (October 17, 1936), 461.

17 The Fascination of Models,' *The Building News*.

18 P. Collins, 'Architectural Modelmaking,' *American Homes and Garden*, vol 12, no 8, 1915, 261; Karen Moon, *Modelling Messages* (New York: Monacelli Press, 2005), 43, 146.

19 McCutchon, 'Architectural Models,' 460.

20 Hobbs, *Pictorial House Modelling*, 10.

21 Kenneth Reid, 'Architectural Models,' *Pencil Points* (July, 1939), 407.

22 Robert Hoyt, 'World's Fair Models,' *Pencil Points* (July, 1939), 420.

23 Edward Hobbs, *Modern Handicraft Materials and Methods* (London: Cassell, 1932), 1.

24 Thomas Bayley, *The Craft of Model Making* (Leicester: Dryad Press, 1938), 9.

25 Harvey, *Models of Buildings*, 116.

26 Bayley, *Craft of Model Making*, 9.

27 Ibid, 7.

28 ICI, *Perspex: The First Fifty Years* (Darwen: Imperial Chemical Industries, 1984), 6.

29 Ibid, 12–14.

30 H. Wahlberg, *1950s Plastic Design* (Atglen: Shiffer, 1999), 5.

31 Jefferey Meikle, *American Plastic* (New Jersey: Rutgers University Press, 1997), 67.

32 Penny Sparke, *The Plastics Age* (London: V&A, 1990), 8; Meikle, *American Plastic*, 41.

33 Meikle, *American Plastic*, 143.

34 Ezio Manzini, *The Material of Invention* (London: The Design Council, 1986), 33.

35 Thorp Modelmakers, 'A History of John B. Thorp,' 6.

36 J. Nunn, 'Models and their Making,' *The Builder*, June 26, 1942, 554.

Chapter 4

V-Section and the Post-War Boom

On October 18, 1955, Kim Allen (the owner of Preview, a modelmaking firm in Westerham, Kent, that specialised in architectural, topographic, and planning models) wrote a letter of thanks to Leslie Bradley, the Director of the Imperial War Museum in London. Bradley had contacted Allen in response to a letter he had received from thirty-year-old Frank Willis, who was seeking work as a modelmaker. The museum had been receiving frequent enquiries from modelmakers since the early-1930s, having commissioned many models of tanks, ships, and aircraft for its exhibits, and with no work presently available, Bradley had forwarded Willis' request to Allen as the latter had been Willis' commanding officer during the Second World War. Allen thanked Bradley for getting the two of them back in touch and promptly employed Willis as a modelmaker, as in his former role as Squadron Leader Allen, Willis had been one the many modelmakers who had carried out secret work under his command at RAF Medmenham in Buckinghamshire.[1]

Frank Willis' post-war move into architectural modelmaking was by no means an exception. The occupational and technical requirements of the war equipped many members of the armed forces with new skills that they were encouraged to put to civilian use once peacetime returned, and the Royal Air Force's training of over one hundred men and women at its top-secret V-Section modelmaking unit to make highly accurate and realistic landscape models provided an unexpected windfall for the profession. As with both Allen and Willis, many of V-Section's modelmakers sought work as architectural modelmakers upon their return to civilian life, bringing their impressive abilities to the profession just as an enormous demand for architectural models during the post-war rebuilding and modernisation of Britain generated a modelmaking boom.

Modelmakers at War

Commercial architectural modelmaking largely ceased as an activity in Britain during much of the Second World War, and at Thorp commissions were almost entirely non-existent between 1940 and 1943. Leslie Thorp managed to keep the company going by finding alternative work producing planning models for the military and making dioramas of major battles to be photographed for use in the daily newspapers, including a two-hundred square feet model of the bombing of Essen. Part of the workshop space at 98 Gray's Inn Road was also turned over to the production of oil burner jets for gas lamps, which were made on a small watchmaker's lathe. Within months of

DOI: 10.4324/9781003298007-5

war being declared in 1939, however, Leslie's staffing levels had halved, falling further to just six modelmakers including himself by the time of the Blitz in 1941, during which a bomb blast on Gray's Inn Road blew out the windows, forcing Leslie to work from the basement of his house in Chiswick for several weeks until the repairs were completed. In Northampton, Harry Clifton, having taken over Twining Models after Ernest's retirement, switched entirely to the production of aircraft and ship recognition models for the armed forces, while also making several experimental models to demonstrate potential camouflage designs to protect factories from bombing, providing just enough work to keep himself employed through the conflict.

With the outbreak of war having created a significant demand for models of all kinds, many commercial modelmakers were awarded contracts to supplement the capacity of hastily established forces workshops.[2] Thomas Bayley, for example, author of the pre-war book *The Craft of Modelmaking* and a tutor at the Ealing School of Art, was commissioned to make training models for the Army, producing a series of detailed dioramas of battle scenes for soldiers to analyse.[3] As the use of such models across the war effort increased, the Royal Air Force in particular quickly began to realise that architectural and landscape models were much easier to understand than maps and drawings, and in 1940 it set up an experimental modelmaking unit at the Royal Aircraft Establishment at Farnborough. The Ordnance Survey had utilised a similar modelmaking outfit during the First World War, producing over one thousand card and canvas relief models based on their own maps,[4] but with limited experience of modelmaking within the armed forces at the start of the Second World War, the architectural modelmaker L. J. Starkey was approached to oversee the unit's creation. Little information regarding Starkey's pre-war work as a modelmaker appears to have survived; however, his position suggests he had been established for some years for his reputation to have brought him to the attention of the military.

Starkey's first appointments to the unit were his two employees, both architectural modelmakers, Donald Lindfield and William Sunter. Noting that professional modelmakers were few and far between even in peacetime, Starkey suggested finding recruits from within the ranks who had been artists before the war. Where this proved challenging, artists, sculptors, and illustrators in civilian life were directly approached to volunteer, and with the briefest of training were given a service rank and commissioned into the RAF.[5] A core unit of nine men in the newly formed RAF Models Unit then began to experiment with making highly detailed briefing and planning models based on aerial photographs of German targets. Their early work was mostly focused on supporting Commando operations, making models that ranged from ports and coastlines to entire cities (Figures 4.1 and 4.2), and their efforts were initially viewed by many in the military as a rather doubtful waste of resources. The overwhelmingly positive response of the Commandos themselves, being able to see the landscapes surrounding their targets in three-dimensions, quickly won over any objections, however.

The original modelmakers working at Farnborough alongside Starkey, Lindfield, and Sunter included Geoffrey Deeley, the head of sculpting at Regent Street Polytechnic; Eric Isherwood, an interior decorator; and Leslie Yeo, a commercial artist. The construction methods adopted for their models were heavily influenced by Starkey, Lindfield, and Sunter's backgrounds, and they would have been familiar to any architectural modelmaker of the time. Various approaches were used depending on a model's scale; however, the principal method was to construct a well-braced baseboard,

Figure 4.1 Model of the coast of France, made by V-Section modelmakers, circa 1943.

Source: Image courtesy The Medmenham Collection.

Figure 4.2 Model of Kiel, Germany, made by V-Section modelmakers, 1942.

Source: Image copyright Imperial War Museum.

then to study the aerial photographs using a stereoscope (twin images were always taken, allowing for an analysis of depth and thus height to be made), which when combined with cartographic information allowed for hardboard contours to be cut out, stacked up, and smoothed with an electrically powered chisel before being coated with a mixture of plaster of Paris and wood pulp (Figure 4.3). The black and white aerial photographs were then soaked in water and stretched over the contoured base before the whole model was painted in colour by hand (Figure 4.4). Trees, roads, and structures were then added, with linoleum used for buildings, and moss and lichen for vegetation.[6] The resulting effect was both highly accurate and extremely realistic, and the experiment at Farnborough was quickly deemed to have been a success. With a rapid increase in demand for models soon following, finding suitable recruits to help expand the unit became an immediate problem, and Starkey turned to women serving in the Air Force, with WAAFs Thea Turner and Gilly Porter as the first female modelmakers to join.

By 1941, the unit had grown beyond Starkey's ability to lead it, and he was retired from service, with Geoffrey Deeley taking command as the unit was transferred to RAF Medmenham (the official name of the hastily requisitioned Danesfield House) in Buckinghamshire. Renamed V-Section, it became part of the highly secretive Central Interpretation Unit, which had been set up to combine the RAF's top-secret photographic interpretation unit with the modelmaking contingent in order to make full use of briefing and planning models based on aerial reconnaissance photography.[7] It was at this point that the skills of the modelmakers were more properly recognised with the creation of a new rank – initially 'Pattern-Makers, Architectural' but by 1944 simply 'Modelmaker.'[8]

Figure 4.3 V-Section modelmakers at work, circa 1944.

Source: Image courtesy The Medmenham Collection.

Figure 4.4 V-Section modelmaker at work, circa 1944.

Source: Image courtesy The Medmenham Collection.

Over the next four years, over one hundred men and women were recruited into the secret modelmaking unit at Medmenham, with artists, composers, window dressers, architects, industrial designers, sculptors, silversmiths, and illustrators among those who were encouraged to join (Figure 4.5). Student Alan East, who was halfway through his architectural studies, was called up in 1943 and quickly found himself being transferred from his work as a radar operator to become a modelmaker at Medmenham.[9] Mary Harrison, an art student from Nottingham before joining the WAAF in 1943, was one of the twenty-one women modelmakers who worked at Medmenham, having seen a notice about a four-week course on modelmaking scheduled to take place at RAF Nunham Park.[10] Here, intensive training was given in advanced modelmaking skills by Pilot Officer Edmund Thring, a general modelmaker and draughtsman who had been an instructor at the Brighton School of Art. Described as a 'sweetly patient man with a merciless eye and inflexible standards of quality,'[11] Thring pushed his recruits hard. Mary Harrison found the mathematics required to understand scale particularly challenging, and there was pressure on everyone to complete their final model, a detailed representation of Newhaven Harbour, to the exacting standards required. On completion of the course, successful recruits found themselves being posted to the modelmaking unit at Medmenham, the top-secret existence of which came as a complete surprise to all of them (Figure 4.6).

In 1942 the modelmaking unit was expanded further with the arrival of the US Army Engineer Model Making Detachment, its three officers and eighty-five men being sent on a shortened version of Thring's training course and put to work alongside their British counterparts.[12] Despite including soldiers with experience working in

Figure 4.5 V-Section modelmakers at RAF Medmenham, circa 1943.

Source: Image courtesy The Medmenham Collection.

Figure 4.6 V-Section workshops, RAF Medmenham, 1945.

Source: Image courtesy The Medmenham Collection.

Hollywood designing and making film sets, the American modelmakers felt they had a lot to learn, viewing the standards at Medmenham to be far superior to what they had achieved in the United States.[13] Other than a brief strike protesting the quality of the base's food, the American modelmakers settled in quickly, and from 1943 onwards the combined British-American modelmaking unit was producing around ten models each week, working in shifts twenty-four hours a day, seven days a week, and had established additional workshops in Egypt, India, and Italy.

Although the models being made at Medmenham were for military purposes, they were essentially architectural models by another name. American V-Section model-maker Leonard Abrams later reflected that the skill of the modelmakers at Medmenham 'lay with the decision of what to include or exclude. Include that which governs vision, exclude that which is distraction,'[14] rather neatly describing the same skills involved in producing an architectural model during peacetime. With the entire outfit having been set up by an architectural modelmaker, the models that V-Section pro-duced continued to be made to their successful template throughout the war. The size and format of the models varied widely from portable campaign planning models at 1:40,000 scale to terrain models up to twenty feet square of entire towns and cities for briefing bombing crews at 1:1,000 scale. In total the V-Section modelmakers made over one thousand four hundred models over the five years of their operation, includ-ing four hundred just for the Normandy landings in 1944.[15] Accuracy was absolutely vital to the Medmenham modelmakers' work; pilots conducting bombing runs on German battleships in the Norwegian Fjords found it impossible to recognise their location using maps, and so V-Section produced a series of lightweight cardboard and canvas models to be carried in their cockpits to help them identify natural land-marks,[16] while larger-scale planning models of the Fjords were used to determine the precise field of fire of the defensive gun emplacements so that exact bearings for the bomber pilots to fly without being hit could be determined[17] (Figure 4.7). V-Section modelmaker Alan East recalled a friend who served on these missions telling him he was convinced that the models had saved the lives of many bombing crews,[18] while the accuracy of the models made of the facilities at Peenemunde in 1943 allowed weapons experts to better discern the development of the German V-weapons, before the same models were used as briefing tools for the bomber crews sent to destroy them.[19]

The pressure for achieving such realism and accuracy was tragically demonstrated by a large model of Dieppe that had shown the sea wall being high enough to provide cover for the Allied tanks that were due to land on the beach, but in reality, it was found to be too low. While the modelmakers were explicitly told after the operation was over that this was the only error on the model, and that overall it had saved countless lives, many of the modelmakers became distressed at the thought that their error might have contributed to some of the three thousand casualties sustained dur-ing the battle.[20] Lines from a poem written by modelmaker Mary Harrison after being shown a photograph of damage caused by a later bombing raid that had been guided by one of her own planning models captured the intense sense of responsibility that they often felt:

How many people have died through me
From the skill at my finger tips?
For I fashion the clay and portray the landscape
As the fliers are briefed for their trips.[21]

Figure 4.7 Model of Sorpe Dam, made by V-Section modelmakers, 1943.

Source: Copyright Imperial War Museum.

By the final years of the conflict the still top-secret work of the modelmakers at Med-menham had come to be viewed by the Allied leaders as having been immensely suc-cessful. Appreciative messages from all three services were regularly passed on to the modelmakers, and General Eisenhower was quoted as saying that 'each of these mod-elmakers is worth a hundred men.'[22] As part of the D-Day preparations V-Section was asked to construct a model of the entire coast of Normandy at 1:5,000 scale.

Comprising dozens of individual panels, when laid together the completed model stretched for over sixty feet in length. Constructed using timber and plaster, the panels were then cast using PVC rubber to create flexible copies that could be painted, rolled up, and shipped directly to the battlefield commanders.[23] On inspection by King George VI, Winston Churchill, and General Eisenhower, the modelmakers were informed that the accuracy of their work was likely to have saved twenty thousand lives in the forthcoming operation.[24]

The Post-War Boom

At the end of the war in 1945, the Central Interpretation Unit was disbanded, although V-Section, returning to its original title of the RAF Models Section, continued with a much-reduced core of eighteen modelmakers before moving to RAF Wyton in 1951, where it remained operational until 1993. In the immediate aftermath of the Second World War the remaining RAF modelmakers found themselves working on civilian projects; Alan East remembers building a large model of the proposed runway layout for London Airport in 1946,[25] demonstrating the interchangeability between their work on military models and more conventional architectural ones. With significant numbers of servicemen and women returning to civilian life at the end of the Second World War, V-Section had effectively trained a sizable population of extremely talented modelmakers who were looking for peacetime applications of their new-found skills. The levels of realism and accuracy to which they had been expected to work were far more advanced than even the established architectural modelmakers such as Thorp and Twining had reached in the inter-war years, and having been initially trained by architectural modelmakers, it was perhaps to be expected that a number of the V-Section modelmakers decided to apply their skills to architectural modelmaking after the war, bringing with them an intensively honed ability to achieve extremely-high levels of realism in their models.

V-Section's inclusion of several WAAFs also provided an important opportunity for women to better establish themselves as commercial modelmakers after 1945, particularly in the case of Margaret Watson. The core of the photographic side of the Central Interpretation Unit had developed from the pre-war aerial photography company Aerofilms, and on the closure of the unit in 1945 the company was returned to private ownership as part of Hunting Aerosurveys. Having seen the commercial potential of V-Section's work, Hunting continued to employ a team of ex-Medmenham modelmakers led by senior WAAF Margaret Watson, who remained at Hunting until the mid-1950s – the first senior position for a woman within the profession. Hunting branded their work as Hunting Aeromodels, and a 1949 brochure for the company promoted their work making detailed planning models from aerial photographs, just as had been the case within the RAF, proudly noting that their modelmakers had been 'trained to work to the limits of accuracy.'[26] Having moved to Borehamwood, Hunting began making models of schools, power stations, and airports, and in 1948 Margaret Watson was photographed showing King George VI and Queen Elizabeth a landscape model of the Balmoral Estate that the Queen had commissioned from them as a silver wedding present for the King.[27]

In addition to Watson and the Hunting modelmakers, V-Section's principle modelmaking instructor, Edmund Thring, set up as an independent architectural modelmaker in London, working until at least the mid-1960s, while Kim Allen established Preview Modelmakers in 1948 having served as both the commander of the V-Section modelshop in Egypt and the main unit at Medmenham, recruiting as many of the V-Section modelmakers as he could, including the aforementioned Frank Willis. Leslie Yeo, Dick Martin, and Nancy Hayes – a further pioneering position for a female modelmaker – were all recruited directly from V-Section to set up the modelmaking unit of the London County Council (LCC) Architects' Department,[28] while just a few years later, newly-recruited LCC modelmaker Mike Karslake found himself being posted to Medmenham in return to run a team of thirty-five modelmakers working on landscape models for the Korean War effort during his national service in 1951, briefly returning to the LCC once more before going on to a successful career as an architectural modelmaker in Southend.[29] Other branches of the military had also been employing dedicated modelmakers, and Alfred Greenside, who had been an Army modelmaker in the Royal Corps of Signals training unit, switched from making models of landing craft and assault ships to making planning models for architects, having established his own modelmaking company in Harrogate.[30] With a huge demand for planning models in the immediate aftermath of the war, all of these former military modelmakers, and more, found that the small-scale models that were required for planning purposes were extremely similar to the models they had been making during wartime, and their experience in creating such precise and ultra-realistic landscape models brought about a significant improvement in the levels of realism in the architectural models they worked on once they entered the profession (Figure 4.8).

Established architectural modelmakers appear to have welcomed the influx of military modelmakers with great enthusiasm, as there was a general sense that while Britain embraced the possibilities of peacetime again the demand for architectural models was bound to increase and that far more architectural modelmakers were going to be needed. In 1945, Peter Wickham's book *Commercial Model Making* was published, aimed explicitly at encouraging more into the profession, noting that:

> [This] book is mainly written for the benefit of those who may be considering the possibilities of model making as a post-war career. No-one can say what post-war conditions may be, but in an age of increased building . . . the model maker's work cannot but be needed.[31]

The popular magazine *Model Maker* observed in 1952 that any hobbyist modelmakers who wanted to take on commercial architectural work would find many opportunities in just their local area,[32] while in the same year, Thomas Hendrick's book *Model Making as a Career* was published as a guide for amateur modelmakers who wanted to become professionals, particularly within architectural modelmaking, 'the branch of the art which is probably in the greatest demand.'[33] Hendrick noted that there were over seventy professional modelmakers listed in the current London telephone directory and gave advice on how to write to companies enquiring about employment. For amateurs, he suggested sending photographs of their work and immersing themselves in books about modelmaking, highlighting how Percival Marshall's company alone had published over one hundred and fifty technical manuals on modelmaking by 1950.[34] Hendrick also outlined the attributes of a good professional modelmaker,

Figure 4.8 Model of a proposed new town at Ongar, modelmaker unknown, 1944.

Source: Copyright Imperial War Museum.

emphasising the importance of improvisation, versatility, and 'flexibility of the imagination,'[35] observing the 'great advantage of men who can turn their hands to different
tools, machines and materials' and that 'it is not always essential to adhere to the use
of any particular material or method of construction provided that the finished article
has a perfect appearance and is strong enough to withstand any reasonable use to
which it may be put.'[36]

The adaptability crucial to successful modelmaking was not something that everyone who approached the profession could handle. As Hendrick warned in his book,
'this flexibility of imagination may prove more difficult to acquire by those tradesmen
who aspire to become model makers after having been engaged in a specific trade for
a number of years.'[37] At Thorp, this had clearly been the case for decades, where a
large number of new recruits lasted barely a handful of weeks, unable to adapt to the
shifting demands of processes and materials that were required of them. In the immediate post-war years Leslie found this problem particularly challenging to deal with,
with twenty modelmakers joining and then leaving in under a year between 1945 and
1950. As architectural commissions began to return after 1943, Leslie found it more
and more difficult to manage the sudden increase in workload, and unlike his father,
whose interests and skills had straddled modelmaking and business equally, Leslie
was much more comfortable purely making models and found the management of
the company a much greater struggle. The return of experienced modelmakers from
their wartime service helped relieve the pressure for a short while, and the return of
Len Hayes in 1946, who had started working at Thorp aged fourteen in 1936 before
being called up for Army service in 1940, proved to be permanent; Hayes became
the company secretary after Florence North's retirement and took over the running of
the shop counter until his own retirement in 1993 and the transfer of the modelshop
side of the business to new owners.

The pressures of running the rapidly expanding business, with staffing levels dou-
bling between 1945 and 1950, began to take their toll on Leslie, and the arrival of a
young wartime movie special effects artist and modelmaker named Ray Pfaendler for
eight months in 1948 clearly made an impact, as a year later Leslie invited Pfaendler to
return to the company as manager, taking over the day-to-day running of the business
and leaving the now fifty-year-old Leslie to concentrate on making models. Pfaendler,
who would later marry Margaret Watson, the former V-Section WAAF leading Hunting Aeromodels, set about modernising the business, overhauling the Edwardian
accounting practices that Leslie had inherited from his father, and embarked on an
intensive marketing push, including a new brochure in 1955 that echoed John Thorp's
own promotional materials from 1906 and 1913. Leslie was nevertheless an accom-
plished modelmaker and worked on many high-profile commissions during the late-
1940s, including a model of the rebuilding of the House of Commons Chamber that
survives to this day and a stunning recreation of the reredos at the east end of St Paul's
Cathedral that had been destroyed during the Blitz (Figure 4.9). Having led the construction of the Liverpool Cathedral model in 1934, Leslie preferred to work purely
in timber, creating intricate mouldings using a miniature French head spindle moulder
that he had designed and built himself.[38]

Twining Models under Harry Clifton also began to win major architectural commissions again, including models for the Hebrew University of Jerusalem in 1944,
Nottingham University in 1949, the redevelopment of Knutsford town centre in 1950,

Figure 4.9 Leslie Thorp making the St Paul's model, 1949.

Source: Image courtesy Thorp Archive, AUB.

and for Greenwich power station in 1952, providing enough work to employ eight additional modelmakers by 1950.[39] Partridge's Models, of whom little information exists relating to their wartime work, quickly began marketing themselves again, sending out a brochure of their pre-war work in 1949 that was once more suspiciously similar to John Thorp's earlier marketing efforts. Entitled *Art of the Model Maker*, the brochure outlined the use of architectural models for public display and in legal cases, noting that models had 'no set limits . . . [their] manifestations are truly remarkable in their interest and variety.'[40] Kenneth McCutchon, having so dramatically demonstrated the potential of Perspex shortly before the outbreak of the war, also found his architectural models increasingly in demand, and trading as McCutchon Studio was employing at least four other modelmakers by 1950.

Due to the flow of V-Section modelmakers into civilian life, by the late-1940s the make-up of the profession had substantially changed. While Leslie Thorp and Harry Clifton continued to lead Thorp and Twining Models respectively, and Partridge's carried on making models after Leslie Partridge's death until the late-1960s, the arrival of McCutchon Studio, Hunting Aeromodels, Preview, and the establishment of the LCC modelmaking section meant there were over four times the number of architectural modelmakers working in Britain compared to the late-1930s, including a growing number of women. The skills of the workforce had also been significantly advanced during the war, with a much greater emphasis on achieving near-photographic levels of realism, and as a result the profession was extremely well-placed to respond to the enormous demand for architectural models that accelerated through the late-1940s and into the 1950s.

While there were plenty of modelmakers to meet this demand, the availability of materials was another matter altogether, with even the most basic materials such as timber and card in desperately short supply. Harry Clifton at Twining Models noted the extreme difficulties he faced in obtaining any modelmaking materials at all during the war itself,[41] and the situation appears to have continued through to the end of the decade; the modelmaker Peter Wickham writing in 1945 that:

> Under the present circumstances, considerable difficulty is likely to be experienced in obtaining any type of tools; and many materials, especially wood of any type, are now in short supply. Generally speaking, however, cardboard is still obtainable in the small quantities needed by the model-maker at the time of writing.[42]

Perspex, despite the enormous capacity of the now no longer needed wartime manufacturing plants, initially remained difficult for modelmakers to obtain in sufficient quantities; modelmaker David Armstrong having recalled the challenge of getting hold of Perspex even in the early-1950s. Making use of the material in small sculptures before he embarked on his modelmaking career, Armstrong found the most accessible source of Perspex to be the broken canopy remains of the seemingly large number of crashed experimental jet aircraft to be found in the fields close to his home: 'In those days planes would crash quite a lot and you could just find the bits of Perspex which was quite a new substance in those days. . . . If there was a crash, I would go and collect the Perspex remains.'[43] Despite the difficulties in obtaining Perspex, its use as a glazing material in architectural models rapidly became the standard as the decade progressed.[44] The lavishly grand and outsized models of the inter-war years must have seemed a distant memory as modelmakers worked hard to locate even small scraps of basic materials, but fortunately, given the materials shortages, the general demand for larger models of individual buildings remained some years in the future as Britain's planners needed to first present their designs for the overall redevelopment of the country's towns and cities before architects could turn their attention to the design of specific buildings.

While there was much wartime damage to repair, the post-war rebuilding program also embraced wider aims, additionally seeking to address the incomplete attempts to improve the quality of British housing stock that had begun during the inter-war years and which had contributed to that period's own modelmaking boom. Combined with the widespread damage and destruction of homes during the Second World War, housing in post-war Britain was in a dismal state. Twenty million people were living in homes that had no bath or hot water, with a fifth of homes in London officially classified as slums.[45] As early as 1941, discussions were being held within government about how to address these problems, and the following year the Ministry of Town and Country Planning was established in anticipation of an imminent end to the war after the entry of the United States into the conflict.[46] With a renewed sense of optimism, pre-war modernist ideas of garden cities and new towns were enthusiastically explored through large planning models such as one made by Leslie Thorp in 1943 of a hypothetical new town to demonstrate the principles laid down by the Ministry's chief advisor, the town planner Patrick Abercrombie (Figure 4.10).

Models were considered the ideal way to communicate the post-war rebuilding plans to the public and were put to effective use in exhibitions such as *Rebuilding Britain* in 1943 and the *Modern Homes Exhibition* of 1946. Public information posters produced by the Ministry of Information highlighted the clean and orderly vision of the future that models were able to portray in stark contrast to the awful ruins of the many bomb-damaged towns and cities across the country (Figure 4.11). A large model of the proposed rebuilding of Coventry, even before the bombings that destroyed much of the city centre, was displayed at an exhibition in 1941, while Harry Clifton at Twining Models was commissioned to make a highly detailed model of a revised proposal for a new city centre in 1943 (Figure 4.12). During a two-week public exhibition in 1945, fifty-seven thousand visitors inspected his model of 'Coventry of the Future.'[47]

Planning models of entire towns quickly became a regular commission for many modelmakers with the newly established town planning departments of the local councils keen to illustrate their ideas in three-dimensions. At the same time, the creation of the National Health Service meant the building of countless new hospitals, planning models of which were also duly ordered, while between 1945 and 1955, two-and-a-half thousand new schools were built, including the new secondary moderns, again adding to the demand for architectural models. As far as housing was concerned, in just six years after the end of the war, some one million new homes were built in Britain, with demand so high for models of these new developments that an inventive company called Bennett Models came up with a postal modelmaking scheme whereby hobbyist modelmakers were paid to make models of bungalows at home, an indication that the demand for such models was outstripping supply.

A further impetus to the post-war modelmaking boom was the large number of models required for the selection, planning, and promotion of the first wave of new towns. The development corporations set up for each new town commissioned large numbers of models of all types and sizes, from early planning models to show the proposed layouts of the towns, to detailed larger-scale models of their town centres and the different types of housing being built. As the development of these towns generated further models during the early-1950s, and the availability of modelmaking materials returned to some semblance of normality, the changes to the modelmaking profession that had taken place because of the arrival of the V-Section modelmakers became especially apparent. The models made for the planning of

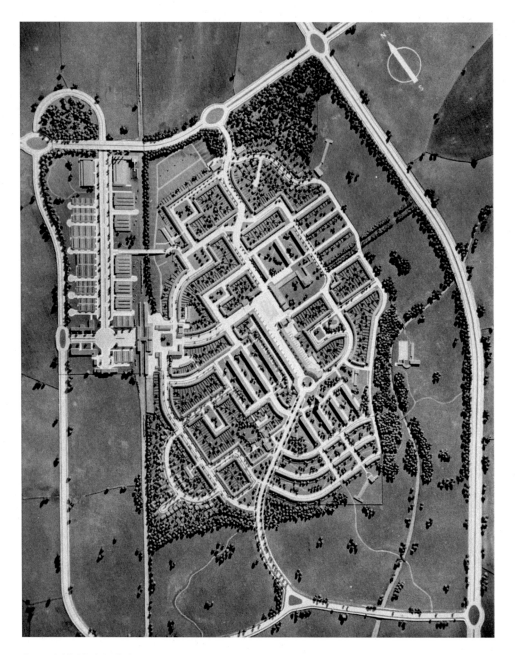

Figure 4.10 Model of a hypothetical new town, made by Thorp, 1943.

Source: Image courtesy Thorp Archive, AUB.

Figure 4.11 Ministry of Information poster, 1943.

Source: Copyright Imperial War Museum.

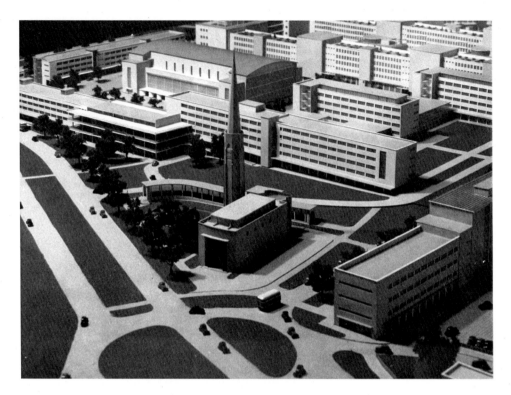

Figure 4.12 Model of Coventry city centre, made by Twining Models, 1943.

Source: Image courtesy Northamptonshire County Archives.

Harlow demonstrate all the hallmarks of the striving for precision and realism that their wartime experiences had instilled. The 1950 masterplan model made by the exhibition and modelmaking firm Cockade was constructed using precisely the same techniques as the wartime topographic models made by the V-Section modelmakers at RAF Medmenham, the model consisting of aerial photographs stretched over a contoured baseboard that gave a highly realistic appearance (Figure 4.13). The seventeen-square-feet model contained several thousand model trees made by dipping panel pins into a mixture of glue, sawdust, and plaster before being painted. Fishing wire was used for hedges and walls, with flock for fields, and strips of beech timber shaped and cut to size for the buildings.[48] The model cost over £700 to make (approximately £28,000 today) and was an unusually expensive outlay in what was ostensibly a period of austerity, signifying how valuable an investment models were deemed to be in successfully communicating such plans to the public. At least twenty larger-scale models were also made of different parts of the town, including a model of the civic centre made by Partridge's Models in 1950 and four highly detailed models of the town centre made by McCutchon Studio (Figures 4.14 and 4.15), who were also filmed by British Pathé in 1955 at work on a model of Harlow's The Lawn, Britain's first post-war high-rise tower block.

Figure 4.13 Planning model of Harlow, made by Cockade, 1950.

Source: Copyright holder unknown, but see Frederick Gibberd, Town Design (London: The Architectural Press, 1962), 161.

While Harlow provided much work for many of the major post-war architectural modelmaking firms, several of the new town development corporations created their own modelmaking departments due to the sheer number of models they required. After completing his national service running the modelmaking section at RAF Medmenham, Mike Karslake spent two years as the in-house modelmaker for the Basildon Development Corporation in the 1950s, while at the same time the architects'

Figure 4.14 Model of Harlow Civic Centre, made by McCutchon Studio, circa 1955.
Source: Image courtesy Essex Record Office.

Figure 4.15 Model of Harlow town centre, made by McCutchon Studio, circa 1955.
Source: Photograph by Henk Snoek. Image courtesy Essex Record Office.

departments of many of the larger towns and cities had also begun to create dedicated modelmaking teams to produce the numerous planning models required for public display, with the commercial architectural modelmakers such as Thorp and McCutchon Studio continuing to work to capacity. The most significant of the new local government modelmaking teams was the one created by the London County Council (LCC).

As has been previously noted, this was established by three ex-Medmenham model-makers and rapidly expanded to become one of the largest architectural modelmaking outfits in the country, pre-empting a trend for many of the larger private architectural practices during the 1980s such as Foster + Partners to operate an in-house model-making workshop. With Leslie Yeo, Dick Martin, and Nancy Hayes all being ex-RAF modelmakers, the models the LCC (and later GLC) Models Section produced were of a very high standard, their V-Section training having instilled a rigorous striving for realism and accuracy. Describing one of the many planning models made of the Roehampton estate, LCC architect John Partridge noted that the model 'not only had all the contours but every tree to scale with its correct position and spread. Never subsequently have I experienced such a design tool at hand. . . . In the 1950s these expensive accurate models were remarkable'[49] (Figure 4.16).

As the 1950s progressed and the planning of the new towns and the rebuilding of bomb-damaged city centres moved into actual construction, larger and more traditional architectural models were increasingly required once more to explain to both the planning authorities and the public what the buildings that were going to occupy these masterplans were going to look like. The use of highly realistic architectural models to communicate the ambitious ideas of a new generation of modernist architects and planners keen to put into action their visions for a better world was exemplified by the 1951 Festival of Britain, which made a clear statement to the public that new buildings constructed in the post-war era were going to be quite different to what had gone before, the architects and planners behind the post-war rebuilding of Britain having fully embraced the principles of modernist architecture. Being a relatively new

Figure 4.16 Model of the Roehampton Estate, made by the LCC Models Section, 1959.

Source: Image courtesy RIBA Collections.

style of architecture in Britain, models were in great demand to present its merits to an often-sceptical public. For modelmakers this created the challenge of effectively representing this new architectural language, as modernist architecture conformed to very different rules.

The 1951 Festival of Britain was intended to play an important role in the rebuilding of Britain in the post-war era, as it allowed the public to not only celebrate Britain's historic achievements but also to experience first-hand the brave new world that was being promised by the reconstruction of Britain's cities and the creation of the spacious new towns. A decision to place three-dimensional exhibits – artefacts, models, and dioramas – as central to the main London exhibition[50] generated a huge amount of work for modelmakers of all specialisms. Thomas Hendrick, in describing the impact of the Festival on the profession, noted that 'with regard to cultural assembly, what greater stimulus can ever have been given to model makers than the 1951 Festival of Britain?'[51] Hendrick was the production manager of Cockade, an exhibition and display company that had been formed by Sir Stephen Tallents and Hugh Casson in 1946 with the aim of creating a consortium of designers and makers to improve the artistic quality of models and displays for the public.[52] Cockade took on a large proportion of the model and display work for the Festival, no doubt through the close involvement of Tallents and Casson in both endeavours, as well as becoming a major provider of architectural models during the 1950 and 1960s.

The Festival itself contained thousands of models of all types and scales, and virtually all the architectural modelmaking firms contributed work, sometimes applying their skills to non-architectural subjects. Thomas Bayley made several models of townscapes, McCutchon Studio and Partridge's Models both submitted many architectural and engineering models, while the general modelmaking firm Shawcraft built a model of London Airport. Hunting Aeromodels made seven architectural models, while Preview and freelance architectural modelmaker Richard Hamilton each provided several large models of the new towns. Cockade itself produced countless models, including an architectural model of the proposed BBC Television Centre, while in Harlow the top floor of The Lawn, the first completed tower block, was given over to a public exhibition as part of the Festival that allowed visitors to compare a large model of the proposed new town with the view of the actual work in progress below.[53] Thorp found substantial work making models of the Festival buildings leading up to its opening, with many planning models of the Festival site on London's South Bank having been commissioned during the design process (Figure 4.17) and further models made specifically for public display in the Festival's office in central London.

With over eight million visitors attending the South Bank exhibition, the models on display were seen by a significant proportion of the British population, and as had been the case with planning models of the rebuilding of war-damaged cities such as Coventry, and of the new towns such as Harlow, they acted as miniature physical embodiments of post-war optimism. As projected improvements to the country's infrastructure were unveiled during the early 1950s, further publicly displayed models explained the plans for motorways, civic buildings, and the modernisation program for Britain's railways, all firmly predicting a brighter more prosperous tomorrow – an association that would later cause problems for the architectural model when the gleam of modernism began to fade in the late-1960s. More immediately, however, was the challenge of accurately and realistically representing modernist architectural styles to the same high standards

Figure 4.17 Model of the Festival of Britain site under construction at Thorp, 1951.
Source: Image courtesy Thorp Archive, AUB.

Figure 4.18 Model of the Sea and Ships Pavilion, Festival of Britain, modelmaker unknown, 1951.
Source: Image courtesy RIBA Collections.

that had been established since the Second World War, with the Festival of Britain marking a watershed moment for the architectural modelmaker. Having served as an important opportunity to present a new style of architecture and design to the public, and to show a vision of how the modernists thought Britain should look, it was clear that few modelmaking commissions in the foreseeable future were going to follow the more traditional styles of the inter-war years and that the established methods of architectural modelmaking needed to change as a result (Figure 4.18).

Following the Festival of Britain the post-war modelmaking boom continued to race ahead, with many commercial modelmakers struggling to keep up with demand. Thomas Bayley wrote in 1959 that many of his former pupils at the Ealing School of Art had gone on to become 'professional model makers of considerable repute and are producing work of the highest quality,'[54] and both Thomas Hendrick's 1957 and Norman Taylor's 1959 books on architectural modelmaking continued the explicit calls made in publications ten years earlier for more individuals to take up the career, so strong was the demand for their work.[55] By the end of the decade, the 'ever increasing importance of the professional model maker in industry' was confidently assured, Norman Taylor writing that:

> Many of Britain's largest industrial undertakings rely on these model manufacturers to supply their model requirements with every confidence, in the knowledge that by doing so they are drawing on countless years of experience in this highly specialized trade.[56]

The addition of the V-Section modelmakers and their intense focus on improving the standards of realism in architectural models had proved to be a tremendous windfall for the profession during the immediate post-war period; however, the expectations that this established quickly began to pose a serious challenge when the demand for relatively small-scale planning models started to be replaced by commissions for much larger, more traditional models of specific buildings. The complication was that having established such high expectations of the degree of realism that could be achieved in architectural models, the new styles of architecture being employed in the rebuilding and modernisation of Britain were using radically different principles, materials, building types, and construction techniques, and as the post-war boom progressed, an urgent need arose for the materials and construction methods of architectural modelmaking to evolve as well. Realistically portraying modernist architecture required a wholescale rethinking of how models were made; however, as Kenneth McCutchon's 1938 schools models made almost entirely from Perspex had already demonstrated, the solution had already been identified shortly before the Second World War.

Notes

1 Kim Allen to L. Bradley, October 18, 1955, letter, Imperial War Museum Archives; Kim Allen to L. Bradley, April 7, 1955, letter, Imperial War Museum Archives; Frank Willis to L. Bradley, October 10, 1955, letter, Imperial War Museum Archives.
2 Thomas Hendrick, *Model Making as a Career* (London: Percival Marshall, 1952), 7.
3 Thomas Bayley, *The Craft of Model Making* (Leicester: Dryad Press, 1938).
4 Ian Pearson, 'Allied Military Model Making during World War II,' *Cartography and Geographic Information Science*, vol 29, no 3 (2002), 227.
5 Leonard Abrams, *Our Secret Little War* (Bethesda: International Geographic Information Foundation, 1991), 15; Taylor Downing, 'Spying from the Sky,' *History Today*, November, 2011, 15.
6 Pearson, 'Military Model Making,' 230.
7 Abrams, *Our Secret Little War*, 22.
8 Alan East, interview with author, January 29, 2019.
9 Ibid.
10 Christine Hallsall, *Women of Intelligence* (Stroud: The History Press, 2012), 129.

11 Abrams, *Our Secret Little War*, 33.
12 Pearson, 'Military Model Making,' 229.
13 Abrams, *Our Secret Little War*, 11.
14 Ibid, 35.
15 Downing, 'Spying from the Sky,' 14.
16 Abrams, *Our Secret Little War*, 40; East, interview.
17 Hallsall, *Women of Intelligence*, 131.
18 East, interview.
19 Abrams, *Our Secret Little War*, 52, East, interview.
20 Abrams, *Our Secret Little War*, 24.
21 Harrison, cited by Hallsall, *Women of Intelligence*, 133.
22 Abrams, *Our Secret Little War*, 27.
23 East, interview.
24 Abrams, *Our Secret Little War*, 59.
25 East, interview.
26 A. Foreman to Curator, IWM, November 3, 1949, letter, Imperial War Museum Archives.
27 John Leatherdale, email to author, November 19, 2018.
28 Mike Karslake, interview with Louise Brady, November 19, 1981, audio recording, Essex County Archives.
29 Ibid.
30 Alfred Greenside to L. Bradley, June 18, 1953, letter, Imperial War Museum Archives.
31 P. Wickham, *Commercial Model Making* (London: Vawser and Wiles, 1945), 6.
32 V. Sutton, 'Making Architectural Models,' *Model Maker*, July, 1952, 490.
33 Hendrick, *Model Making as a Career*, 8.
34 Ibid, 38.
35 Ibid, 26.
36 Ibid.
37 Ibid.
38 Thorp Modelmakers, 'A History of John B. Thorp,' 1983, 10, Thorp Modelmaking Archive.
39 Stan Buck, *Ernest Twining: Model Maker Artist & Engineer* (Ashbourne: Landmark Press, 2004), 103.
40 Partridge's Models, *Art of the Model Maker* (London: Partridge's Models, 1949).
41 Buck, *Ernest Twining*, 102.
42 Wickham, *Commercial Model Making*, 8.
43 David Armstrong, interview with Louise Brady, September 23, 1999, audio recording, Ove Arup Architecture Interviews, British Library.
44 A. Forman, *How to Make Architectural Models* (London: The Studio, 1946), 46; P. Wickham, *Modelled Architecture* (London: Percival Marshall, 1948), 41.
45 Barry Turner, *Beacon for Change* (London: Aurum, 2011), 8.
46 Alan Powers, *Britain: Modern Architectures in History* (London: Reaktion, 2007), 75.
47 Buck, *Ernest Twining*, 102; David Kynaston, *Austerity Britain* (London: Bloomsbury, 2008), 166.
48 Frederick Gibberd, *Town Design* (London: The Architectural Press, 1962), 161.
49 John Partridge, 'Roehampton Housing,' in *Housing the Twentieth Century Nation*, eds. Elaine Harwood and Allan Powers (London: Twentieth Century Society, 2008), 117.
50 Helen Atkinson, *The Festival of Britain: A Land and its People* (London: I.B. Taurus, 2012), 46.
51 Hendrick, *Model Making as a Career*, 4.
52 Thomas Hendrick, 'The Achievements of Cockade,' in *A Tonic to the Nation*, eds. M. Banham and B. Hillier (London: Thames and Hudson, 1976), 163.
53 Atkinson, *Festival of Britain*, 186.
54 Thomas Bayley, *The Craft of Model Making (Fifth Revised Edition)* (Leicester: Dryad Press, 1959), 5.
55 Thomas Hendrick, *The Modern Architectural Model* (London: Architectural Press, 1957); Norman Taylor, *Architectural Modelling and Visual Planning* (London: Cassell, 1959).
56 Taylor, *Architectural Modelling*, p. xii.

Chapter 5

The Modern Architectural Model

In 1957, modelmaker Thomas Hendrick's comprehensive practical guide to architectural modelmaking, *The Modern Architectural Model*, was published by the Architectural Press in London. The title Hendrick chose for his book neatly encapsulated the scale of the radical changes in architectural modelmaking that were taking place at the time, not only referring to modern approaches to making architectural models but also the fact that they were models of modern architecture. Compared to the heavy timber and card models of the inter-war years, the post-war 'modern' architectural model that Hendrick described was notable for one significant difference: the use of plastics. The widespread adoption of these synthetic materials by architectural modelmakers during the post-war era enabled new lightweight construction methods, higher levels of technical precision, and perhaps most importantly, an increased sense of realism through finer detail, better paint finishes, and fully transparent windows. In discussing the impact of plastics on architectural modelmaking, Hendrick wrote that 'the use of these materials has done more to facilitate the methods of construction and to improve the finish of architectural models than any other substance or method.'[1]

The tentative explorations of plastics in architectural modelmaking during the late-1930s had largely been driven by a desire to find cheaper and lighter materials to counter the unsustainable size and complexity of models that had been fuelled by the over-enthusiasm of both the first generation of professional architectural modelmakers and clients overawed by the attention such models commanded. The Second World War and the period of austerity that followed had ultimately forced a solution to the problem, as it was not until the 1950s that both the materials and funds became available to even consider a return to such lavish large-scale architectural models. With the rebuilding of Britain's towns and cities having instigated a sudden demand for planning models that were ideally suited to the skills of the newly demobbed V-Section modelmakers, the Festival of Britain had made it clear that the buildings that were to populate these plans were going to be of a very different style to what had gone before. As the modelmaking boom of the 1950s continued to unfold, the freshly invigorated and expanded profession found itself drawn to plastics such as Perspex once more, not to solve a problem of weight and cost but as a solution to the much more basic issue of how to make models of modernist architecture to the standards of realism that were now expected.

DOI: 10.4324/9781003298007-6

Meeting the Challenges of Modernism

Modernism had begun to spread through European architecture from the turn of the century, however Britain lagged behind for several decades. The first examples of modernist buildings in Britain were built in 1925, with the movement only properly becoming popular within architectural circles here during the late-1930s.[2] The influence of Edwin Lutyens and Giles Gilbert Scott – both of whom were prolific commissioners of models from John Thorp – along with the garden city movement, had steered the architectural style of the country in a different direction, particularly regarding housing. By the outbreak of the Second World War, only nine hundred modernist houses had been built out of a total of four million new homes, as throughout the 1930s modernist architecture in Britain had largely been restricted to public buildings.[3] Despite a growing interest in the movement, house buyers simply wanted to live in more traditionally styled dwellings with gable roofs, half-timber façades, and lattice windows, as exemplified by the popularity of the mock-Tudor style in the inter-war years.[4]

While modernist architecture was perhaps slow to catch on with the public in the 1930s, within British architectural schools it had virtually swept all other forms of architecture aside, largely inspired by the arrival of several prominent modernist architects from Europe and through the spread of Bauhaus teaching approaches that embedded both modernism and the architectural model as central to architectural education. Erich Mendelsohn and Serge Chermayeff had arrived in Britain in 1928, while Berthold Lubetkin and Denys Lasdun formed the Tecton Group in 1932. Walter Gropius arrived in 1934 and formed a partnership with Maxwell Fry, while Marcel Breuer arrived the following year and went into business with F. R. S. Yorke. Le Corbusier was a frequent visitor to London in the 1930s, and by 1933 the Modern Architecture Research Group (MARS) had been established in London to promote the ideas of architectural modernism.[5] Students at the major architectural schools during the 1930s, particularly at the Architectural Association (the AA) and the Liverpool School of Architecture, openly embraced the modernist movement, and increasingly through the decade the architectural journals' reporting of their graduation shows was accompanied by photographs of their final project models, all in the modernist style. A 1938 exhibition by the MARS Group was similarly filled with models demonstrating the clean lines of modernist architecture (Figure 5.1), and by 1942 it was regarded that modelmaking had become an essential part of the curriculum at most of the schools of architecture in Britain, 'a necessity in the process of present-day architecture' due to its unfamiliar forms.[6]

Initially there had been a polarising debate between two factions of the modernist movement in Britain – the 'new humanists,' who drew from a softer Scandinavian form of modernism, and the harder modernists, who were inspired by Le Corbusier.[7] This was particularly noticeable within the LCC's architects' department, where different groups who were split between admirers of Alvar Aalto and of Le Corbusier were given free rein to experiment, often within the same development.[8] The Roehampton estate, for example, incorporated a 'softer' low-density mix of point blocks – narrow blocks of flats surrounded by grassed areas – and low-height maisonettes

Figure 5.1 Models at the MARS exhibition 'New Architecture,' 1938.

Source: Image courtesy RIBA Collections.

with traditional pitched roofs, alongside the 'harder' more slab-like complexes that were reminiscent of Le Corbusier's *Unite* designs. By the early 1950s, modernism had come to dominate British architecture, and the urbanist high-density views of Le Corbusier's followers had largely won the argument. As historian David Kynaston has described the consequences of this debate, 'the future was to be modern, urban, vertical, and communal, and unambiguously so.'[9] A high-rise housing boom had begun, with blocks as tall as seventeen floors under construction in East London as early as 1950 and various attempts to fully realise Le Corbusier's concept of *La Ville Radieuse* passing through the planning system, such as the 1958 proposal for 'High Paddington' above the station's goods yard. The model of the proposed vertical township of over eight thousand people was constructed by Hunting Aeromodels and became a lightning rod for protests against the development led by John Betjeman.[10]

For architectural modelmakers the adoption of modernist architectural styles in the rebuilding of post-war Britain meant they were facing a double demand. Not only were enormous numbers of models required to communicate the rebuilding and modernisation plans to the public, but the newness of the style of architecture being used led to a further demand to explain the architecture itself. Kenneth McCutchon had noted as early as 1936 that due to the 'growth of new materials and new methods of construction [of buildings] giving rise to new values in the questions of space and scale, the use of models is increasing in popularity.'[11] In 1942, the British architect Price Nunn wrote that 'the potentialities of the model for publicising the aims of architecture are high, especially in present times, when the popular interest in the future shape of our buildings is so intense' and that drawings were unable to 'convincingly convey to clients unaccustomed to the them the effects which modern architecture is designed to produce.'[12] The complex combinations of asymmetrically arranged masses that were common features of modernist architecture were particularly difficult to understand in plan and elevation drawings, with models – and photographs of models – becoming 'almost a necessity for both architect and client.'[13]

Realistically representing the elements that comprised modernist architecture in model form was not an easy task, and with the demand for realism having been bolstered by the impressive achievements of the ex-RAF modelmakers working on planning models, an urgent practical need arose for modelmakers to find new methods of construction that could more realistically portray the new materials, construction methods, and visual language of the buildings being designed. The materials used in buildings had begun a wholesale shift from brick and stone to glass, steel, and concrete. Steel-framed construction methods allowed for much more open expanses of glass to be used, while entirely new forms of building such as high-rise blocks of flats posed a double challenge to architectural modelmakers. Large numbers of windows across multiple floors left little room to hide any internal bracing, and the solid construction approach favoured by Thorp and many other modelmakers before the war, where card façades were applied to solid timber blocks, simply could not be used to effectively represent these new building types. By the early-1950s, the crispness demanded by modernist architecture, with sharp corners and clean lines, had forced a radical rethinking of model construction and finishing techniques. Crucially, modernist architecture had embraced concepts of light and air, with internal spaces intended to be flooded with light from the outside during the day, while at night buildings almost became glowing boxes, in complete opposition to the heavy masonry walls featured in more traditional architectural styles. Modernism demanded a completely different balance of solid wall to glass, and transparency consequently became a hugely important requirement for architectural models (Figure 5.2). As Kenneth McCutchon had realised before the Second World War, Perspex, produced as a rigid and optically

Figure 5.2 Model of Magnet House, made by Nick Quine, 1963.

Source: Image courtesy AMI/David MacKay.

clear sheet, was ideally suited for representing this new modernist aesthetic, and by the early-1950s it was once again commercially available in large enough quantities for modelmakers to utilise, just as the demand for architectural models intensified as the post-war boom moved from planning models to larger-scale models of individual buildings in the new modernist style.

The Plastics Revolution

The increased commercial availability of Perspex came at precisely the right time for modelmakers facing demands for models of building designs that would otherwise have been almost impossible to convincingly make using timber and card. Its transparency and innate transformability instigated a series of shifts in construction methods that ultimately resulted in the widespread adoption of the all-Perspex approach that had been explored by McCutchon's school models in 1938. By the end of the Second World War, Perspex production had reached nearly two thousand tons a year, the war effort having fuelled the rapid development of both the casting process and refinements to the material's chemical composition, becoming even clearer, stronger, and less prone to shrinkage and deformation.[14] Mechanised production had replaced the original hand-pouring approach, and by the late-1940s ICI had a large number of factories dedicated to the production of what was by then a much more refined plastic, for which its main application in aircraft canopies had been substantially reduced. ICI was therefore keen to find new uses for its material and so began an active period of promotion to various industries. In 1945, an exhibition was held by ICI in Birmingham to showcase the material to architects, industrial designers, and manufacturers, with the British Plastics Federation holding a similar exhibition in London in the following year, both shows encouraging potential peacetime applications of Perspex.[15] The first major industry to make use of Perspex after the war was the lighting industry, with ICI producing pigmented and opal sheets especially for their use.[16] This success quickly spread the use of Perspex to signs and shop fascias. Modelmakers had become aware of the potential uses of Perspex before the war, as McCutchon's use exemplifies, and as early as 1941 other innovative uses by craftsmen and designers were being demonstrated in various art colleges, while its availability in large blocks had already attracted the attention of sculptors.[17]

As Kenneth McCutchon's 1938 school models had so effectively demonstrated, Perspex was well suited for use in architectural models to represent glazing, and it was its transparency that first attracted modelmakers to its potential as a material solution to the problem of realistically portraying modernist architecture. The more modelmakers began to work with the material, however, it became apparent that Perspex's potential was far more extensive than just its transparency. By the late-1940s Perspex's reputation as a vital material for architectural modelmaking had been firmly established, Peter Wickham noting that:

> Of the transparent plastics, Perspex is the best known, and has many virtues, being quite clear; easily worked and fitted, and very light. The snags about Perspex are its high cost, and the fact that it is not, at present, available below 1/16th inch for thickness.[18]

By 1952, Perspex was an 'essential part of the modelmaker's stock,' being able to be bent and formed into 'almost any shape imaginable.'[19] Overall, Perspex's intrinsic adaptability proved to be an excellent match for the modelmaker's requirements. It could be cut on a circular or band saw with ease, sanded quickly, and could be polished clear after machining. As a thermoplastic it could be bent to fit over a mould or former when heat was applied, after which it retained its new shape. The precision with which Perspex could be cut or shaped was considerably higher than with either card or timber, and its dimensional stability meant that two pieces cut to size by a machine tool would invariably join with no visible gap, a light sanding removing all trace of the edges of Perspex sheets where two met at a corner of a model. Solvents such as dichloromethane could be used to weld it together, and its ability to be machined with existing woodworking tools made it a highly attractive choice for modelmakers. Taking paint well further added to Perspex's list of admirable qualities, and by 1947 its use in the construction of both hobbyist model kits and professional models of cars and boats had become widely established.[20] A rapidly expanding branch of modelmaking – that for aircraft models – was also making extensive use of Perspex in both design and display models, and it was clear by this point that Perspex offered far more to the modelmaker than simply being a glazing replacement as Thomas Bayley had first suggested, although its transparency remained a crucially beneficial property (Figure 5.3).

In terms of practical advances in the construction and quality of architectural models, Perspex went through several phases of use. Initially, Kenneth McCutchon's all-Perspex models from 1938 were an exceptional approach to the use of the material that most architectural modelmakers did not widely adopt until the mid-1950s. Particularly in the late-1940s, when materials were still difficult to come by, Perspex was generally only used as a direct replacement for glass and mica as a glazing material. Norman Taylor enthused in 1959 that 'there are a hundred and one uses for Perspex in model making, but the first one which comes to mind for the architectural modeller is the representation of glass in model windows.'[21] Actual transparent window representation was quite rare in architectural models both before and immediately after the Second World War. For small-scale models, solid timber blocks with card façades were still the norm, although for larger-scale models a hollow plywood carcass with internal bracing to prevent warping was also used.[22] Windows on these types of models were often represented by applying strips of coloured card or paper to the plywood exterior before being covered with a suitable clear material, usually mica, celluloid, or – after 1945 – Sellotape. Card facings were then applied over the top of this, with window apertures carefully cut out. Where the interior of a building needed to be seen, apertures were cut into the plywood with a fretsaw, and small strips of mica, glass, or celluloid were placed behind the opening. Perspex was a natural replacement for these materials, but the approach left many unsatisfactory compromises, as Thomas Hendrick observed in 1957:

> In the first place, unless the scale of the model is so great that the thickness of the plywood forms a true representation of the width of the reveals, the proportions are badly out, particularly if the plywood has to receive an additional layer of card to provide a suitable surface for the exterior colour treatment. Looking at the walls from the inside, what is to be done about the edges of the glass or Perspex?

(probably oozing beads of Scotch glue). The answer is that the thickness of the walls must be further increased by the addition of another layer of card on the interior to form a trim and flush surface around the window.[23]

This approach, while tidying up the visible interior of the model, was not only complicated to construct and unnecessarily time-consuming, but it further increased the

Figure 5.3 Perspex model of a Brussels office tower, made by Nick Quine, circa 1961.

Source: Image courtesy AMI/David MacKay.

thickness of the walls beyond what was true to scale. The solution, as Hendrick further noted, was to use Perspex for the entire structure, just as McCutchon had demonstrated in 1938. The Perspex walls could then be clad with either plywood or card façades with windows cut into them, leaving the Perspex underneath completely clear. Window bars could be scribed into the Perspex and paint rubbed into the grooves to simulate the appearance of frames. This combination of a Perspex structure and card facings proved to be highly successful, and by the mid-1950s pre-printed brick papers and rub-down transfers were adding extra realism to the representation of different materials such as concrete, brick, and tile. The modelmakers at Thorp under Leslie's leadership rapidly switched to this approach as standard, while McCutchon Studio, which by the mid-1950s had become one of Thorp's largest competitors – likely advantaged by Kenneth McCutchon's early adoption of Perspex before the war – became well known for their impressive models of the proposed new terminal for London Airport that used a combination of both approaches to wall and glazing construction. Highly publicised models such as these demonstrated the degree to which Perspex could so enticingly represent modernist architectural designs with their openness and transparency. Being able to see into buildings also greatly improved the sense of realism in architectural models, while the inclusion of internal lighting helped encapsulate modernism's idea of architecture as forms assembled in the light. The technical precision with which pieces of Perspex could be cut, engraved, sanded, and attached to one another also allowed for cleaner and often invisible joins between component parts, further improving their overall quality (Figure 5.4).

The use of Perspex walls with card facings remained a widely used approach to model construction until the late-1980s, particularly so within in-house modelshops such as those maintained by the LCC and other local councils. This was partly due to the cleanness of construction. The cutting and assembly of Perspex walls required only the most basic of workshop machinery – circular and band saws, a sanding disk, and pots of dichloromethane to weld the pieces together. Card, being either painted by hand with inks and watercolours or furnished with brick papers and rub-downs, required no messy or potentially toxic paints, cellulose-based paint having become the norm in commercial architectural modelmaking workshops during the 1950s.[24] For modelmakers such as Thorp and McCutchon Studio, however, card was gradually replaced with high-impact polystyrene sheet (HIPS) during the 1960s. Having been developed by BASF in the 1930s, HIPS was a brittle, opaque, and low-cost plastic that came in a variety of thicknesses down to less than 1 mm and was very easy to cut with a scalpel; being able to be sanded and heat bent, it was a far more durable material than card and could take cellulose paint well. The ability to spray-finish architectural models further increased their levels of realism (Figure 5.5).

Perspex also opened entirely new methods of model construction, and consequently allowed architectural models to express elements of designs that had previously been impossible. As early as 1949 the architectural practice ARCON had made use of a largely clear Perspex model to show the interior arrangement of floors and spaces in a proposed church design, while in 1957 Thorp produced a remarkable concept model for a proposed design for the Barbican in London that used stacked layers of Perspex sanded to give a frosted appearance, the first known example of what was then a startlingly modern take on the traditional wooden block model, and which today has become a commonplace method of representing building masses during early design

Figure 5.4 Perspex and card model, made by Thorp, circa 1960.

Source: Image courtesy Thorp Archive, AUB.

stages for planning or competition purposes (Figure 5.6). In the same year, Thomas Hendrick commented on the development of fluorescent Perspex, sheets of which had a characteristic neon glow when left unpolished, further opening new possibilities for highlighting surfaces in cutaway sections of models,[25] and which later led to the development of new creative styles in the 1990s with the introduction of the laser cutter.

While the use of Perspex in creating more abstract models such as Thorp's frosted block model would not be fully exploited for several decades, Perspex's main influence

Figure 5.5 Model of Poole General Hospital, made by Thorp, 1963.
Source: Image courtesy Thorp Archive, AUB.

Figure 5.6 Perspex concept model of the Barbican, made by Thorp, 1957.
Source: Image courtesy Thorp Archive, AUB.

during the 1950s and early-1960s was to enable the new more lightweight and open forms of modernist architecture to be realistically portrayed. A consequence of this was that the interiors of models became much more visible, requiring not just a rethinking of how internal walls could be loadbearing but also a reconsideration of how much detail could be included. Largely determined by the budget of whoever was commissioning a model, at the very least all internal floors in a curtain-walled office building were expected to be included, and for more expensive models, interior walls, furniture, lift doors, staircases, and more could be included – every detail adding additional time and costs to the building of a model (Figure 5.7).

Figure 5.7 Model of St Martins Lane, made by Nick Quine, circa 1962.
Source: Image courtesy AMI/David MacKay.

Perspex's transparency and sheer adaptability, being able to be machined in a variety of ways and finished through moulding, engraving, painting, and laminating to represent a diverse range of other materials, meant that by the end of the 1950s it was the principal material used by professional architectural modelmakers in Britain. The mixing of materials that had been the hallmark of the first generation of professional modelmakers such as John Thorp and Ernest Twining settled down during the post-war era into a suite of materials that could be applied to different purposes, but less often within a single model. Differing rates of thermal expansion and contraction encouraged modelmakers to limit the number of materials used in a model, especially given Perspex's impressive dimensional stability compared to timber. Balsa, plywood, and hardboard were still used for baseboard construction, with beech, sycamore, and mahogany strips used for facings, while Perspex, polystyrene sheet, and card became the dominant materials used for the buildings themselves. In 1972 it was noted that within modelmaking 'modern plastics – in only twenty years – have usurped the roles of many ancient materials,'[26] and just a few years later plastics manufacturers were keen to note that 'modelmakers have developed construction methods in which plastics materials are used almost to the exclusion of all other.'[27] Ray Pfaendler at Thorp wrote in 1966 that 'the wide variety of thermoplastics and thermosetting plastic materials now available have greatly increased the scope of modelling techniques, and made possible the production of almost any free form shape or pattern,'[28] and the sheer versatility of plastics such as Perspex and polystyrene sheet was such that modelmakers rarely found themselves looking for additional materials, instead focusing

Figure 5.8 Model of Centre Point, made by Nick Quine, 1963.

Source: Image courtesy AMI/David MacKay.

their attention on improving the quality and detail of their models. For the architectural modelmaker, the shift to plastics was taking place at a time when, as the plastics industry journal *Beetle Bulletin* observed:

> Plastics materials are impinging on almost every art and craft, [and] it is not surprising that the professional modelmaker – who is both artist and craftsman – is making more and more use of them to satisfy exacting demands for both accuracy and realism imposed by architects and planners.[29]

The resultant improvements in quality and realism in professionally made architectural models during the 1950s and early-1960s is clear in photographs of models from the period. Nick Quine, who in 1959 embarked on what was to be a fifty-four-year career as an architectural modelmaker in London, adopted plastics from the very start, with striking models of buildings such as Magnet House, Tolworth Tower, and his 1963 model of Centre Point all made almost exclusively from either Perspex sheet or injection-moulded plastic parts from his own metal tooling (Figure 5.8).

The precision and realism of Quine's models dramatically illustrated how significantly the introduction of plastics had advanced architectural modelmaking in Britain, and while Quine went further than most in making his own accessories for his models, most modelmakers continued to take advantage of the modelshop that fronted Thorp's premises at 98 Gray's Inn Road, which by the mid-1950s was supplying modelmaking materials including Perspex and polystyrene sheet to other modelmakers and architects across London. Thorp's range of cast white metal figures and vehicles, produced at various standard scales, began to be seen on almost every architectural model made in the country. With the added availability of pre-made scale-model trees and flock powder during the 1950s, as well as softer plastic foams that could be carved and shaped with hand tools, even more realistic natural landscapes could be modelled (Figure 5.9). The wide availability of such new materials

Figure 5.9 Model for Vickers Engineering, made by Nick Quine, circa 1965.

Source: Image courtesy AMI/David Mackay.

and accessories also greatly increased the efficiency of model construction, as while a model such as Twining's 1934 diorama of Bournemouth described in Chapter Three involved the hand-making of two thousand vehicles, it was now possible to purchase them ready-made, vastly reducing the time needed to complete a model to such realistic standards.

A Modernised Profession

By the start of the 1960s, architectural modelmaking in Britain had undergone a period of rapid evolution, the use of Perspex having revolutionised the construction of architectural models and opened new possibilities for the levels of quality, technical precision, and realism that could be achieved, all of which further fuelled the demand for models during the second half of the post-war modelmaking boom. With new modelmakers using new materials to represent new forms of architecture, new processes and ways of working went hand in hand. In a typical modelmaking workshop such as at Thorp or McCutchon Studio, the use of machine tools became ever more dominant as the shift to hard plastics ruled out the use of more traditional hand tools except for the construction of timber baseboards (Figure 5.10).

Crucially, the profession had demonstrated its ongoing adaptability, having accepted the changes that it faced during the post-war era with enthusiasm, and doggedly maintained John Thorp's original focus on the needs of the model rather than holding an attachment to any particular process or material. Robert Hoyt's 1939 observation of 'ingenious adaptation' as a crucial element of architectural modelmaking had become a much-paraphrased description of the modelmaker's process during the 1950s, with Norman Taylor remarking that modelmakers 'are usually noted for their ingenuity and ability to adapt unusual materials to their own particular requirements,'[30] and Thomas Hendrick writing that 'new and improved materials and methods are evolved daily and the eager hunter of information will be rewarded by discoveries which will save him time and money in addition to improving the construction and appearance of his models.'[31] In 1955, a Thorp brochure proudly noted that they were 'constantly applying new methods, materials and ideas for the even better realisation of your needs,'[32] and in 1959 Thomas Bayley summarised a change of emphasis in the role of the modelmaker that had emerged, noting that:

> Whereas in the past little more was expected of the model maker than that he should produce a true to scale model of whatever was presented to him, one can now expect, and indeed demand, models which are both artistically designed and of superb craftsmanship.[33]

The complexity of architectural models had in many ways returned to the heady days of the inter-war years boom, as while their size remained much more modest, the levels of detail being included and the need for individual floors and even whole interiors to be realistically portrayed required valuable time and money; the modelmakers at Thorp found themselves increasingly working in smaller

Figure 5.10 Thorp workshop, 1952.

Source: Image courtesy Thorp Archive, AUB.

scales to offset the general rise in costs that the greater complexity of models brought about.[34] Ever since the early days of John Thorp's workshop, most architectural models had been team efforts, groups of between two and five modelmakers working on any single project depending on its demands. Unlike in the United States, where during the 1950s modelmaking had been industrialised with an almost Fordist attitude of dividing tasks into specific roles, leading to a single modelmaker employed just to make trees working on multiple models at the same time,[35] in Britain modelmakers were expected to turn their hand to whatever tasks a particular model required. This kept adaptability and diversity central to the modelmaker's experience, with change something to be embraced with curiosity and enthusiasm.

With the post-war boom continuing into the early-1960s, and the demand for architectural models remaining high, the profession continued to thrive. Alongside Thorp, modelmakers such as McCutchon Studio, Cockade, Preview, Twining Models, Nick Quine's company Architectural Models International, Partridge's Models, Hunting Aeromodels, and the Models Section of the LCC Architects' Department all continued to expand, the larger organisations employing over twenty modelmakers each. Further companies began to open around the country, sometimes just single modelmakers working on their own, taking advantage of a demand for models that was beginning to spread beyond just London. Mike Karslake, having set up on his own studio after leaving the Basildon Development Corporation in 1956, quickly found work making models for the oil industry – the discovery of the North Sea oil field having created a need for models of both oil rigs and land-based processing plants.[36] By the end of the 1960s, Karslake was employing seventeen modelmakers and had won the Queen's Award to Industry. At the LCC Models Section, an average of fifty models were being made each year, with major civic projects such as the Royal Festival Hall, the South Bank redevelopment, Elephant and Castle housing, plus dozens of new school buildings each year providing ongoing work. The LCC's job records provide evidence that their modelmakers were constantly working to capacity, with additional models being commissioned from Thorp and McCutchon Studio on a regular basis.[37]

At Thorp, Ray Pfaendler, who had been hired to manage the company under Leslie's ownership in 1950, continued his modernisation of the business (Figure 5.11).

Figure 5.11 Ray Pfaendler working on a model, circa 1960.

Source: Image courtesy Thorp Archive, AUB.

While Leslie had been very much a strong believer in the value of traditional materials and techniques, Pfaendler saw the benefit of the 'considerable advances over the last twenty years in the techniques of precision [that modelmakers] can bring to bear,'[38] and with an interest in mechanical models encouraged the inclusion of lighting panels and moving parts in the more complex models the company made. In 1957 Leslie instigated an apprentice training program that took on teenagers between the ages of sixteen and nineteen for a three-year period in which they learned the skills of architectural modelmaking. Hugely successful, over fifty trainee modelmakers passed through the program over the next thirty years, and during the 1960s the staffing at Thorp continued to grow, with a steady core of experienced modelmakers remaining in place until the early-1980s.

Leslie Thorp retired from the business in 1964, and with Florence North having died some years prior, Leslie, as the sole owner, handed day-to-day responsibility to Ray Pfaendler. Just two years later Leslie died and Pfaendler purchased the business, accelerating his modernisation program and changing the name of the company from 'John B. Thorp' to 'Thorp Modelmakers.' An entirely new suite of mills and lathes, vacuum forming machines, and pantograph engraving and scaling machines were installed, the last of which longstanding Thorp modelmaker Alec Saunders remembered with fondness:

> It was like a locksmith's key engraver. You could make copies and change the scale of objects. If we did an airport, for example, we would take an Airfix jet and we would put half of it on a panel and follow this roller over it, and it would produce half in a block of [Perspex], then register it and turn over the other half of the fuselage and create the other side. You'd get a perfect scaled aircraft.[39]

Pfaendler successfully rebranded the business with a new corporate image and developed marketing materials in the form of brochures, leaflets, and even complementary scale rulers to be given to potential clients, echoing John Thorp's own innovative efforts some sixty years prior. With John having instigated a system of photographing every model the company made before it left the workshops, Pfaendler turned to the acclaimed architectural photographer Henk Snoek, whose dramatically composed black and white images captured a drama in the company's models that highlighted the quality of their work (Figure 5.12). A push for overseas commissions also proved to be especially productive, with work flowing in as a result of foreign investment projects in the Middle East and Africa, while the continued growth of British commissions such as for the Barbican Centre, Ramsgate Hoverport, and the NatWest Tower (Figure 5.13) pushed the volume of models Thorp produced each year to well over two hundred and fifty. By 1964, sales had risen to £30,000 a year (roughly £500,000 today).[40]

Throughout the post-war boom the architectural model continued to prove its worth as an indispensable tool for both the architect and planner alike; local authorities began to insist that any scheme submitted for planning approval be accompanied by a model. Architectural modelmaking in Britain was on a high, Thomas Bayley having noted in 1959 that 'considerable progress has been made in the craft of model making: not only has the demand for models greatly increased but a more informed appreciation of their qualities is being shown.'[41] Ray Pfaendler wrote in 1966 that

Figure 5.12 Model of the Phoenix Development, made by Thorp, 1965.

Source: Photograph by Henk Snoek. Image courtesy Thorp Archive, AUB.

due to the architectural model's continued success, 'there is likely to be an increasing emphasis on professional skill and finish.'[42] Central to this success was undoubtedly the use of Perspex in allowing modelmakers to successfully adopt new methods of construction that captured the feel of modernist architecture during the expansive demand for architectural models during the post-war boom. The consequences of this shift, however, were to outlast both the boom and modernism itself, as while Perspex was ideally suited for modernist architecture, the approach of building a hollow Perspex core clad with layers of card or polystyrene sheet was suitable for almost any form of architecture – modernist or otherwise. The 'modern' architectural model, as Thomas Hendrick had described, was seemingly here to stay (Figure 5.14).

The changes to architectural modelmaking that took place during the 1950s and 1960s were not altogether welcome, however. The close associations with modernist utopian visions that the model developed during the optimism of the post-war rebuilding efforts, and the realism that Perspex enabled, were to cause significant problems when modernism, realism, and plastics – despite all they had done to improve the quality of the architectural model – began to rapidly fall out of fashion in architectural circles during the late-1960s. As that decade drew to a close, the standing of

Figure 5.13 Model of the NatWest Tower, made by Thorp, circa 1969.

Source: Image courtesy Thorp Archive, AUB.

Figure 5.14 Model of a Jamaican hotel, made by Thorp, 1969.

Source: Image courtesy Thorp Archive, AUB.

the professional architectural modelmaker suddenly came under attack as a brewing conflict between the visionary ideals of the architect and the commercial realities of property development came to a head, with the modelmaker unexpectedly caught in the middle.

Notes

1 Thomas Hendrick, *The Modern Architectural Model* (London: Architectural Press, 1957), 34.
2 Alan Powers, *Britain: Modern Architectures in History* (London: Reaktion, 2007), 13.
3 Juliet Gardiner, *The Thirties* (London: Harper Collins, 2011), 354.
4 Martin Pugh, *We Danced All Night* (London: Vintage, 2009), 71.
5 Powers, *Britain*, 40; Barry Turner, *Beacon for Change* (London: Aurum, 2011), 34.
6 J. Nunn, 'Models and their Making,' *The Builder*, June 26, 1942, 553.
7 John Partridge, 'Roehampton Housing,' in *Housing the Twentieth Century Nation*, eds. Elaine Harwood and Allan Powers (London: Twentieth Century Society, 2008), 116.
8 Peter Carolin, 'Sense, Sensibility and Tower Blocks,' in *Housing the Twentieth Century Nation*, eds. Elaine Harwood and Allan Powers (London: Twentieth Century Society, 2008), 106.
9 David Kynaston, *Family Britain* (London: Bloomsbury, 2010), 280.
10 Ibid, 284.
11 Kenneth McCutchon, 'Architectural Models,' *Architects' Journal*, 84 (October 17, 1936), 459.
12 Nunn, 'Models and their Making,' 553–4.
13 Kenneth Reid, 'Architectural Models,' *Pencil Points* (July, 1939), 407.

14 H. Perry, 'A More Heat-Resistant Acrylate Material,' *British Plastics* (October, 1943), 254.
15 'Exhibitions,' *British Plastics*, vol 17, no 198 (November, 1945), 479; 'A London Plastics Exhibition,' *British Plastics*, vol 18, no 210 (November, 1946), 488.
16 ICI, *Perspex: The First Fifty Years* (Darwen: Imperial Chemical Industries, 1984), 26.
17 V. Yarsley and E. Couzens, *Plastics* (London: Pelican, 1941), 116; ICI, *Perspex*, 28.
18 P. Wickham, *Modelled Architecture* (London: Percival Marshall, 1948), 46.
19 Thomas Hendrick, *Model Making as a Career* (London: Percival Marshall, 1952), 19.
20 'Models and Moulding,' *British Plastics*, vol 19, no 222 (November, 1947), 174.
21 Norman Taylor, *Architectural Modelling and Visual Planning* (London: Cassell, 1959), 29.
22 Hendrick, *The Modern Architectural Model*, 59.
23 Ibid, 66–67.
24 Taylor, *Architectural Modelling*, 149.
25 Hendrick, *The Modern Architectural Model*, 223.
26 J. Newman and L. Newman, *Plastics for the Craftsman* (London: George Allen & Unwin, 1972), 1.
27 'The Small World of Malcolm Allan,' *Beetle Bulletin*, 39 (1976), 6.
28 Ray Pfaendler, 'Architectural Models,' *The Architectural Review* (July, 1966), 5.
29 'The Small World of Malcolm Allan,' 2.
30 Taylor, *Architectural Modelling*, 23.
31 Hendrick, *The Modern Architectural Model*, 26.
32 Thorp Modelmakers, 1955, brochure, Thorp Modelmaking Archive.
33 Thomas Bayley, *The Craft of Model Making (Fifth Revised Edition)* (Leicester: Dryad Press, 1959), 5.
34 Pfaendler, 'Architectural Models,' 4.
35 Teresa Fankhanel, *The Architectural Models of Theodore Conrad* (London: Bloomsbury, 2021), 32–33.
36 Mike Karslake, interview with Louise Brady, November 19, 1981, audio recording, Essex County Archives.
37 *Models Job Record*, GLC Models Section, 1969, GLC Collection, London Metropolitan Archives.
38 Pfaendler, 'Architectural Models,' 1.
39 Alec Saunders, interview with author, March 13, 2018.
40 *Annual Accounts 1964*, Thorp Modelmakers, Thorp Modelmaking Archive.
41 Bayley, *The Craft of Model Making*, 5.
42 Pfaendler, 'Architectural Models,' 5.

Chapter 6

A Fall From Grace

In February 1969, *The Architect and Building News* published a withering attack on the architectural model by *The Daily Telegraph's* architectural correspondent John Chisholm. Written at a time when concerns were being raised about the quality of buildings that had been erected during the commercial boom of the late-1950s and early-1960s, Chisholm put the blame squarely on presentation and marketing models made by professional modelmakers (Figure 6.1). Noting that 'hardly a project of any consequence rose from the ground unaccompanied by a prestige model,' he argued that 'the apparently infallible honesty of the beautifully executed scale model has seduced planning committee, board of directors and the general public.'[1] Chisholm even went as far to suggest that buildings were designed as they were simply because they were easier to make in model form, stating that:

> A cynical theory was once advanced that most of the rash of commercial building of the fifties was designed not by architects at all, but by one of the three or four large model-making companies operating at the time. After all, the repetition of apparently identical buildings clad in large glazed areas . . . and the acres of flat roofing did make their 'model' construction much easier.[2]

In Chisholm's view, professional modelmakers, working for commercial clients, were responsible for the poor state of architecture in Britain at the end of the 1960s. Architectural models, Chisholm was adamant, should be made by architects themselves to develop their ideas, not to sell those designs to other people. The problem, Chisholm argued, was two-fold: that models were powerful tools of seduction, and that the realities they portrayed were at best unobtainable, and at worst dishonest. In striving for realism, architectural models were in fact being unrealistic. The snapshots of the future they presented were too precise, too clean, and too optimistic:

> Planning committees the length and breadth of the land were sold on the contents of hundreds of Perspex boxes enclosing the dust-free atmospheres of miniature 'true-to-scale' worlds of shopping centre, office redevelopment or point block housing project: A utopian climate where mini bays of exposed aggregate concrete wall cladding, shining sheets of aluminium and brightly coloured infill panels retained their original colouring and texture protected for ever from the corrosive effects of climate and smog ridden air.[3]

DOI: 10.4324/9781003298007-7

Figure 6.1 Marketing model made by Thorp, 1965.

Source: Image courtesy Thorp Archive, AUB.

What Chisholm had articulated in his article was a realisation that the utopian fiction of the model was always unfavourably contrasted by the reality that followed. As Christophe van Gerrewey later described, the architectural model is ultimately a realisation of 'what architecture promises, yet can never attain,'[4] with Chisholm further remarking that:

> Perhaps one of the saddest experiences of present-day life is to see a prestige model on display . . . as pristine and bright as the day it was proudly unveiled before the board of directors, while about it the all-too-familiar reality of the dream stands – stained and tatty.[5]

By the late-1960s, the future that the architectural models of the post-war boom had been predicting had become the present, and the reality did not look at all like the models had suggested. By being too concrete in their predictions, in being too realistic in terms of detail, scenery, and inhabitation, architectural models were starting to be seen as giving a false impression of what a proposed building would be like. In capturing the idea of the building in its idealised state, models were creating a fantasy that a real building could never live up to. For Chisholm and others in the architectural profession, this was an almost criminal act, and a backlash against realism in architectural models was well underway that would severely damage the relationship between modelmakers and architects for the next two decades.

The high standards of quality and realism that emerged because of the post-war boom in architectural modelmaking had by the late-1960s become a hallmark of the profession in Britain. The introduction of Perspex had proven to be the ideal material to represent the modernist architecture adopted for the rapid rebuilding and modernisation of Britain's war-damaged towns and cities, its transparency and versatility revolutionising architectural model construction and the levels of detail and technical precision that were possible to achieve. Clear glazing, fine details, complex paint effects to represent brick or concrete, miniature trees and shrubs, and pedestrians and road vehicles all added to a sense of realism that conveyed a more confident prediction of what a proposed development would be like (Figure 6.2).

For the professional architectural modelmaker, the strive for ever-greater realism had been the driving force behind their work since John Thorp had first set up shop, and architectural commentators had long praised the results of their efforts. Chisholm's views were therefore not allowed to pass without comment from understandably surprised and offended architectural modelmakers. J. K. Adams, in a letter to the editor published the following month, wrote that the accusation that modelmakers were dictating the design of buildings that could be easily be made in miniature was 'the biggest load of rubbish I have seen in print.'[6] Adams further pointed out that the purpose of a model was to 'show how expertly the architect has dealt with his brief,'[7] suggesting that architects might better look at their own work than that of the modelmaker when apportioning blame for poor-quality architecture. Modelmaker George Rome Innes, who was working at Arup Associates at the time, later reflected on Chisholm's article, noting that it was 'a bit much to blame it on the models.'[8]

Figure 6.2 Model of a residential development, made by Thorp, 1970.
Source: Image courtesy Thorp Archive, AUB.

The broader observations Chisholm made regarding the gap between the utopian vision of the model and the reality that followed were issues that came to dominate architecture's thoughts on the model throughout the 1970s; however, and over the following decade, more and more articles began to be published that continued these criticisms. Several contributors to the American publication *Great Models* expressed the same concerns, with one architect echoing Chisholm's claim that modelmaking was in effect responsible for poor-quality architecture, noting that modelmaking techniques had led to the design of buildings with 'mono-chromatic designs with cut-out elevations,'[9] while Romaldo Giurgola summarised his concerns about realistic models by saying that including detail to please the layman's eye turned the model into 'a mockery of the building.'[10] In the same year, another architect commented that 'architectural models can tell the truth, but they can also tell partial truths, and even lie,'[11] while Richard Pommer in *Idea as Model* described presentation models as 'propaganda for persuading clients.'[12] Even Ray Pfaendler, managing director of Thorp, had written in 1966 that 'models are open to the objection that miniatures are themselves attractive and so tend to get accepted for the wrong reasons,'[13] while an American publication on architectural modelmaking techniques warned that models 'should not be abused by over-presentation, misrepresentation, or the use of gimmicks.'[14]

From the late-1960s onwards, realism in architectural models became a highly contentious issue for architects in a way that had rarely been a concern before. In part this was caused by a frustration of the architect that the model created a better reality than the actual finished building, which meant models could be embarrassing reminders of what they had predicted. Equally, the model's association with the grand modernist projects of the post-war era and their perceived failure compounded a sense that the model had over-promised and architects had under-delivered. Whereas the architectural models of the post-war boom had been confidently predicting a better future, it was manifestly clear by the end of the 1960s that those predictions had been wrong. More generally, there was also the model's growing association with commercial property development, something that was frowned upon by discerning architects of the 1960s, and the reality of the situation whereby the main commissioners of architectural models were no longer architects but developers, with the model's function having increasingly shifted from one of communication to one of sales (Figure 6.3).

Figure 6.3 Thorp Modelmakers promotional stand, 1965.

Source: Image courtesy Thorp Archive, AUB.

Selling Utopia

The role of architectural models as sales tools has been fundamental to their success since their invention, and while models are perhaps more regularly described as communicating architectural ideas, that communication has often been for the purposes of convincing others to support projects with either permission or financial investment, and, from the mid-twentieth century onwards, to purchase space in the resultant building. In 1919 an American article championed the architectural model as the most effective means of giving a client a concrete idea of an architect's intentions,[15] with *The Building News* recommending in 1924 that models be used for advertising purposes.[16] A year later, the American modelmaker LeRoy Grumbine described how successfully an architectural model can help an architect sell his design. An architectural model, he wrote, 'creates a desire on the part of the client, who sees a beautiful creation without the exercise of imagination. He wants it. His mind is on the thing itself, not the cost. . . . The client is much better satisfied because he sees what he is buying before he buys.'[17] Kenneth McCutchon observed in 1936 that the ability of models to sell an idea was 'fully understood by . . . committees, who know that subscriptions and donations come more freely when a model is at hand to give concrete shape to a projected scheme.'[18] Clients, he continued, liked to 'know what they are getting for their money – a point that is profitable for the architect to keep in mind.'[19] Edward Hobbs wrote the following year that 'whatever one may feel about house models in estate agents and builders' offices, the acid test is, does the model attract clients and help to make sales?'[20]

The model's success as a sales tool was due to the same reasons that explained its success as an explanatory device: 'Few people can resist the appeal of a good model.'[21] As architect Price Nunn commented, 'The architect of to-day has come increasingly to realise the usefulness of the model . . . to demonstrate to his client his intentions and purposes in a form the latter can easily understand.'[22] In the post-war era, the role of models to aid with commercial sales came to the fore, and by the 1970s it was noted that 'models are excellent tools for public relations [and] fund raising.'[23] Realism was seen as a key part of the sales pitch:

> The miniature world is infinitely real and believable: it is easy to imagine oneself down in . . . the clean new environment where it is always summer. It is increasingly necessary to sell ideas; clients need to be persuaded.[24]

The aim of a good marketing model was to be able to produce a photograph that was indistinguishable from the real thing,[25] and the increasing use of photomontage whereby photographs of architectural models were carefully added to photographs of the proposed location became the forerunners of today's highly realistic computer-generated renders (Figure 6.4). Architectural models, as had been the accepted intention from John Thorp onwards, were supposed to be as realistic representations of actual buildings as was possible. They were, after all, aimed at communicating architectural information to non-architects, their strength being their almost universal comprehension as a miniature representation of a proposed reality. By the time Chisholm launched his broadside against the professionally made architectural model in 1969, however, it was no longer the architect who was setting the parameters of that reality,

Figure 6.4 Photomontage of a model and an actual street scene, made by Thorp, 1977.
Source: Image courtesy Thorp Archive, AUB.

with the property developer having become the main commissioner of architectural models from the workshops of Thorp, McCutchon Studio, and others.

The scale of private property development had been growing since before the First World War, when cheap land prices had fuelled the rise of large building firms such as John Laing, Costain, George Wimpey, and Taylor Woodrow during a period when the RIBA had banned speculative architectural practice, leading to the bulk of the new homes built in the inter-war years being designed by unqualified assistants or copied from pattern books.[26] Models of these developments for display at exhibitions such as the *Daily Mail* Ideal Homes Exhibition were therefore ordered directly by the developers, architects having been largely bypassed in the design of privately funded housing. Most architects remained happy to work within the public sector, and after the Second World War the rebuilding efforts provided plentiful work for an entire generation of eager modernist architects. By the 1960s, however, the abandonment of building controls in 1954 had led to a speculative property boom fuelled by private finance. The developer became a key source of funding, and architects found themselves subservient to their commercial aims. Photographs in newspapers, magazines, and journals began to appear that all showed an eerily similar composition – 'powerful men in suits staring down, or pointing, at a small-scale model with cardboard blocks set across it'[27] (Figure 6.5).

Developers acted as catalysts for building projects, with an aim to 'take land and improve it with bricks and mortar so that it becomes more useful to somebody else and thus more valuable to [them].'[28] Few were concerned with the aesthetics of the buildings they commissioned, being instead focused on extracting the maximum possible profit from the land they had purchased: 'What developers want from architects is a service. They need functional buildings designed to a certain price, usually the lowest possible.'[29] For idealistic post-war architects this was not a particularly

Figure 6.5 Executives inspecting a model of Southampton Docks, made by Thorp, 1966.

Source: Image courtesy Thorp Archive, AUB.

attractive market to be operating in. For ambitious young architects who wanted to get things built quickly, however, commercial development was an appealing option, as architects who did work for developers found themselves responsible for enormous numbers of new buildings. It has been estimated that between fifty and seventy-five percent of all speculative office blocks built in London following the Second World War were designed by a mere ten firms, and of the twenty-two thousand registered architects in Britain in 1969, fewer than five thousand were in private practice, local councils being the principal employers at the time.[30] Leading the design of speculative commercial buildings were the architect Richard Seifert, his partner George Marsh, and the developer Harry Hyams. By the mid-1960s, Seifert and Partners had designed major developments such as Centre Point, Magnet House, and the Tolworth Tower (Figure 6.6), having grown the business from a staff of twelve to over two hundred in just ten years, turning over thirty million pounds a year. Modelmaker Nick Quine built his business producing many dramatic models of their designs, becoming notable for his highly impressive all-Perspex realisations, while the sheer volume of model work Seifert and Partners commissioned also provided extensive work for Thorp throughout the 1960s and 1970s.

During the post-war boom architectural models had rapidly become a central marketing tool for the developer, both to sell space in their buildings to prospective clients and to secure the initial investments needed to build them. An estate agent

Figure 6.6 Model of the Tolworth Tower, made by Nick Quine, 1962.

Source: Image courtesy AMI/David MacKay.

for one of the major 1960s developers was asked how he sold a site to his employer and the answer was revealing: 'I usually have a model made. He loves a model, you see. When he sees it, he usually says "I like that." I've almost never known him to say he didn't like one.'[31] As large-scale commercial developments such as the first covered shopping centres built by Arndale, Hammerson, and Laing took shape in the mid-1960s, models began to appear once more in town centres just as they had done to explain the post-war rebuilding programmes. This time, however, the developments were commercially led and being sold for the financial benefit of the developer rather than for the social benefit of rebuilding a community. As a result of the model's success in communicating the developers' plans, commercial development became an increasingly large proportion of the profession's business, and at Thorp their marketing efforts began to be directed at developers as potential clients rather than architects.

A consequence of this change towards developer-led model commissions was a shift in the relationship between modelmakers and architects, and between architects and the model. Even while criticisms such as Chisholm's of highly realistic sales models were being aired, the professionally made architectural model was moving further away from architects' control; modelmakers simply responded to the needs of their increasingly dominant clients, the developers, who continued to order highly realistic models that the public could easily understand. Such models soon became associated with gaudy colours and what many architects termed a 'model railway' aesthetic. High levels of realism in a model were viewed as not reflecting the creative work of an architect, and instead were deemed to be aimed at cultivating associations with childhood miniatures to sell property. As architects tried to distance themselves from the commercial realities of property development, 'the less palatable realism in models became.'[32]

With the standing of realistic models rapidly declining within the architectural profession, architects nevertheless continued to look to the model as a surrogate for their idealistic visions, but it was clear that the kinds of models being produced by commercial modelmakers such as Thorp were no longer meeting their requirements. For architects, models had long been seen as 'the natural territory of vision, perfectly adapted for projecting futuristic, visionary proposals, however intrinsically unbuildable they may be.'[33] Architectural modelmaker Richard Threadgill has described how 'a model is architecture at its purist, untouched by building regulations and door handles. It is the ultimate expression of an architect's intentions.'[34] As a favoured medium of modernists such as Le Corbusier and Mies van der Rohe, models also quickly gained strong associations with that ideological and architectural movement. For the visionary architects behind these designs, the model was often as close to reality as they could get, the world not yet fully prepared to embrace their ideas. The model, as architecture in an ideal state, was therefore utopian by its very nature. A journalist visiting Thorp once remarked that they were 'struck immediately by the fact that the world one is entering is illusory; a perfect, miniaturized version of the world as it should be.'[35] The connection between the architectural model and ideas of an ideal or better future had been growing since the inter-war years, when modernism become the dominant ideological force within British architecture. Driven by a 'clear and pure vision,'[36] modernist architects saw architecture as the language through which they could express their ideas of a better world.[37]

Through John Thorp's 1930 model of Charing Cross, Ernest Twining's model of
F. R. S. Yorke and Marcel Breuer's proposal for a concrete city of the future, and Partridge's model of the Quarry Hill Estate in Leeds, the inter-war years had seen an intensive period of modernist utopian models gracing magazine covers and being featured
in exhibitions; the model was becoming a surrogate for eager architects frustrated by
a lack of opportunity to build in a country still sceptical of their ideas. In post-war
Britain, architectural models had then become intimately bound to the enthusiasm
of building a better future and moving away from the memories of war. The town
planning models made to communicate the post-war reconstruction plans were all
fundamentally utopian in nature, projecting visions of an ideal Britain, while during
the late-1950s and 1960s, Thorp was commissioned to produce a number of widely
publicised models of highly speculative architectural projects for the Pilkington Glass
Age Committee, including Geoffrey Jellicoe's Motopia in 1959, Sea City in 1968, and
the Crystal Tower in 1961 (Figures 6.7, 6.8, and 6.9). Visionary and unshrinkingly
utopian in nature, these were all schemes that were never actually intended to be built,
instead being concepts for discussion and inspiration.

By the late-1960s, however, as John Chisholm's criticisms reveal, the growing utopian associations of the architectural model were causing as much concern as their
association with commercial development. As a safe playground in which architects
could project their ideas of a better future, the model world was seductive to both
architects and the public at large. For many modernist architects more models were

Figure 6.7 Model of Motopia, made by Thorp, 1959.

Source: Image courtesy Thorp Archive, AUB.

Figure 6.8 Model of Sea City, made by Thorp, 1968.
Source: Image courtesy Thorp Archive, AUB.

made than actual buildings, leading to suggestions that they had lost touch with the complexities of reality through their occupation of the utopian worlds their models afforded. Arthur Drexler in his criticism of modernist architecture commented that the 'model generated its own truth,'[38] describing how the world of the model became a surrogate for reality and the focus of their attention. Actual buildings, he claimed, became superfluous copies of models.[39]

The sense of deception and betrayal that Chisholm expressed in his article was therefore perhaps less to do with the architectural model itself and more to do with the faith architects held in their own abilities to deliver the perfect world models portrayed. By being so confidently precise about how a future building would look, surrounded by clean streets and green trees, realistic architectural models left no room for ambiguity or interpretation. The models constructed by Thorp, McCutchon Studio, Nick Quine, and the local government modelmaking departments such as at the LCC were pinning architects down to a very detailed vision of a future that could never possibly come about. Architects were increasingly being criticised for the quality of buildings erected during the post-war era, with the general public having become disillusioned with both

Figure 6.9 Model of the Crystal Tower, made by Thorp, 1961.

Source: Image courtesy Thorp Archive, AUB.

modernist architecture and architects themselves.[40] The failure of the modern movement to deliver the improvements it had promised put the very competence and expertise of architects in the spotlight,[41] and by the 1970s the presumptions of the modernist generation of architects were increasingly viewed as lacking an appreciation of the growing community-centred and environmental concerns of the public.

The Contested Nature of Realism

While architecture wrestled with its internal crisis of confidence and began to reconsider its relationship with the architectural model, professional modelmakers remained largely unaffected by the debate surrounding them, continuing to produce highly realistic models for developers and the commercially oriented architectural practices who supplied them with their building designs. As the 1970s progressed, however, the number of dedicated modelmaking firms began to decline. With Cockade, Twining, and Partridge's Models having closed in the 1960s and McCutchon Studio shutting its doors in 1974, Thorp's dominance within the industry ballooned once more, employing over forty modelmakers by the end of the decade. Alec Saunders, on starting his apprenticeship with Thorp in 1973, recalled that at the time there was very little competition and that most other architectural modelmakers were working independently as sole traders.[42] Despite the dire financial circumstances of the early-1970s leading to a drastic reduction in the demand for architectural models for building projects planned for Britain, the closure of some of the older modelmaking firms and an increase in overseas commissions concentrated what work was available, keeping modelmakers such as Thorp, Mike Karslake, Nick Quine, and John Piper far busier than might have been expected. Both Thorp and Karslake picked up a considerable volume of work from the petrochemicals industry as the North Sea oil boom necessitated models of refinery plants and oil rigs (Figure 6.10). Malcolm Allan, a former carpet designer, set up L. S. Angus and Company, a modelmaking firm in Glasgow targeted specifically at the offshore oil industry, while other major infrastructure projects such as the Thames Barrier and the Humber Bridge generated a further need for large and impressive models.

Under Ray Pfaendler's leadership Thorp also actively switched its attentions to gaining foreign commissions, with work from Africa and the Middle East accounting for three quarters of its annual income by the end of the decade.[43] With Thorp witnessing an expanding demand for work in Nigeria, Ray Pfaendler also took the innovative step of appointing a company agent there in 1975. In that same year, only twenty-one out of eighty models the company made were for British-based projects, and between 1977 and 1980 thirty-five models alone were made for the growing Saudi Arabian architectural practice Zuhair Fayez and Associates. With the European approach to architectural modelmaking at the time largely based around in-house modelshops within architectural practices and American commercial modelmakers primarily catering for their internal market, British modelmakers – and Thorp in particular – were effectively the only modelmakers available to serve the demand for architectural models for international clients. It was not until the 1980s that the property boom in Hong Kong fuelled the establishment of architectural modelmaking companies in Asia, and not until the 2000s that major firms began to open in China, India, and the Middle East. Until then, the demand for models from newly emerging

Figure 6.10 Model of a North Sea oil rig, made by Thorp, 1974.

Source: Photograph by Henk Snoek. Image courtesy Thorp Archive, AUB.

economies beyond Europe and North America, largely for marketing purposes, pre-dominantly fed into Thorp and other UK-based modelmakers. Consequently, Thorp's turnover more than doubled because of major projects such as models of the Tarbela Dam in Pakistan and the Yanbu city masterplan in Saudi Arabia (Figure 6.11).

Figure 6.11 Model of Yanbu, made by Thorp, 1978.
Source: Image courtesy Thorp Archive, AUB.

British commissions continued to be received during this period, however, with significant models of designs for Kodak's headquarters in Hemel Hempstead (Figure 6.12), IBM's Greenock offices, and Seifert and Partners' Liverpool redevelopment concept (Figure 6.13) among many hundreds of British projects that the company worked on by the end of the decade.

Figure 6.12 Model of the Kodak headquarters, made by Thorp, 1970.

Source: Photograph by Henk Snoek. Image courtesy Thorp Archive, AUB.

Figure 6.13 Model of a proposed redevelopment of Liverpool Docks, made by Thorp, 1967.

Source: Photograph by Henk Snoek. Image courtesy Thorp Archive, AUB.

The apparent prosperity and stability at Thorp during the 1970s were far removed from the turmoil that the architectural profession itself was undergoing, insulated from the raging debates over their relationship with the architectural model due to the company's heavy reliance on developers rather than architects for its British commissions. Its shift to foreign work had also largely offset the decline in British building projects that was severely affecting architecture's prospects. Most architectural commissions during the previous decades had come from the public sector, but by the end of the 1970s that source of funding had largely collapsed. The property market crash of 1973, the quadrupling of oil prices, soaring inflation, and the three-day week all put enormous pressures on public sector budgets, with the quality of new buildings suffering as a result, for which architects were perhaps unfairly blamed.[44] In 1976, the International Monetary Fund insisted that the Labour government cut its capital expenditure programme, and with further spending cuts under the Thatcher government from 1978, the public sector's role as a patron of British architecture was severely impacted.[45] A consequence of this for the architectural profession was a dramatic shift from public to private sector employment. Architects were suddenly at the mercy of commercial forces, with a rapid growth in private practice taking place. Due to the combination of the critical reaction to modernist architecture's poorly received legacy, the economic collapse, and the shift from public to private employment, architects were experiencing 'a diminished, if not extinguished, respect'[46] from a public that held little trust in their ability to improve the urban environment. Publications such as *Crisis in Architecture*[47] and *Why is British Architecture so Lousy?*[48] summarised the state of feeling within the profession.

At the same time, a lack of building opportunities during the 1970s saw many architects turn to theoretical and conceptual work. Nigel Coates noted how the 1970s forced architects to find 'other ways of making architecture. . . . The question was, can you be an architect without building? That was the game.'[49] As ideas of representation, symbolic meaning, language, and abstraction were embraced, the writing of Charles Jenks, Philip Johnson, and Robert Venturi promoted a more art-based view of the discipline,[50] and architecture began to position itself as a broad cultural field rather than as just the designing of buildings.[51] Part of this included a re-thinking of the value of the artefacts architecture produced, leading to an acceptance of texts, images, and models as being valid forms of architecture alongside actual buildings. An increased sense of value being assigned to other architectural outputs was perhaps inevitable during a decade with limited opportunities to build; however, this new position helped to provide some clarity around architecture's desires for what architectural models should be. If architecture was not necessarily just about buildings anymore, then neither, surely, was the architectural model.

This line of thinking was encapsulated in two American publications, *Idea as Model*[52] and *Great Models*,[53] which focused on the conceptual nature of architectural models and their ability to transcend ideas of representation. Could models be conceptual devices in their own right rather than mere surrogates for buildings? Could they be considered both objects of artistic appreciation and tools for generating ideas within the design process? The shift in thinking that *Idea as Model* expressed was summarised by the architect Peter Eisenman: 'We do not seek to assemble models of buildings as propaganda for persuading clients, but rather as studies of an idea of architecture,'[54] while in *Great Models*, the architect Michael Graves was adamant that 'we make models of ideas not real buildings.'[55] During the 1970s, architects increasingly came to embrace this view, helping to resolve the question of what architectural models were for. Their visionary, idealistic nature was confirmed, with an understanding that models did not necessarily have to represent anything that was intended to be built.

By the end of the decade, the combination of a general dislike of commercial development and their associated realistic marketing models, the model's ability to reveal the flaws in utopian modernist ideology, and architecture's rethinking of architectural models as models of ideas rather than of buildings had given depth to John Chisholm's reactionary view that professionally made architectural models were in some way growing distant from architecture's own concerns. In using realism to project false ideas about not only how a building would look but what architecture itself was now considered to be, their ability to seduce and distort was targeted for criticism. By carefully excluding adjacent buildings or showing mature planting that would not reach that state for several decades, models were argued to be manipulating their audiences.[56] Perspex in particular was highlighted as a problem – being clearer than glass, it made buildings look far more transparent than they ever could be.[57] By the early 1980s, Chisholm's view of realism in presentation models, emboldened by the rethinking expressed in *Idea as Model*, had become entrenched within much of architectural discourse, the architect Piers Gough describing architectural models as being 'by and large a vehicle for fraudulent seduction. How many clients have been sold garbage, how many town centres ruined by a childlike delight in the twee characteristics of the model?'[58] Such models were still seen as being ideally suited to the marketing of buildings because of their 'effectively seductive charms,'[59] however this was not something that architects particularly wanted to be associated with. 'To seduce and to illude [sic]: after all, isn't that the technique normally used by businessmen?'[60] A newspaper article on architectural modelmakers noted how 'trees, people and street furniture help distract attention from a controversial building;' the author went on to describe how an architectural model was:

> [A]s much a rhetorical device as a watercolour perspective garnished with sunny skies and balloon-toting happy families. The tricks of the trade are more diverse, the persuasive potential extended into three dimensions. Reality is embellished.[61]

The backlash against realism in architectural models that gathered pace within the architectural profession during the 1970s and early 1980s was therefore predominantly a reflection of architecture's internal deliberations – a dislike of both commercial architecture and the profession's own increasing reliance on property developers as clients, a reminder of the flaws of their utopian ideas, and a consequence of a rethinking of what the architectural model was in an increasingly conceptual manner. What this view of realism illuminated was a change in architecture's perception of the model and what it should represent, with realistic developers' models being seen more as models of buildings than of architecture itself. What had also become clear was that although modelmakers such as Thorp were thriving by tending to the demands of developers and overseas clients, the types of models they were offering simply no longer met many architects' needs. While property developers were content with impressive and highly realistic models, architects were not. Having become more pluralistic and critically aware, the architectural profession now wanted the architectural model and its makers to follow suit. Consequently, architectural modelmaking, while still commercially successful, found itself detached from architecture itself, wedded instead to the sales and marketing needs of the developer. As the 1980s dawned, however, a shattering of Thorp's dominance as the leading architectural modelmaker in Britain created an opportunity to address these issues, with architecture's direct relationship with professionally made models restored through the legacy of an influential architectural practice's own modelmaking workshop whose reach was set to instigate the biggest change to the making of architectural models since the profession began.

Notes

1 John Chisholm, 'Rehearsal for Reality,' *The Architect and Building News*, February 27, 1969, 24.
2 Ibid.
3 Ibid.
4 Christophe van Gerrewey, 'What Are Rocks to Men and Mountains? The Architectural Models of OMA/Rem Koolhaas,' in *Models: The Idea, The Representation, and Theory*, eds. Bas Princen and Krijn Koning, *Oase* 84 (2011), 36.
5 Chisholm, 'Rehearsal for Reality,' 24.
6 J. K. Adams, 'Letter to the Editor,' *Architect and Building News*, March 27, 1969, 41.
7 Ibid.
8 George Rome Innes, interview with author, April 18, 2019.
9 Graham Hartman, 'Some Observations on the Influences of Architectural Models,' in 'Great Models,' *The Student Publication of the School of Design North Carolina State University*, vol 27, 1978, 31.
10 Romaldo Giurgola, 'Modelling,' in 'Great Models,' *The Student Publication of the School of Design North Carolina State University*, vol 27, 1978, 68.
11 S. Abercrombie, 'Creative Playthings,' *Horizon*, July, 1978, 79.
12 Richard Pommer, 'The Idea of "Idea as Model",' in *Idea as Model*, ed. Kenneth Frampton and Silvia Kolbowski (New York: Rizolli, 1981), 3.
13 Ray Pfaendler, 'Architectural Models,' *The Architectural Review* (July, 1966), 1.
14 John Taylor, *Model Building for Architects and Engineers* (New York: McGraw Hill, 1971), 11.
15 E. Parker, 'The Model for Architectural Representation,' *Architectural Forum*, April 30, 1919, 119.
16 'The Fascination of Models,' *The Building News*, March 28, 1924, specially reprinted copy of the original article made by John Thorp, Thorp Modelmaking Archive.
17 LeRoy Grumbine, 'The Use of Scale Models as an Aid to the Architect,' *The Western Architect*, June, 1925, 59.
18 Kenneth McCutchon, 'Architectural Models,' *Architects' Journal*, 84 (October 17, 1936), 459.
19 Ibid.
20 Edward Hobbs, *House Modelling for Builders and Estate Agents* (London: The Architectural Press, 1937), vii.
21 P. Wickham, *Commercial Model Making* (London: Vawser and Wiles, 1945), 5.
22 J. Nunn, 'Models and their Making,' *The Builder*, June 26, 1942, 553.
23 Taylor, *Model Building*, 11.
24 J. Rawson, 'Small Beginning: Modelmaking,' *Architects' Journal* 191 (January 17, 1990), 63.
25 Ibid, 69.
26 Peter Hall, *Cities of Tomorrow* (Oxford: Blackwell, 2002), 76.
27 Andrew Marr, *A History of Modern Britain* (London: Macmillan, 2007), 76.
28 Oliver Marriott, *The Property Boom* (London: Abingdon Publishing, 1989), 25.
29 Ibid, 28.
30 Ibid, 27.
31 Tovey, cited by Marriott, *The Property Boom*, 28.

32 Karen Moon, *Modelling Messages* (New York: Monacelli Press, 2005), 132.
33 Ibid, 103–4.
34 Richard Threadgill, 'Modelmaking,' *Architects' Journal* 186, July 1, 1987, 79.
35 L. Knights, 'A Model to Build On,' *OS Weekly*, September 11, 1980, 6.
36 Peter Blake, *The Master Builders* (New York: Norton and Company, 1976), iv.
37 Ibid, xv.
38 Arthur Drexler, *The Architecture of the Ecole des Beaux-Arts* (London: Secker and Warburg, 1977), 15.
39 Ibid, 27.
40 Alastair Goobey, *Bricks and Mortals* (London: Century Business, 1992), 28.
41 Elaine Harwood and Alan Powers, *The Seventies: A Lost Decade of British Architecture* (London: Twentieth Century Society, 2012), 11.
42 Alec Saunders, interview with author, March 13, 2018.
43 Thorp Modelmakers, 'A History of John B. Thorp,' 1983, 11, Thorp Modelmaking Archive.
44 Harwood and Powers, *Seventies*, 12.
45 Goobey, *Bricks and Mortals*, 29.
46 C. Croft, 'David Rock: "Architecture is the Land of Green Ginger" or "Form Follows Culture",' in *The Seventies: A Lost Decade of British Architecture* eds. Elaine Harwood and Alan Powers (London: Twentieth Century Society, 2012), 67.
47 M. MacEwan, *Crisis in Architecture* (London: RIBA Enterprises, 1974).
48 N. Silver and J. Boys, *Why is British Architecture so Lousy?* (London: Newman, 1980).
49 Nigel Coates, cited in Maria Neilson, 'Form Follows Culture: Architectural Models in London 1970–1990,' (MA diss., Royal College of Art, 2013), 58.
50 Harwood and Powers, *Seventies*, 19.
51 Christopher Davies, *Thinking about Architecture* (London: Lawrence King, 2011), 11.
52 Kenneth Frampton and Silvia Kolbowski, *Idea as Model* (New York: Rizolli, 1981).
53 Suzanne Buttolph (ed.), 'Great Models,' *The Student Publication of the School of Design North Carolina State University*, vol 27, 1978, 68.
54 Peter Eisenman, 'Preface,' in *Idea as Model*, eds. Kenneth Frampton and Silvia Kolbowski (New York: Rizolli, 1981), 3.
55 Michael Graves, 'Thought Models' in Suzanne Buttolph (ed.), 'Great Models,' *The Student Publication of the School of Design North Carolina State University*, vol 27, 1978, 43.
56 Moon, *Modelling Messages*, 115.
57 Ibid, 164.
58 Piers Gough, 'Model Makers,' *Architects' Journal* 177 (April 27, 1983), 30.
59 P. Scuri, 'Skyscraper Business,' *Domus* 660 (April, 1985), 25.
60 Ibid.
61 Janet Abrams, 'Models of their Kind,' *Independent*, August 26, 1988, 18.

Chapter 7

The Arup School

By the start of the 1980s, Thorp had occupied its position as the dominant architectural modelmaker in Britain for almost a century. For all the criticisms of the realistic models made by professional modelmakers that had been levelled over the previous decade, from John Chisholm's disgust at the 'infallible honesty of the beautifully executed scale model'[1] to Piers Gough's description of the model as a 'vehicle for fraudulent seduction,'[2] the reality for companies such as Thorp was that while architects were increasingly unhappy with the types of models they were producing, in most cases it was the developer who had the money to commission them, and thus the creative control. The growing disconnection between architects and professional modelmakers was clearly not sustainable, but the economics of the relationship appeared stuck in favour of the developer's needs (Figure 7.1).

It was during the 1980s that this conflict was ultimately resolved, with the shifting economic and competitive circumstances of both architectural modelmaking and architecture itself providing an opportunity for the profession to expand its focus to encompass both the expressive, visionary needs of architecture and the realistic, commercial needs of property development. At the heart of this change was the influence of the in-house modelmaking workshop at Arup Associates, which – through its creative use of timber rather than the plastics favoured by commercial modelmakers such as Thorp – transformed the way architectural models could be made.

Timber and the Rise of the Arup Modelshop

Accompanying architecture's backlash against realism in architectural models that had characterised the 1970s was a turning away from the materials that had done so much to advance the illusion of reality in the first place – plastics. With the major commercial modelmakers continuing to serve the needs of their developer clients with high-quality realistic models, plastics, in the form of Perspex and polystyrene sheet, had remained the default materials used in professionally made architectural models throughout the decade. Timber had not been entirely forgotten as a material, however, having found its place in helping to highlight the juxtaposition between concepts of old and new. By using timber for the existing buildings on a model and plastics for the proposed development, the eye could be drawn to the realistically painted Perspex buildings, with the simpler, more abstract timber buildings receding into the background. This shorthand of timber for existing buildings and plastics for new ones had become an effective part of the modelmaker's communicative toolkit, the contrast

DOI: 10.4324/9781003298007-8

Figure 7.1 Marketing model made by Thorp, circa 1965.

Source: Image courtesy Thorp Archive, AUB.

between the two materials' qualities symbolising the difference between the existing urban context and the excitement of the new development.

Despite the dominance of plastics in professional modelmaking, timber had nevertheless remained the material of choice for architects and architectural students making their own models throughout most of the post-war era in Britain. After an initial flirtation with Perspex's abstract potential, on a symbolic level plastics quickly became associated not only with architecture's growing dislike of the highly realistic developer's model but also broader cultural associations with mass-production and cheap, poor-quality goods. Polished timber, on the other hand, had come to signify quality and exclusivity. Compared to more traditional materials, the synthetic plastics, in contrast to their utopian associations of the inter-war years, had come to be seen as being of inferior quality. Rather more practically, plastics such as Perspex were also difficult to cut without workshop machinery and required painting to achieve even the simplest finish. This meant the making of models using plastics within an architect's office required a significant investment in equipment.

In the same way that card had become the material of choice within drawing offices in Britain during the late-nineteenth century, so it was that during the post-war era balsa wood became increasingly favoured in both local government architects' departments and, perhaps more significantly, the makeshift studios of a new generation of independent architects starting their careers in the 1960s and 1970s, including James Stirling and Norman Foster. Easy to cut and work with, the simple, abstracted style balsa presented quickly became fashionable, marking a return to a less detailed and more ambiguous form of architectural model that spoke more of the process of design than it did a finished building. As publications such as *Making Models in the Drawing Office*[3] and the discussions featured in both *Idea as Model* and *Great Models* make clear, architects on both sides of the Atlantic during the 1970s were championing the use of sketch models during the design process, and presentation models made using balsa wood therefore provided a continuity of approach that appealed to architects engaging with theories of representation and language following the critical introspection of the profession that was taking place at the time. What timber models offered overall was a highly attractive alternative to the contested realism of fully painted Perspex models that were the mainstay of professional modelmakers. Without having been expressed as such at the time, the growing use of timber models by architects themselves was a clear sign that they had already found the solution to their concerns regarding realism and the changing nature of what an architectural model should be; however, it was not so much timber as a material that was the solution, but the abstraction and ambiguity it engendered.

With architects instinctively drawn to timber models, it was perhaps inevitable that as the first private in-house modelmaking workshops were established in Britain during the 1960s, timbers rather than plastics were initially favoured. At the time, very few architectural practices other than the local council architects' departments had in-house modelshops, mainly because few private practices were large enough to warrant one, with most architects still working in the public sector. In America, both I. M. Pei and Mies van der Rohe had established in-house modelmaking workshops during the 1950s, but in Britain it was not until the late-1970s and early-1980s that architects such as Hugh Casson, Norman Foster, and Richard Rogers followed suit. In 1964, however, Robert Kirkman began his modelmaking career, establishing an in-house workshop for the architect Denys Lasdun. With limited facilities available in Lasdun's offices, a small conference room was emptied and turned into a basic studio. No machinery was installed, and every model was made from balsa wood, using just a steel rule and a scalpel.[4] Kirkman applied his previous experience in advertising and a keen eye for photography to his work, intending to produce models primarily for use in publicity shots. For three years Kirkman made hundreds of models for the practice, including many variations of Lasdun's designs for the National Theatre as the project developed (Figure 7.2). Made from a single material and without any use of applied colour, Kirkman's models were clear to understand despite eschewing any attempt to represent the specific textures and materials that the real buildings would employ. Photographed in black and white, the balsa wood models appeared appropriately monumental, with the focus on pure form suiting their brutalist designs.

Moving to the architects' department of Southwark Council for seven years before setting up his own architectural modelmaking company, Kirkman's exquisite timber models drew far more architects as clients than developers, attracted by his own view of architectural modelmaking as an art form, striving to make models that were much more expressive than those that his larger competitors such as Thorp were offering.[5]

Figure 7.2 Model of the National Theatre, made by Robert Kirkman, 1965.

Source: Image courtesy Robert Kirkman.

At the time it was taken for granted that a realistic model would sell an idea to the public while a more abstract model would not. For one project Kirkman had made 'a very aesthetic Perspex and wood model, and just before the weekend [the architect] said "Could you make it look more realistic for the developer?" I disowned it, took my name off it.'[6] What became obvious to Kirkman was that developers were simply concerned with selling their buildings, with little interest in making miniature works of art, and where possible he avoided taking commissions from property developers for precisely that reason.

While Kirkman was working for Denys Lasdun, an even larger in-house modelmaking workshop had been established at Arup Associates, where in 1961 David Armstrong (Figure 7.3) was hired by Ove Arup and Philip Dowson to replace an earlier freelance modelmaker with whom Dowson had clashed. Armstrong had trained as a cabinet maker and after his national service ended in 1951 was making a meagre living selling small timber sculptures. When a friend who worked at Arup suggested he might be a good candidate to take over the modelmaking position, he met with Dowson, who commissioned him to make a hardwood model of the nuclear physics laboratory at Oxford University as a trial. Having no workshop facilities at his flat in Holland Park, Armstrong struggled with the commission and initially swore he would

Figure 7.3 David Armstrong in the Arup workshop, circa 1980.

Source: Image courtesy Roger Hillier.

never make another model again, but he was impressed by the care and interest the architect Peter Foggo had shown in his work, calling by every other day to check his progress, and so Armstrong decided to accept the company's offer to become their first in-house modelmaker.[7] His second model was for a block of flats in Bracknell, and then major work on models of the Sydney Opera House quickly followed.

Armstrong was given a clear brief from Philip Dowson to make 'beautiful things made out of lovely woods. And in that he was quite right; the finished [realistic] model can look quite stark and dead.'[8] Dowson was adamant that Arup's models should be made from hardwoods rather than balsa, which meant a fully equipped workshop was required. Armstrong was initially resistant to this, preferring to maintain a hand-made feel to the models, however he rapidly embraced the benefits of machine tools, if only for their increased efficiency as the modelshop's workload grew.[9] Exploring the qualities of different timbers, Armstrong developed a palette that included yellow and red cedar, pine, and sequoia, with Perspex reluctantly used wherever glazing was

Figure 7.4 Model of Leicester University, made by the Arup Modelshop, 1966.

Source: Image courtesy Roger Hillier.

required, as well as for fine detailing and structural support on more complex models (Figure 7.4).

As the modelshop at Arup grew, Armstrong deliberately steered clear of employing anyone who had already worked as an architectural modelmaker, as he specifically wanted to avoid people who had 'come through the model railway aesthetic' of realistic models,[10] and so Julian Thompson (an ex-RAF fitter), librarian Tina Miller, graphics graduate Roger Hillier, and architectural clerk George Rome Innes joined the team during the first ten years. This helped preserve the approach to architectural modelmaking that Armstrong had established.

Noting that the commercial modelmakers in London were almost exclusively working in Perspex, Armstrong was acutely aware that Arup's models were a departure from what was going on elsewhere,[11] demonstrating a highly nuanced artistic understanding of both the model's purpose and the visual composition required to make it a success. He resisted including too much detail in their models, noting that while some architects couldn't bear to see anything left out, 'this has the effect of mixing too many colours together: the result looks like mud.'[12] Observing that most models were designed to communicate a specific point, Armstrong recommended that 'any detail which does not contribute to this point weakens the impact of the model' and should be omitted.[13] With an on-site materials library, the Arup modelmakers could compare different timbers, plastics, and metals, opening up new avenues of experimentation when composing the appearance of a particular model.

Working in the Arup modelshop during the 1960s and 1970s was an altogether different experience to working at one of the established modelmakers such as Thorp, McCutchon Studio, or even the LCC's models section. As an interdisciplinary practice combining both architects and engineers, Ove Arup's vision for how a company should be run was very progressive, led by a personal conviction that their efforts should be driven by a desire to make the world a better place. The modelshop became known for its rather wild Friday lunches, where the team would draw in others from across the practice for lively discussions about left-wing politics and philosophy.[14] This progressive and philosophical culture was also evidenced in their approach to modelmaking, with Philip Dowson having reflected that the modelshop's success was largely due to their making models which 'did not attempt to produce a false reality but to represent the underlying form and nature of the architecture itself.'[15] Referring to their models as 'beautiful objects in their own right,' Dowson noted how a 'whole genre has developed, and the quality of both imagination and craftsmanship that has been brought to this area of Arup's work has in turn influenced what we have done as designers.'[16]

Many of Arup's models were made with the principle aim of being photographed, and with the trend for striking black and white architectural photography instigated by Henk Snoek still dominant, their models were made using carefully selected combinations of hardwoods that would produce strong tonal contrasts with prominent grain lines.[17] There was also a less-well-acknowledged practical reason for favouring timber models, however, in that they were much easier to alter than a model made from Perspex. With much of the Arup modelshop's work being a constant dialogue with architects and engineers, final models were rarely that. With a timber model, however, 'if you use water-based glues, you just spit on it and it fell apart.'[18] Not all models were left as bare timber either. George Rome Innes remembered Philip Dowson asking for a white model of Goodwood racecourse, but the team instead produced a painted model with very pale accents of colour. Upon seeing the model, 'Dowson said "lovely white model," because he knew what he wanted but it was not what he said.'[19] Roger Hillier recalled an intense dislike of painted models, however, noting that 'if anyone wanted anything painted, we usually had a hissy fit.'[20]

For over thirty years the Arup modelshop continued to produce many hundreds of creative and abstract models for projects such as the Aldeburgh concert hall (Figure 7.5). As with Robert Kirkman's models, Arup treated their models as objects to be admired, attending to the aesthetics of what they were making as much as to those of the proposed building they were representing. With the engineering arm of the firm employed by many of the leading architects during the late-1970s and early-1980s, the modelshop also produced models for architects such as Richard Rogers, Renzo Piano, and Norman Foster before they had established their own dedicated modelshops as their practices grew. A consequence of this was that the Arup in-house style began to be circulated among a much wider audience, leading to architects enquiring whether they could obtain models from the Arup modelshop on a commercial basis.[21]

Figure 7.5 Model of Aldeburgh concert hall, made by the Arup Modelshop, 1966.
Source: Image courtesy Roger Hillier.

Following this trend, Thorp began to experiment with balsa wood models during the early-1970s (Figure 7.6), but developers only rarely commissioned them when they wanted a model to give the impression that a new development wouldn't overwhelm an existing street scene, with both the proposed building and its surroundings being rendered in neutral timbers. In a typical year less than five percent of Thorp's models were made in this way, the rest overwhelmingly relying on plastics.

What both the Arup in-house workshop and Robert Kirkman were separately offering throughout the 1960s and 1970s was an alternative language for architectural models that directly appealed to architects' evolving understanding of what an architectural model should be. The abstraction that timber models engendered, while still finely made and complex creations, turned them into more ambiguous suggestions of what was to come – expressions of ideas, impressions rather than promises. Being an in-house modelmaking workshop, however, Arup's approach to

Figure 7.6 Balsa model made by Thorp, 1970.

Source: Image courtesy Thorp Archive, AUB.

making models remained very much restricted to their own architects, and with Robert Kirkman deliberately choosing to keep his own business operating on a smaller scale, opportunities to commission more abstract models were severely limited in the face of the larger commercial modelmakers' preference for realism. This situation finally changed when a downturn in business at Arup in the late-1970s led to the modelshop staff being encouraged to look for new jobs should redundancies be forthcoming, resulting in Arup's creative and abstract modelmaking techniques being shared with a new generation of modelmakers studying at the Medway College of Art in Rochester.

A Model Education

Until the 1960s, the only way to receive any form of training in architectural modelmaking was through employment. Commercial modelmakers were actively on the lookout for hobbyist modelmakers who could make the sometimes difficult transition to working to tight deadlines and with much greater efficiency than a pastime allowed, with Robert Kirkman having secured his position with Denys Lasdun as a result of the balsa wood model aircraft he had made in his spare time.[22] Thorp's three-year apprenticeship that offered on-the-job training had begun in 1957, but could only take on three people at any one time. By the late-1960s, however, a three-year diploma in modelmaking was being taught at the Medway College of Art, offering the first formal education route into the profession. The course was established by John Gaylard, who had been teaching the modelmaking components of the display and exhibition design, three-dimensional design, and woodworking diplomas at the college since the early-1960s, and by 1968 a specific modelmaking course was being offered within a vocational crafts diploma.[23] In 1970 the embryonic course was moved from its original base at Free School Lane to the new campus next to Fort Pitt grammar school on a hill overlooking Chatham and Rochester.

By the late-1970s, the Industrial Modelmaking diploma, as it had become, was looking for a specialist architectural modelmaker to join the team of tutors, and Gaylard advertised the position. Arup modelmaker Tina Miller saw the advert for the teaching position at Medway and showed it to her colleague George Rome Innes, who duly applied.[24] Innes was not initially keen on the job but saw it as good interview practice, and to his surprise he was offered a two-day-a-week contract teaching architectural modelmaking on the course.[25] Despite the downturn in work, Arup agreed to release him for those hours while still paying him his full-time salary: 'Arup's attitude was that we must give back to the world, so I went down to Medway and started teaching.'[26] By then a highly skilled architectural modelmaker with a decade's experience, Innes was clear that he wanted his students to appreciate the artistic skills of modelmaking as well as the technical processes of making them so they could fully explore the creative potential of the practice.[27]

Through Innes' connection to Arup, modelmaking students at Medway also began taking up short-term work placements at the company, and later with Robert Kirkman as well, and as a result the late-1970s and early-1980s saw a new generation of architectural modelmakers entering the profession who had been taught to develop their artistic skills rather than just the technical proficiencies of making realistic models. Richard Armiger gained his diploma from Medway in 1978 and, after a period of working at Arup and then establishing an in-house modelshop for Hugh Casson, started his own company Network Modelmakers in 1982. Soon after he himself began a period of teaching architectural modelmaking on the newly established modelmaking course at St Albans College of Art and Design (now the University of Hertfordshire), further spreading the 'Arup School' approach. Graduating in the same year as Armiger were Nick Grace, who worked at Arup for many years before also moving into teaching, and Tim Price, who established his own architectural modelmaking company in Kent. In 1981, Robert Danton-Rees graduated from Medway, setting up the London architectural modelmaking firm Capital Models in 1994. Neil Vandersteen graduated from Medway in 1985 and recalled that there 'was a wave of people who came out of Medway into architectural modelmaking at that time.'[28] After a period of freelancing for a number of firms including Robert Kirkman's, Vandersteen then joined the in-house modelshop at Foster + Partners in 1989, where he consciously pushed to make 'really beautiful models,' just as he had learned from Innes.[29] The following year Ben Moss graduated from Medway, and after starting his own teaching career set up the modelmaking HND at Bournemouth and Poole College of Art and Design (now Arts University Bournemouth) in 1992.

Through these modelmakers the Arup approach to architectural modelmaking instigated by David Armstrong in their in-house modelshop in the 1960s began to percolate through the wider profession. When Neil Vandersteen joined Foster + Partners, the modelshop had been run by Chris Windsor for over a decade, but Windsor had recently moved to a second dedicated workshop at Norman Foster's home, leaving a small team of five working at Foster's offices in Portland Place. No one working there had a formal modelmaking background, and with the most experience Vandersteen was placed in charge of the team. Most of the models being made at Foster + Partners at the time were sketch models using polystyrene sheet, Perspex, plywood, and Rohacel – an expanded acrylic foam. Over time, however, Vandersteen's training helped the modelshop expand the range of creative approaches that it applied to its presentation models, becoming a highly important creative influence on the profession during the 1990s and beyond.

While Arup had favoured timber over plastics in its models, the legacy of Innes' teaching at Medway was to open up the stylistic palette of architectural models by re-introducing timber alongside Perspex and to embrace the abstract potential that timber allowed. Whereas plastics had become the default choice of material by post-war modelmakers in their pursuit of realism, the modelmakers emerging from Medway in the early-1980s were taking a very different approach, making much more considered creative choices as to which materials suited the needs of a particular model to convey its messages in a more abstract form. This diversity in modelmaking matched the broadening of architectural styles that had emerged during the 1970s, with high-tech, a classical revival, and postmodernism with its 'indulgent complexity'[30] all standing in contrast to the puritan austerity of modernist architecture. A new generation of architects that included Nicholas Grimshaw, Terry Farrell, Jeremy Dixon, Richard Rogers, and Norman Foster were starting to gain fame, and they presented a highly diverse range of approaches and styles. The graduating modelmakers from Medway were perfectly trained to meet their needs, but the overwhelming dominance of Thorp and its commercially prudent focus on realistic models for its developer clients stood as a major obstacle for modelmakers such as Armiger and Danton-Rees in establishing their own businesses. In 1981, just two years short of its centenary, however, Thorp's dominance was unexpectedly broken, and a space was created for the new generation of Arup School modelmakers to launch their careers.

Creative Opportunities

In 1980 Thorp was a confident business in high spirits. Under Ray Pfaendler's leadership the company's pursuit of foreign business, particularly in the Middle East, had paid off spectacularly, and the company had just completed an enormous model of Kuwait City as it might look in the year 2000 (Figure 7.7). Built at 1:1,000 scale, the model took six months to build and was so large that the company rented a dedicated temporary workshop in Hammersmith, kitting it out with an entirely new suite of machine tools just for the project. Two modelmakers were sent to Kuwait to do a full survey of the existing city, taking over three thousand photographs. Built in forty sections, the completed model included thousands of buildings and over twelve thousand palm trees.

Figure 7.7 Model of Kuwait under construction at Thorp, 1979.

Source: Image courtesy Thorp Archive, AUB.

The following year, however, things suddenly turned sour. With profits high, several of Thorp's most experienced modelmakers, each with around twenty years at the company, had become frustrated with Pfaendler's leadership and the fact that even as directors of the company, their shareholding percentages remained very small. Stephen Fooks had just started his apprenticeship with the company, and on his third day at 98 Gray's Inn Road a tearful Pfaendler gathered the staff to inform them that the three directors had left and were starting their own competing business, Kandor.[31] Having lost his most experienced modelmakers, Pfaendler was devastated, and over the next few months more and more modelmakers handed their notices in, simply telling Pfaendler they were moving on, trying to spare his feelings by not saying they had been hired by the new company.[32] Kandor was able to launch itself thanks to the market knowledge and experience of the former Thorp directors and quickly grew to the extent that by 1985 the firm was employing twenty modelmakers and had established itself as a major player in the industry in direct competition with Thorp. Stephen Fooks soon moved to Kandor as well, noting that with so many staff having transferred to the new company, 'for a long time Kandor replaced Thorp because they pretty much were Thorp' in terms of the modelmakers who worked there.[33]

Pfaendler, meanwhile, attempted to rapidly employ new staff as the company had just secured its largest-ever contract, worth over £200,000, for a model of the Great

Figure 7.8 Modelmakers at Thorp working on a model of Mecca, 1982.

Source: Image courtesy Thorp Archive, AUB.

Mosque of Mecca (Figure 7.8). Completing the model became an issue of pride for Pfaendler and the few existing modelmakers who remained at Thorp, including Alec Saunders. The eight-metre-square model took twelve months to complete and required the hiring of specialist painters to reproduce the marble effect on the cast resin elevations, but with the remaining team having pulled together to finish it to an exceptional standard, Pfaendler was confident that the company's future was secure and could carry on.

While Thorp's almost total dominance over the profession was ended by the Kandor split, the business continued to remain healthy, producing thousands of models over the next two decades before its eventual purchase by the general modelmaking firm Atom in the late-1990s. Thorp was nevertheless soon eclipsed by both Kandor and another rapidly growing new competitor, Pipers, purchased from its founder John Piper by Barry McKeogh in 1977 and which quickly overtook Thorp in terms of turnover and reputation. With the Thorp-Kandor split having created a space in which new competing firms could thrive, the early-1980s consequently saw a major restructuring of the profession. Alec Saunders is adamant that had the split not taken place, the industry would be in a very different place today, noting that it served to lower prices and encourage competition: 'It started a snowball effect, just from that one action. What it did is spawn this sort of feeling among modelmakers that they could be a bit more adventurous.'[34] A renewed sense of entrepreneurialism emerged within the profession, with multiple new modelmaking companies setting up business as the decade progressed, and at Pipers a similar split soon occurred when Lee Atkins, Martin Giddons, and Kevin Mullane, all modelmakers at the firm, left to set up 3DD in 1988. The new company gained a reputation for producing high-quality models within very tight deadlines. Early clients included architects such as SOM, Swanke Hayden Connell, and Terry Farrell (Figure 7.9), before the directors made a conscious effort to specialise in working for developers rather than architects, as the time pressures were far more manageable.

In the same year that 3DD launched, Tetra Modelmakers was formed by three architecture graduates from the Architectural Association, quickly becoming known for their creative and impressive models that appealed directly to architects, while in Bristol the general modelmaking company Amalgam opened in 1984, becoming a favoured supplier of architectural models to Norman Foster. By the middle of the decade, Unit 22, established by the architect Don Shuttleworth in 1983, was also growing into a distinguished maker of competition and concept models, including many notable projects for Jan Kaplicky at Future Systems (Figure 7.10), and as the profession rapidly expanded an attempt was even made to establish a Modelmaker's

Figure 7.9 Model of The Peak, made by 3DD, 1992.

Source: Image courtesy 3DD.

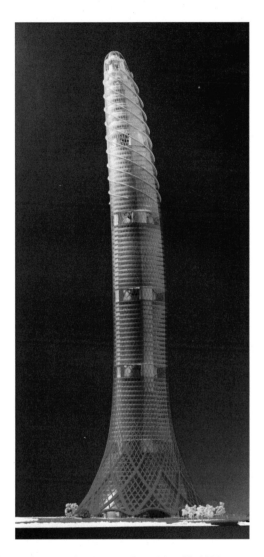

Figure 7.10 Model of Future Systems' Big Bird, made by Unit 22, 1998.

Source: Image courtesy Unit 22.

Association, offering regular meetings and a magazine to help build the profession's standing and improve communication, but its high fees led to a rapid demise.

Of all the opportunities that the breakup of Thorp's dominance created, the most significant was the chance to offer the 'Arup School' approach to modelmaking on a much larger commercial basis. The Medway graduates who had studied under George Rome Innes were perfectly suited to take advantage of architecture's desire for a less-realistic approach to modelmaking that better reflected its revised understanding of what architectural models should be representing. While Thorp, Kandor, 3DD, and

Pipers continued to focus their attention on the lucrative developers' market, the fragmentation and expansion of the industry provided the space for other modelmakers to directly target the differing needs of architects. The leading modelmaker to apply the lessons of the 'Arup School' in this way and to set a new standard for architectural models over the next two decades was Richard Armiger and his company Network Modelmakers. While working at the Arup modelshop after his graduation from Medway, Armiger had observed a string of young architects, 'all Knighted or Lords now,'[35] entering competitions where they had teamed up with Arup for the engineering work. 'Jump ahead and the same young architect is doing another project and he knocks on the door of the modelshop and says "remember me? I have this project . . . " but if it's not under the Arup umbrella, we can't make it. But maybe Richard can, he's a freelancer.'[36]

Through these kinds of introductions, Armiger began to pick up work from architects such as David Chipperfield, Nicholas Grimshaw, Jan Kaplicky, and Jeremy Dixon. Crucially, Armiger noted that each architect's work was unique, and so no single style of model would suit all of them. As a result, Armiger established Network Modelmakers with the idea of replicating the Arup experience, but for a variety of different architects each with their own unique styles. 'I could be like an in-house modelshop for all of them, so David Chipperfield with all his timbers and occasional use of colour, and Jan Kaplicky with the super automotive finishes, and Eva Jiricna and her black models. And so I went on to develop a model vocabulary for all these people.'[37]

The differing approaches required by Armiger's clients meant he was constantly adapting his own methods to suit their needs, and rather than developing a single style of modelmaking that was defined by a particular visual signature or material choice, Armiger's work came to be defined by adaptability itself. Whereas an architect commissioning Thorp or Kandor for a model would do so knowing exactly what they wanted and what they would get, architects who approached Armiger were generally less certain about what they wanted stylistically, when what they really wanted was Armiger's skill in developing a style that was right for their project. Experimenting constantly and adapting to meet the needs of each client, Armiger's individually styled abstract and creative models perfectly matched their desire for models that represented looser concepts and ideas rather than finished buildings.

In architectural model photographer Andrew Putler's opinion, Richard Armiger had 'one of the best palettes of all modelmakers,'[38] and the two began to collaborate with Putler, photographing Armiger's models to be used either by his clients in competition submissions or to send to the architectural press as publicity. Putler was by this point already a noted music photographer who had made his name capturing dramatic images of the 1970s rock and roll scene and met Armiger through freelance work photographing models Armiger had made for a marketing agency. More and more model work began to pour in, and a distinguished second career as a model photographer took off. Putler remembers this as a fascinating time, noting that for young architects, 'the only way they could get their head above the parapet was to enter international competitions, and they needed photography and they needed models.'[39] Putler's model photography quickly became highly sought after, and within a few months he had several journal covers to his name. As the more creative models made by Armiger and photographed by Putler began to be featured more regularly in the architectural press, so their visibility increased further (Figure 7.11), sparking

Figure 7.11 Model of Big Blue, made by Network Modelmakers, 1992.

Source: Photography by Andrew Putler. Image courtesy Andrew Putler.

curiosity among other modelmakers keen to follow suit.[40] Through Armiger's work, aided by Putler's photography, the 'Arup School' approach to architectural model-making quickly spread, just as the demand for models skyrocketed once more as the British economy suddenly upturned after the doldrums of the previous decade.

In 1986 the 'Big Bang' – the deregulation of the London stock markets that rapidly turned London into a global financial capital – brought about a wholesale change to the fortunes of the property market. Enormous levels of foreign investment in London property, combined with a need for additional office space for the growing financial services, generated a massive property boom. The total volume of office space in London doubled between 1985 and 1993,[41] creating an extensive demand for both the services of architects and for architectural models. As part of their wider economic plans, the government had also established sixteen Enterprise Zones in 1981 to stimulate regional development. Exempt from land taxes and most planning constraints, these provided attractive incentives for property developers with land prices deliberately kept below market value.[42] In 1982 the Isle of Dogs Enterprise Zone became the semi-private London Docklands Development Corporation, which spent £800 million on land purchases, reclamation, and transport links. Three years later, SOM's master-plan for Olympia and York's Canary Wharf development was unveiled, adding two and a half million square feet of office space to the capital, with developments in the city of London contributing a further sixteen million square feet.[43] Further projects such as Broadgate, Ropemaker Place, Albion Gate, London Wall, plus the demand for out-of-town shopping centres such as Lakeside, Merry Hill, and Hatfield Galleria (Figure 7.12) provided excellent opportunities for young architects seeking to build their reputations and to test out the new architectural styles that had emerged in the wake of modernism. Capitalism had become the great new patron of architecture, and there was considerable competition between architects who were all seeking architectural models to help them stand out.

At the same time, a further change in government policy created an additional demand for architectural models through the active encouragement by Michael Heseltine as Minister for the Environment to run architectural competitions as a way of fostering competition between architects and to drive both innovation and value for money. Making models for architectural competitions required a great relationship of trust between an architect and their chosen modelmaker to understand and interpret their vision. Such models were by necessity very creative and highly abstract, and competition models offered an ideal opportunity to explore the role of models as expressions of ideas rather than of proposed buildings. For Richard Armiger they were an 'epicentre for creativity,'[44] the design so ill-defined at such an early stage in the process that a realistic model was usually not an option. Often there would be no drawings at all to work from, sometimes just a conversation with the architect, and so abstraction was partly a way of covering the fact that the design had not been completed, while also appealing directly to the architect's vision in a more conceptual manner without tying them to a concrete prediction of a building. With the actual material choices of the building rarely being determined so early on either, this often dictated the use of either polished or frosted Perspex, unpainted timber, or monochromatic white models.[45] Additionally, the competition organiser would usually set a specific scale for the models submitted, which made it even more imperative that each architect's model stood out.

Figure 7.12 Model of Hatfield Galleria, made by Thorp, 1992.

Source: Image courtesy Thorp Archive, AUB.

In 1982 Robert Kirkman produced the competition model for Terry Farrell's design for the BBC Radio Building extension. 'Farrell did a nice scheme and I did the model, but he was tight for money, and so I made a small model of just the site. I think it must have been about a £3000 fee for the model.'[46] The competition came down to two finalists, Farrell and Norman Foster, who ultimately won. For Kirkman, it was clear why Foster had won – his model was spectacular. 'His modelmakers had modelled from Oxford Circus right down to Regent's Park, all of that street, the buildings going out for three rows either side.'[47] The model included the whole of the existing BBC building, with Foster's glass extension 'sitting like an absolute jewel. It was under-lit and must have cost something like thirty or forty thousand pounds. It was sheer presentation; Foster didn't mess about.'[48] The following year Kirkman made the model for ABK's winning submission to the competition to design the extension to the National Gallery in London (Figure 7.13). Made in Sycamore and balsa wood with Perspex glazing, the model quickly became an unwitting lightning rod for intense criticism of the design by the Prince of Wales in his notorious 'Carbuncle' speech to the RIBA.[49] Several years later the competition was re-run, Kirkman again making a model for one of the submissions, this time for CZWK, which again was rejected. A third competition was then won by Robert Venturi and Denise Scott Brown, and it was their design that was eventually built.

Figure 7.13 Model of ABK's design for the National Gallery extension, made by Robert Kirkman, 1984.

Source: Image courtesy Robert Kirkman.

A crucial turning point proved to be the 1991 competition held at the Venice Bien-nale to design the Venice Gateway, a new bus station for the city. Modelmaker Rich-ard Armiger was commissioned to produce the architectural models for four different British architectural practices that were submitting entries; each of the architects – Eva Jiricna, Harper MacKay, Weston Williamson, and Dixon Jones – having pro-duced radically different designs. The challenge for Armiger was to make each model distinctive without imposing his own house style, using different combinations of materials together to create visual and textural contrasts in highly abstracted ways that reflected the architects' personalities as much as they did the designs of the pro-posed buildings. For each submission Armiger created an entirely unique look using different materials (Figures 7.14, 7.15, 7.16, and 7.17). 'Weston Williamson had a tiny budget and asked how we could do the model for hardly any money,'[50] and so the architects made the context buildings for the model while Armiger produced the base and the model of their entry, a high-tech design that required a lot of vacuum-formed polystyrene and metal etchings. For Harper MacKay's design, Armiger made use of Rohacel, birch veneer, and frosted Perspex with realistic trees to offset the model's yellow colour. With Eva Jiricna's model, Perspex was back-sprayed a dark grey to create the effect of water. 'Hers was an intense steel and glass structure and so we did this model all in black with silver details,'[51] and Armiger created the complex roof

Figure 7.14 Model of Harper MacKay's design of the Venice Gateway, made by Network Modelmakers, 1991.

Source: Photograph by Andrew Putler. Image courtesy Andrew Putler.

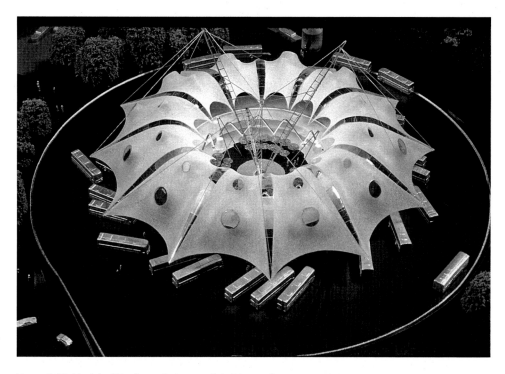

Figure 7.15 Model of Eva Jiricna's design of the Venice Gateway, made by Network Modelmakers, 1991.

Source: Photograph by Andrew Putler. Image courtesy Andrew Putler.

Figure 7.16 Model of Weston Williamson's design of the Venice Gateway, made by Network Modelmakers, 1991..

Source: Author's Collection..

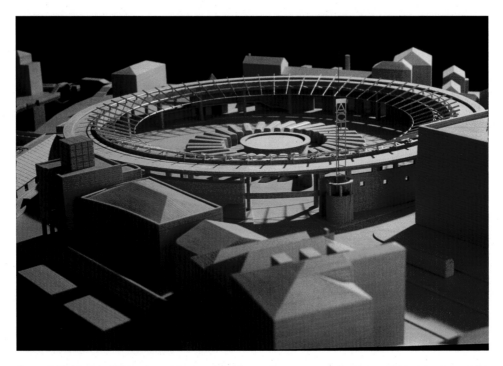

Figure 7.17 Model of Dixon Jones' design of the Venice Gateway, made by Network Modelmakers, 1991.

Source: Photograph by Andrew Putler. Image courtesy Andrew Putler.

structure using heat-bent Perspex carefully masked and sprayed silver. For Dixon Jones' competition-winning entry, Armiger used a simple all-timber palette to blend the design into the surrounding buildings, which also served to draw attention to the stainless-steel roof details.

The different creative approaches evident in the Venice models stood in stark contrast to the all-or-nothing realism that had dominated the previous decades. That one modelmaker was able to produce four abstract models in radically different styles, at the same time, and for the same competition brief demonstrated just how broad the modelmaker's palette had become, offering architects precisely the individualistic and abstract models they had been wanting in place of the ongoing pursuit of realism that the developer-focused firms such as Thorp were attending to.

The Legacy of the Arup School

By the start of the 1990s, the 'Arup School' of architectural modelmaking had become deeply embedded within the profession. After his retirement, David Armstrong reflected on the Arup modelshop's legacy, noting that while 'old fashioned firms like Thorp would make the painted plastic model extremely well,' the new companies that came through Arup and Medway chose a different approach, 'and still it goes on.'[52] Due to the spreading of Arup's creativity and abstraction through George Rome Innes' teaching at Medway, the breakup of Thorp ending the company's dominance within the industry, and Richard Armiger's success in applying that approach to architectural competition models during the 1980s property boom, the range of styles present in professionally made architectural models in Britain expanded significantly. With architects having largely rejected realistic models, and yet developers continuing to find them extremely successful, it was vital that for the model to remain relevant to both sets of clients architectural modelmakers could not simply provide either highly realistic painted Perspex models or abstract timber ones, as a demand existed for both. In addition, purely timber models, such as had become the hallmark of the Arup modelshop, presented a distinct style of their own, and for modelmakers this created an additional challenge as the new generation of architects attempting to make their name in the early 1980s were in fierce competition with one another and they all wanted models that reflected their own style rather than the modelmaker's.

As a result of the changes that took place during the 1980s, both the profession of architectural modelmaking, and the model itself, were radically changed. Thorp, despite losing its dominant position over the profession, continued to thrive, and while its output dipped from over one hundred models in 1982 to only forty in 1984, business rose again to seventy-five models in 1987 and almost entirely for British-based developments rather than the overseas commissions that had been the mainstay of its business over the previous decade. With Thorp's near-monopoly broken, however, the ballooning demand for architectural models that accompanied Britain's property boom was largely absorbed by the newer companies that established themselves during the 1980s. Overall, a clear divergence had taken place, with Thorp, Kandor, Pipers, 3DD, and Nick Quine's AMI dominating the market for developers' marketing models and Network Modelmakers, Unit 22, Robert Kirkman, and Tetra gaining a strong reputation for their more expressive competition models. Through Richard Armiger the Arup approach to modelmaking continued to be refined and passed on to further modelmakers during the 1990s, with both Millennium Models' and A Models' founders having been trained by Armiger, and who continued to work creatively in collaboration with architects in an extension of the 'Arup School' of modelmaking well after the original in-house modelshop had closed. Larger architectural practices such as those of Norman Foster and Richard Rogers had already begun to expand their own in-house modelmaking workshops based on Arup's approach, and the growing number of modelmaking courses being taught at Rycotewood College, Hertfordshire College of Art and Design, Sunderland Polytechnic, Barking College, Northbrook College, Hounslow College, Bourneville College, and Bournemouth and Poole College of Art and Design all embraced the Arup approach to architectural modelmaking in their teaching.

Two schools of thought now existed within the profession – the Thorp, Kandor, and Pipers approach of producing models for marketing and sales purposes that drew from the long tradition of pushing the boundaries of technical precision and realism that plastics had enabled during the immediate post-war era (Figure 7.18), and the 'Arup School' employed by Network Modelmakers, Robert Kirkman, Unit 22, and others, that embraced a creative drive for experimenting with materials and abstraction (Figure 7.19). Both approaches proved to be equally valid, the profession having

Figure 7.18 Model of the Post Office Headquarters, made by Thorp, 1975.

Source: Image courtesy Thorp Archive, AUB.

Figure 7.19 Model of Luton Arts Centre, made by 3DD, circa 1995.
Source: Image courtesy 3DD.

successfully adapted to serve the now differing demands of architects and developers. No longer pursuing a single desire for ever-increasing realism, architectural model-makers had come to recognise the importance of tailoring and adapting every process to a specific model's – and a specific architect's – needs.

By the end of the 1980s, architectural modelmaking in Britain was no longer solely focused on a relentless pursuit of realism, instead embracing a spectrum that extended from the highly realistic at one end to the abstract and artistic at the other. This broadening of styles required greater levels of creativity, with one commentator noting that 'good architectural modelmakers need to be inventive with an obsessive interest in detailed work.'[53] Modelmaker Christian Spencer-Davies has described how the creative process of modelmaking became more like that of cookery and the art of mixing two things together that 'suddenly make something that's greater than either of them.'[54] Selecting a contrasting range of materials, colours, and textures had become crucial to the success of a more abstract model: 'That's the creative bit, putting two or three things together to create a palette that works.'[55] Through the influence of the Arup approach to architectural modelmaking the profession had found a way to reconcile the conflicting expectations of the developer and the architect, and the damaging criticisms levelled by John Chisholm in 1969 during the profession's fall from grace could finally be put to rest. In just a single decade architectural modelmaking in Britain had been completely transformed, with the number of companies tripling between 1980 and 1995, each finding its own niche along the spectrum of creative styles that now existed. As the 1990s continued to unfold, however, the profession was to face yet another period of radical change as the introduction of computer-aided manufacturing processes forced the profession to adapt once more as it suddenly found itself confronted with the upheaval of the emerging digital age.

Notes

1 John Chisholm, 'Rehearsal for Reality,' *The Architect and Building News*, February 27, 1969, 24.
2 Piers Gough, 'Model Makers,' *Architects' Journal* 177 (April 27, 1983), 30.
3 E. A. Brown, *Making Models in the Drawing Office* (Richmond: Draughtsman & Allied Technicians' Association, 1971).
4 Robert Kirkman, interview with author, April 29, 2019.
5 Ibid.
6 Ibid.
7 David Armstrong, interview with Louise Brady, September 23, 1999, audio recording, Ove Arup Architecture Interviews, British Library.
8 Ibid.
9 David Armstrong, 'Model Making at Arups,' *The Arup Journal*, November, 1966, 2.
10 Tina Miller, interview with author, April 30, 2018.
11 Armstrong, interview with Louise Brady.
12 Armstrong, 'Model Making,' 3.
13 Ibid.
14 Miller, interview.
15 Phillip Dowson, 'Introduction,' in *Arup Modelshop*, brochure, Arup Associates, 1990.
16 Ibid.
17 Miller, interview.
18 George Rome Innes, interview with author, April 18, 2019.
19 Ibid.
20 Roger Hillier, interview with author, April 30, 2018.
21 Richard Armiger, interview with author, October 12, 2018.
22 Kirkman, interview.
23 Ken Houghton, email to author, March 26, 2018.
24 Miller, interview.
25 Innes, interview.
26 Ibid.
27 Ibid.
28 Neil Vandersteen, interview with author, March 26, 2018.
29 Ibid.
30 P. Goldberger, 'Post-Modernism: An Introduction,' *Architectural Design*, April, 1977, 257.
31 Stephen Fooks, interview with author, May 8, 2018.
32 Ibid.
33 Ibid.
34 Alec Saunders, interview with author, March 13, 2018.
35 Ibid.
36 Ibid.
37 Ibid.
38 Andrew Putler, interview with author, June 7, 2019.
39 Ibid.
40 Ibid.
41 Alan Powers, *Britain: Modern Architectures in History* (London: Reaktion, 2007), 223.
42 Peter Hall, *Cities of Tomorrow* (Oxford: Blackwell, 2002), 394.
43 Ibid, 396.
44 Armiger, interview.
45 Christian Spencer-Davies, interview with author, June 6, 2019.

46 Kirkman, interview.
47 Ibid.
48 Ibid.
49 Graham Stewart, *Bang! A History of Britain in the 1980s* (London: Atlantic Books, 2013), 268; Kirkman, interview.
50 Armiger, interview.
51 Ibid.
52 Armstrong, interview with Louise Brady.
53 J. Rawson, 'Small Beginning: Modelmaking,' *Architects' Journal* 191 (January 17, 1990), 64–65.
54 Spencer-Davies, interview.
55 Ibid.

Chapter 8

Digital Efficiencies

On March 22, 1996, the University of Hertfordshire held a conference dedicated to the future of modelmaking. With the institution's modelmaking diploma course in the process of becoming a full degree, it was a sign of the profession's growing confidence and maturity, but while the presented papers adopted a fairly upbeat tone there was an unavoidable sense of anxiety surrounding the event, reflected by the dominant subject being discussed: rapid prototyping.

While the introduction of computer-aided design and computer-aided manufacturing (CAD/CAM) processes to architectural modelmaking had been slowly gathering pace over the course of the previous decade, the second half of the 1990s saw the wholesale change of many of the established processes of the profession with new automated tools replacing a significant proportion of manual work, bringing dramatic increases in efficiency and opening up new possibilities in the making of architectural models. Computer numerically controlled (CNC) machining and laser cutting were rapidly being adopted as standard processes, and while any period of major change is likely to cause some anxiety, it was the arrival of commercially affordable 3D printers and other forms of rapid prototyping that generated the most concern. The availability of machines that could produce fully assembled scale models from digital files raised legitimate questions about the future role of the modelmaker. In his opening speech to the conference, Brian Holder outlined a range of potential futures that included the disappearance of modelmaking altogether, the marginalisation of small firms unable to afford new technologies, models being replaced by screen-based media, and what he felt to be more likely, 'nothing much changes at all, but a few small things change a lot.'[1]

The perceived threat of rapid prototyping and the increased quality of computer-generated images were also causing considerable concern within the architectural profession, and for both the modelmaker and the architect the late-1990s was a period of opportunity, uncertainty, and most of all, change. As one architectural historian has remarked, 'no advance in technology has had a more lasting and far-reaching impact on the work of the architect and the modelmaker than the arrival of the office computer.'[2] The analogue processes of architectural design, including drawing and modelmaking, appeared to be under imminent threat as computer-aided design swept through the architectural profession, the desktop computer 'turning the tools that served generations of architects and were a hallmark of their profession into antiquated museum pieces.'[3] Drawing by hand on paper was quickly replaced by drawing on a screen, and architects began to ask themselves whether physical models, despite

DOI: 10.4324/9781003298007-9

Figure 8.1 Model of Embankment Place, made by Pipers, circa 1988.
Source: Image courtesy Pipers Model Makers.

their tangible presence and effectiveness in communicating a design (Figure 8.1), were about to be replaced by virtual ones. For architects, the transition from analogue to digital working proved to be what one commentator described as a 'brutal and all-encompassing upheaval. From conception to implementation, no part of the architectural design process remained unchanged.'[4] In 1994 the American architectural writer Thomas Fisher summarised the uncertainty that was keenly felt by many, writing that 'one of the storm clouds on the horizon for modelmakers is the computer' and that 'some in the profession, however, see it only as a matter of time, perhaps within a decade or so, before computer technology advances to the point where it can surpass the quality of what is now done by hand.'[5]

For architectural modelmakers in Britain, the broader concerns over physical models being replaced by virtual ones were relatively short-lived, however. With the arrival of high-quality computer-generated images the initial assumption had been that architects and developers would commission these instead of models. However, the reality turned out to be far less damaging, most modelmakers observing that their clients quickly realised that digital images and physical models served entirely different purposes.[6] Several architectural modelmaking firms including Pipers, Thorp, and 3DD experimented with offering virtual models and animated fly-throughs to brace themselves for a potential loss of demand for physical models during the early-1990s, but few modelmakers ever seriously pursued the idea as they had been hearing the same arguments for over a decade. As early as 1981 the modelmakers at Arup had been invited to watch a presentation about computer-generated imagery and 'were told with a gleam in some people's eyes that this would replace us.'[7] Shown digitally animated walkthroughs inside virtual buildings, the modelmakers noted that they already had periscope cameras that could do the same with physical models and came away unconvinced that these basic computer graphics were an imminent threat to their work.

By the time of the Hertfordshire conference in 1996 the major concern within architectural modelmaking was no longer the possibility of models being replaced by computers but instead that models could be made by computers, rapid prototyping and 3D printing seemingly the technologies that might ultimately make the professional modelmaker's role redundant. In 1992 the Association of Professional Model Makers (APMM) had been established in the United States specifically to address this threat, and yet (as the presentations at the Hertfordshire conference illustrate) the mood in Britain by 1996 was cautiously optimistic if a little uncertain. Ian Mitchell, a lecturer on the HND in Modelmaking at the university, had just returned from the third APMM conference and noted that in the United States 'advances in technology are being embraced, rather than being seen as the death knell of the model making profession.'[8] Summarising the mood of both the APMM conference and that of the Hertfordshire gathering, Mitchell continued:

> If we look back less than a decade ago when CAD/CAM and CNC mills seemed set on usurping the role of the modelmaker or at least to bring about a re-skilling, it is easy to see how this was a natural scepticism about change. We can now see that the worry was over the damage these systems might do to us rather than, how can these new developments be used to our advantage and create more opportunities for the future?[9]

Modelmaker Trevor Crout also spoke optimistically at the conference that 'the future of modelmaking I believe will make the best use of new materials and technologies to speed up and enhance the traditional hand crafted model,'[10] commenting that he felt it unlikely that computers would ever fully replace the human element of the process. This optimism was shared by many within the profession,[11] as despite the enormous upheaval of the digital revolution that was taking place, and with rapid prototyping looming on the horizon, by the middle of the 1990s, architectural modelmakers had become extremely used to change.

The Drive for Efficiency

As a result of the break-up of Thorp's dominance and the introduction of the 'Arup School' of modelmaking, by the 1990s the profession had been greatly expanded, supported by thriving HND courses in modelmaking at Bournemouth, Hatfield, Rochester, and Sunderland. New companies such as Kandor, Unit 22, Network Modelmakers, 3DD, and Tetra were tending to the demands for both highly realistic models for developers and more abstract and creative models for architectural competitions using new styles, new approaches, and new materials. The profession had nevertheless been severely battered by the economic recession of 1989–1991, however, with soaring inflation and collapsing demand squeezing the finances of many companies to the extent that jobs were cut and wages left unpaid.[12] Robert Kirkman found his turnover halving,[13] while Thorp's directors took the noble but costly approach of attempting to ride out the recession without making any redundancies. This had a major long-term consequence for the business, as with a strong cash reserve because of their successful overseas push during the 1970s and 1980s, the expectation had been that the downturn in business would be short, but by the time the economy began to pick up again from 1992 onwards, those savings had been spent. Ray Pfaendler had also reached retirement age and in 1995 he sold his interest in Thorp to the family-run general modelmaking company Atom. With Thorp's future secured, the company soon sold 98 Gray's Inn Road and moved to a purpose-built studio in Sunningdale, named the John Thorp Building after its founder, just a short walk from Atom's own premises in the Berkshire village.

The changes of the previous ten years, whether through the pressures of the recession or simply through increased opportunities for competition within the massively expanded profession, had very much placed efficiency at the top of everyone's agenda. For all the developments that had taken place since John Thorp first began making models in the 1880s, the basic tools and processes of architectural modelmaking had remained remarkably consistent throughout, as whether working with timber or plastics, machine tools such as the band saw, circular saw, and sander were necessities in any modelmaking workshop. Even the daily use of the scalpel by hand had continued for over a century, transferring from cutting card and paper to soft plastics such as polystyrene sheet. Improved motor-driven machine tools, particularly during the interwar years, had brought about improvements to the quality of architectural models, but fundamentally the equipment in an architectural modelmaker's workshop in the 1980s would have been recognisable to anyone working in Thorp's workshop in the 1920s (Figure 8.2).

The unaddressed problem was that in the interim architectural models had become vastly more complicated and time-consuming to make. Whether meeting the demands for ultra-realism or creative abstraction, architectural modelmaking was a very costly activity, and just as the need for new materials during the 1930s had sparked the modelmaker's sense of adaptable curiosity, so too did the tantalising potential of new computer-aided manufacturing processes. While there was still a genuine concern that rapid prototyping might ultimately replace the modelmaker in some manner, at the time of the 1996 conference this was a prospect that remained a relatively safe distance in the future, and for most architectural modelmakers digital technologies offered a vital means of increasing the efficiency of their basic processes, and, perhaps just as importantly, offered an escape from the sheer drudgery of much of their day-to-day work.

Despite more creative and abstract models having become increasingly commonplace during the 1980s, for the majority of architectural modelmakers the bulk of their work continued to be making fully realistic marketing models. These required a large amount of detail, and, crucially, a lot of windows to cut out, which was one of the most laborious tasks involved in making an architectural model (Figure 8.3). Modelmaker Lee Atkins recalled the effort involved in cutting just a single window out of a sheet of Perspex: 'If you were cutting out windows you were on the pillar drill cutting out a hole for each window and then using a fretsaw with V-blocks to hold

Figure 8.2 Thorp workshop, 1986.

Source: Image courtesy Thorp Archive, AUB.

them and file them out.'[14] Even when using softer ABS sheet and a hand-held power tool such as a Dremel, window cutting remained an incredibly time-consuming task as each window needed a hole drilled in one corner, then a power tool inserted to cut all four sides out before being filed and sanded square.[15] On a building with several hundred windows this was an enormous task, and the process was made even more time-consuming due to the multiple layers required to make a building's façade. A clear Perspex sheet for the glazing had to be scribed and inked with a ruling pen to create window bars, and then the window apertures in the façade of the building had to be cut out of either Perspex or ABS. High Impact Polystyrene Sheet (HIPS) could only be used for façades if being cut by hand, as the drill bits would melt the plastic.

Figure 8.3 Model of Paddington Basin, made by Unit 22, 1999.
Source: Image courtesy Unit 22.

With HIPS, drawings had to be plotted onto each sheet, scored, and then cut out using a scalpel, a process that could take days on a larger model, as Alec Saunders recalled: 'You knew that elevation. You started it in the morning and you were still doing it when you went home. Everything was so labour intensive.'[16]

If the building had a brick façade, the process was even more arduous as the material had to be cut and engraved by hand. A typical job for an apprentice modelmaker was to spray a basecoat and apply a speckle effect to mimic brickwork, then align the sheet on a drawing board and engrave brick lines every one or two millimetres depending on the scale. On a large model, this process alone might take two or three days.[17] For tall buildings floor plates would be made by taping sheets of Perspex together and then scoring the outline of the floors onto the top sheet using a scalpel and ruler before running the whole stack through a band saw and then filing and sanding each sheet to the precise shape required. For a building with twenty or thirty floors, even ensuring that the holes in each plate for any columns to pass through were correctly aligned could be an exercise in itself (Figure 8.4), as a modelmaker had to make sure each hole was drilled vertically through the stack, and rarely was a drill bit long enough to complete the task in one batch.[18]

Figure 8.4 Architectural model made by 3DD, circa 1995.
Source: Image courtesy 3DD.

Although the introduction of more abstract approaches to architectural modelmaking had widened the stylistic palette of the model, the standard processes of making a realistic presentation or marketing model out of Perspex and polystyrene sheet had been in place since the early 1950s. By the 1990s neither the materials nor the tools used in architectural modelmaking had fundamentally changed in over forty years, and as the decade progressed the task of the modelmaker became even more challenging as the design of buildings began to embrace more organic forms that were extremely costly to produce as models using existing methods. Models such as those for Future Systems' designs for the Birmingham Selfridges and The Earth Centre proved to be extremely difficult to make, the latter requiring several hundred individual roof segments to be vacuum formed, cut out, filed and sanded, sprayed, and then attached to the model[19] (Figure 8.5).

With the digital revolution sweeping through architects' offices, and computers beginning to appear in modelmaking workshops to handle business accounts and basic word processing tasks, there was an increasing sense that the processes involved in architectural modelmaking were outdated and inefficient. While rapid prototyping at the time was far from being able to produce anything near to the quality of the models being made by hand, the speed with which 3D printers could produce

Figure 8.5 Model of The Earth Centre, made by Unit 22, 1997.

Source: Image courtesy Unit 22.

components stood in stark contrast to the analogue methods of the modelmaker's traditional tools. Ultimately, it was a hunger for increased efficiency and a desire to be released from the drudgery of repetitive processes that first attracted architectural modelmakers to CAD/CAM processes. As Ian Mitchell noted during the middle of this transition at the Hertfordshire conference in 1996, 'The great advantage . . . is that these model makers free themselves to create beautiful models that are extremely accurate, and they can spend far more time finishing the model to a higher standard than they ever had time to do before.'[20] To gain those efficiencies and freedoms, however, meant investing in highly expensive computer-controlled machines and learning to use complex computer-aided design software, applying the adaptable nature of modelmaking to new extremes in embracing a wholesale shift from analogue to digital ways of working that revolutionised how architectural models were made.

CNC Machining and Laser Cutting

Computer numerically controlled workshop machinery had been available since the mid-1970s; however, high costs meant that initially only the largest firms could countenance their purchase, and it was not until 1984 that Thorp spent £12,000 on their first computer-controlled Bridgeport milling machine. Operated using a keypad and computer monitor, the movement of the machine's bed could be programmed by entering a coded set of coordinates. Thorp had purchased the machine to assist with engraving brickwork and cutting window openings out of Perspex, and it made an immediate difference as, while not necessarily quicker, it was far more accurate than cutting by hand.[21] Early CNC milling machines had to be carefully programmed and could be extremely complicated to use, but their advantage was that once programmed the machines did all the cutting and engraving automatically, freeing the modelmaker's time to be spent on other tasks. At Pipers a hand-operated Newing-Hall pantograph was converted to computer control in 1988, and by 1989 desktop CNC machines had become available that were offering 0.1mm cutting precision. Trevor Crout, the in-house modelmaker at the architectural practice GMW, purchased one to replace the hand-scribing of brick and window details entirely.[22] Nick Quine at Architectural Models International bought a CNC in 1994 for £26,000,[23] while in 1995 the Bridgeport machines at both Thorp and Kandor were converted to operate from CAD files produced on a desktop computer rather than from commands manually typed into the machine. Drawing the outlines of the windows to be cut or brick lines to be engraved in Autocad, the software then converted the drawing into cutting commands automatically, further speeding up the process.

CNC milling machines were useful, if expensive, tools for architectural modelmakers to adopt, as they were extremely accurate and removed the drudgery of cutting and engraving building façades. With Perspex, ABS, HIPS, and most timbers all able to be machined, the existing materials of the modelmaker could remain constant while the tools used to cut them became automated. As both the CAD programs and the milling machines themselves became more advanced, the process became even quicker, and with the ability to draw complex shapes in Autocad and other CAD programs that could be accurately machined by the CNC, it also became easier for modelmakers to create models of more complex architectural designs. For those who could afford the huge outlay, CNCs became the main cutting tool in the workshop, enabling significant time-savings through the automation of basic repetitive tasks, and one of the immediate benefits that Atom's purchase of Thorp brought about was access to their extensive suite of CNC machines.[24]

Other than for very organic shapes that might need to be carved from a single block, however, most architectural models were assembled from flat surfaces. CNCs, with their large vertical movement, were over-specified for most modelmakers' needs, and it was for this reason that the use of CNCs rapidly transitioned into the use of laser cutters. Having been in industrial use since the 1970s, the first recorded use of a laser cutter in architectural modelmaking was by the architectural practice SOM in New York in the early-1980s,[25] with the California-based architectural modelmaking firm Scale Models Unlimited developing and selling its own brand of laser cutters, LaserCAMM, in 1989.[26] Costing over $100,000 at the time, such laser cutters were nevertheless rapidly adopted by American architectural modelmakers, Akiko Busch noting in 1991 that it was the 'tool that perhaps has most changed the model maker's trade.'[27] As the use of laser cutters became increasingly widespread across a number of industrial applications, suppliers of computer-driven machine tools also began to sell them, and this is likely the means by which modelmakers in Britain first became aware of their potential; Neil Merryweather recalled attending a trade show in London in the mid-1990s with the intention of purchasing a CNC machine but was instead more interested by the laser cutters on display beside them.[28]

The first known architectural modelmaking firm in Britain to make extensive use of a laser cutter was Presentation Unit, a small but highly regarded firm that had become well known for their impressively detailed model of Mies van der Rohe's design for Mansion House Tower in London, unveiled after a two-year construction period in 1982 (Figure 8.6). Being very technologically savvy, by 1986 the company had invested in their first CNC machine, and by 1990 the firm had a CAD suite with several desktop PCs running a bank of CNC mills and engravers.[29] In the same year the company followed Scale Models Unlimited and announced plans to introduce their own desktop laser cutter with the aim of selling it commercially; however, while this plan does not appear to have come to fruition, Presentation Unit were certainly using laser cutters for their own models perhaps as many as five years before the rest of the profession in Britain.

Figure 8.6 Model of Mansion House Tower, made by Presentation Unit, 1982.

Source: Image courtesy RIBA Collections.

Until the mid-1990s, Presentation Unit remained a pioneering user of laser cutters in Britain, and few others in the profession were even aware they had the equipment. By 1995, however, more and more modelmakers were hearing about the potential of the technology. When upgrading their Bridgeport CNC to operate directly from a desktop computer, the modelmakers at Kandor found that the company supplying the equipment was now also selling laser cutters.[30] Simon Hamnell at Millennium Models recalled an engineer they were working with visiting their workshop and asking why they were still cutting plastics by hand. 'He said "make a laser; I'll go and buy the bits and you can use that instead." That planted the seed, realising we could do it much more easily with a laser.'[31] For Hamnell the investment in a laser cutter was ultimately a commercial decision to speed up their processes to match their competitors:

> Already people like Pipers and Kandor had invested in CNC milling, probably some five or six years previously, and where we were bidding for work against them we would lose out every time. Once you go and see who sells them and they do a demonstration, you see there is no question about it.[32]

Following Presentation Unit's early adoption of the laser cutter, the growing in-house modelshops at Foster + Partners, Richard Rogers Partnership (later RSHP), and KPF were the next to follow suit. This was undoubtedly due to architectural practices having sufficient capital to invest in what were still very expensive machines, being much larger businesses than the commercial modelmakers. The modelmaking workshop at the Richard Rogers Partnership took ownership of their first machine in 1995,[33] with Millennium Models following in 1996. Kandor, Pipers, 3DD, and Thorp then quickly followed, with many other commercial modelmakers purchasing laser cutters by the end of the decade.

For smaller companies such as A Models and Unit 22, specific laser-cutting bureau services proved to be invaluable alternatives as they allowed them to sub-contract the work on a job-by-job basis. Zone Creations set up as a fabrication bureau in 1999, purchasing two LaserCAMM laser cutters from Scale Models Unlimited in the United States. For Christian Spencer-Davies at A Models it was an extremely useful service that allowed them to gain use of the technology without the associated investment costs.[34] Don Shuttleworth at Unit 22 was also using Zone Creations until he decided to purchase one for the company in 2000, and many smaller firms continue to use bureau services today, with Robert Kirkman having made a conscious decision not to buy a laser cutter specifically because of the attractive economics of using bureaus rather than purchasing one himself.[35] Robert Danton-Rees at Capital Models sent his early laser-cutting jobs to Pipers, but by 2000 he had purchased his own and quickly found other modelmakers coming to him with their own laser-cutting jobs as their popularity spread.[36]

The rapid adoption of the laser cutter was eased by the suitability of the modelmaker's existing principal materials – timber, and more significantly, Perspex – to be used in the machines. As one modelmaker noted, despite the change in cutting tools, 'we used the same materials; we just used three times as much.'[37] Despite its relatively high cost, Perspex was ideally suited for laser cutting, and with polystyrene sheet (HIPS) unsuitable for use in the machines due to its low melting point, the typical construction method of cladding clear Perspex with HIPS façades quickly shifted to an all-Perspex approach. While most timber veneers and thin plywood were suitable for laser cutting, the laser left a visibly burnt edge on timber that put many modelmakers off using the equipment with the material, although at KPF darkened edges and engraving lines on timber models became a popular style.[38]

The time and accuracy gains that the laser cutter brought about were immediately apparent, having dramatically improved the efficiency of architectural modelmaking, and the weeks spent engraving brick lines and cutting individual windows out by hand were reduced to hours or even minutes. As the process sped up, so too did the accuracy of the parts being produced, and just as Ian Mitchell had predicted, more time was freed up to spend on finishing models to an even higher level of quality (Figure 8.7). Fears were expressed at the time, however, that the automation of any part of the modelmaking process would put modelmakers out of a job, though these were quickly found to be misplaced.[39] The main concern was over the loss of hand skills from the profession, but when reflecting on the length of time it took to cut out windows and scribe brick lines by hand, modelmakers quickly recognised the laser's benefits, and their initial caution proved unwarranted. While automating an intensely dull portion of their daily work, the components that the laser cut out still needed to be sanded, sprayed, and assembled by hand, but the efficiency gain meant that a whole job was now much quicker to complete, with a model that would require eight people working on it for a month suddenly needing only four, freeing the others to complete separate commissions.[40]

Figure 8.7 Model of Geneva Airport, made by Millennium Models, 2016.

Source: Photograph by Grant Smith. Image courtesy Simon Hamnell.

With the shift from hand cutting to laser cutting, many architectural modelmakers found themselves needing to learn entirely new skills to replace those no longer being called for. Rather than cutting out pieces of Perspex by hand, they had to draw them on the computer first. The shift to using CAD, first for those modelmakers who had purchased CNC machines and then more generally when laser cutting became widely adopted, was an incredibly rapid change that saw some modelmakers being left behind; Adam Burdett at Unit 22 recalled a freelance modelmaker who he had to stop using simply because they couldn't use a computer.[41] Initially computers were used to receive digital drawings from clients, first on compact disk and then later by email, before being printed out to be plotted by hand onto Perspex and timber. This then quickly progressed to editing the original CAD drawings to select the lines that needed to be cut, which were then sent directly to the laser cutter. A further early use of CAD was in the production of etching drawings. At the architectural practice KPF, the first use of CAD in the modelmaking workshop was to replace hand-drawn drawings that were printed as photographic negatives and sent off to be used in photo-etching processes. The speed and accuracy of computer-drawn templates dramatically improved the quality of the etches they received back from the supplier.[42]

Stephen Fooks witnessed the rapid arrival of desktop computers in the workshop at Kandor, observing that 'within about a year we'd gone from a couple of computers to having one on each desk,'[43] while at the Richard Rogers Partnership under head modelmaker Jackie Hands it was quickly realised that everyone needed their own computer as queues were beginning to form at the sole workstation used to create the drawings for the laser cutter.[44] Learning how to use the software took time, although to become proficient in drawing two-dimensional façades for laser cutting took considerably less time than it did to master the cutting of façades by hand. As such, the quality of work from a novice modelmaker was much improved, enabling them to become more skilled in a relatively shorter space of time.

Throughout the early-2000s more and more architectural modelmakers invested in laser cutters, and despite the initial expense they quickly proved their worth, with the productivity gains they brought about more than offsetting the cost of the investment. With new virtual methods of architectural representation increasingly competing against the model during this period, the leap in efficiency the laser cutter afforded helped the architectural model to maintain its relevance and to keep up with the increasingly complex architectural designs that CAD programs were enabling architects to create. Within just a few years the laser cutter had become one of the main tools of the profession, described as an 'essential tool of modern modelmaking.'[45] Models could now be produced to a higher standard, more quickly, and at a lower cost, the precision and speed of the modelmaker's new digital tools having more than answered their desire for efficiency.

Modelmaking in the Digital Age

By the start of the new millennium the simmering anxiety around the potential threat of rapid prototyping expressed at the 1996 Hertfordshire modelmaking conference had been largely mitigated by the successful adoption of both the CNC and the laser cutter with such positive results. Architectural modelmakers had adapted to the world of CAD drawings and digital manufacturing processes with relative ease, and with the profession

Figure 8.8 Model of Kings Cross Station, made by Millennium Models, 2008.

Source: Photograph by Andrew Putler. Image courtesy Simon Hamnell.

experiencing yet another boom due to the PFI-funded government expansion of schools and hospitals, most architectural modelmakers were too busy making models to worry about the increased availability, lower costs, and higher quality of 3D printers that were entering the market. Ultimately even these proved to be yet another type of highly valuable tool to help modelmakers meet the changing demands of architectural design.

The adoption of advanced 3D computer modelling software had enabled architects to develop new forms that would previously have been extremely difficult to conceive, let alone draw using pen and paper (Figure 8.8). With the ability to create complex organic surfaces, many architects began to experiment with architectural designs that were quite difficult to understand when viewed on a two-dimensional screen. John Blythe, a partner at Foster + Partners, has noted that while computers allowed an architect to gain a good overall feel for a design on a screen, the way complex curves were projected was never as smooth as on a model.[46] The use of physical models to test and verify the complex forms computer software had become capable of generating remained a vital part of the design process at many architectural practices, and a significant challenge for architectural modelmakers was how to effectively reproduce these highly complex shapes in model form. Alec Saunders at Thorp remembered the shift change required as CAD software began to move from 2D to 3D design:

T. P. Bennett, who had won the contract to refurbish London Bridge Station, their computer had designed the buildings above the station to be supported on these

very organic columns that grew out through the platforms and split off, supporting the offices above. They sent us the files, and I was thinking how are we going
to make a model of this?[47]

The increased complexity of architectural geometry was the principal factor that
drove the adoption of 3D printing by architectural modelmakers during the first
decade of the twenty-first century. Multi-axis CNC machines could carve reasonably
complex shapes out of foam or timber, but the availability of more-affordable 3D
printers made a significant difference to what a modelmaker could achieve. As the
technology used to design buildings developed, so too did the processes used by modelmakers to represent them: 'Go back ten years or so and [architects] were unable to
easily create that kind of sophisticated architecture. The architect's work changed, so
therefore we changed.'[48] As with the initial adoption of the laser cutter, the in-house
modelmakers within the large architectural practices had the resources to invest in the
new technology first. Foster + Partners was an early pioneer in the use of 3D printing
during the late-1990s, with the complex geometry of 30 St Mary Axe marking the
first time the in-house modelshop made use of the process,[49] in this case commissioning Malcolm Nichols Ltd to print the building's external structure in four cylindrical
parts (Figure 8.9).

As a process, 3D printing (the by-then more commonly used term for the various
methods of rapid prototyping) had already been in use for a decade before Foster +
Partners first adopted it for architectural modelmaking, with product designers using
the technology to produce prototypes of their designs much more quickly and accurately than had previously been the case when made by hand. Modelmakers specialising in product models were therefore the first to raise the alarm regarding 3D
printing's potential to make the modelmaker redundant, but for architectural modelmakers their arrival coincided with the increasing complexity of architectural designs
that would have been almost impossible to produce accurately by hand.

Just as had been the case with the adoption of the laser cutter, for many architectural modelmakers, their first encounter with 3D printing was using specialist
bureaus. Unlike the laser cutter, however, which effectively replaced older ways of
working, for most architectural modelmakers the 3D printer was initially used only
when specific models required complex parts, and so outsourcing their occasional
use was a much more economical approach than buying machines themselves. Mike
Fairbrass at RSHP began using the Royal College of Art, as they had a range of different 3D printers at quite an early stage: 'We would print components and there
would be quite a lot of hand finishing of them, and then they would be sprayed and
installed into a model and you would never know what had been 3D printed, lasered,
or hand finished.'[50] The use of 3D printers dictated that modelmakers learned not
just how to draw in two-dimensions using CAD software for preparing drawings for
laser cutting but also how to use three-dimensional modelling software. This provided
another challenge for firms looking to use the technology, but it was soon realised that
the benefits outweighed the negatives. As 3D printers became even more affordable,
commercial modelmakers then began to purchase them, and rather than replacing
the modelmaker, as had initially been feared at the Hertfordshire conference in 1996,
3D printers ultimately proved to be just another highly useful tool. When combined
with the existing suite of CAD/CAM equipment at the modelmaker's command, 3D

Figure 8.9 Model of 30 St Mary Axe, made by Foster + Partners, 1998.

Source: Photograph by Richard Davies. Image courtesy Foster + Partners.

printing was able to push the quality and realism of architectural models even further, allowing for bespoke details and more organic architectural forms (Figure 8.10).

The use of 3D printing in architectural models quickly became fashionable as a signifier of the latest technology, and architectural modelmakers found clients specifically

Figure 8.10 Model of Baku, made by Millennium Models, 2014.

Source: Image courtesy Simon Hamnell.

asking for 3D printed components, or even fully 3D printed models, when other methods were actually more cost-effective. 'When it first started happening there were things we could have done easier and cheaper with a piece of model board and needle files, but they wanted it 3D printed,' Base Models' Matt Driscoll recalled.[51] While most modelmakers continued to finish the 3D printed parts so they merged seamlessly into the rest of a model, a growing trend emerged whereby architects and even some developers requested the prints remain unfinished, this despite the visual appearance of all but the most expensive 3D printing methods being quite coarse. The point was to be able to show the inclusion of this new technology, and a fashion for wholly 3D printed architectural models was successfully exploited by dedicated 3D printing firms such as Lee 3D and Hobbs 3D (Figure 8.11). At one architectural practice the

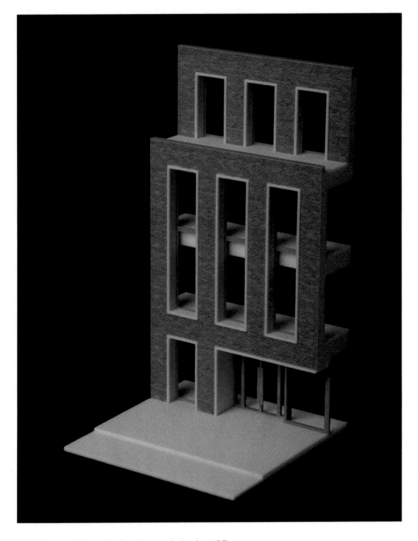

Figure 8.11 3D printed sample façade, made by Lee 3D.

Source: Image courtesy George Lee.

3D printer was kept out in the main studio rather than in the modelmaking workshop, on display as 'a flag of how up to date a practice we were using 3D printers.'[52]

When left in their unfinished states, 3D printed components mostly remained white or translucent, creating a visual appearance that has been described as a 'de-stylised aesthetic,'[53] in that as exact reproductions of computer data 3D printed models are 'essentially an output of information, not a created object.'[54] Fundamentally, it was this exactness of the 3D printed building that prevented the widespread replacement of their handmade counterparts. Architectural models, as Neil Merryweather has pointed out, are not replicas of building designs, but representations: 'You can't just take your digital building model and hit print; it needs the skill of the modelmaker to interpret it.'[55] Purely on a practical level, the reduced scale of architectural models forces a considerable degree of abstraction – while the level of detail possible on smaller-scale models dramatically improved due to the use of CAD/CAM processes, there remained a considerable amount of full-size detail that needed to be removed from a 1:100 scale model as it would be impractical to reproduce, and, on a more artistic level, would distract from the overall message the model was trying to communicate. As Karen Moon has described, every model is a construct that is the 'result of a series of choices about what to show and what not to show,'[56] and it was the lack of human input that limited the popularity of purely 3D printed architectural models. One modelmaker described the look of entirely 3D printed models as being 'really soulless, like ghosts of models,'[57] and by 2015 the demand for visibly 3D printed models had fallen dramatically as the novelty of the process wore off, with clients seeking more expressive models that showed elements of human craftsmanship rather than digital perfection.

For most commercial architectural modelmakers producing high-quality presentation models, the impact of the 3D printer, despite its seemingly revolutionary potential, was ultimately less significant than the introduction of the laser cutter, and while undeniably useful the concern that the technology would replace the modelmaker had fallen out of most modelmaker's minds within just a few years after their widespread introduction. 3D printing was more enthusiastically embraced within in-house modelmaking workshops, where the ability to print quick yet detailed iterations of developing architectural designs made them a viable alternative to the traditional card-and-foam sketch model. At Make Architects, modelshop manager Paul Miles described overseeing a team of four human modelmakers and fourteen robot ones – the practice making extensive use of a suite of Ultimaker 3D printers (Figure 8.12): 'They don't go on holiday or call in sick. It means we can run twenty-four hours a day in effect.'[58] At PLP Architecture a similar in-house set-up was developed with early-stage massing and study models being printed out overnight using 3D printers, with more traditional modelmaking processes being used the further towards completion a design became.[59]

A consequence of the efficient and relatively clean processes of 3D printing was an expansion of the number of modelmaking workshops within architectural practices during the second decade of the twenty-first century, closely echoing how the introduction of card had helped to shift modelmaking from within building construction workshops to architectural drawing offices a century and a half earlier. As was the case then, developments in modelmaking processes allowed for a cleaner workspace, making the activity more suitable for inclusion in the office environment of an architectural practice. Foster + Partners had maintained in-house modelmaking workshops employing professional architectural modelmakers since the 1970s, and while

Figure 8.12 Ultimaker 3D printers at Make Architects, 2018.
Source: Author's Image.

several other practices such as SOM, Richard Rogers Partnership, and KPF followed suit in the 1990s, from the millennium onwards the number of in-house modelshops increased dramatically, reaching around thirty by 2020. The use of laser cutters and 3D printers also served to lower the barrier to entry for freelance modelmakers to establish businesses for themselves, with dozens of smaller dedicated architectural modelmaking firms setting up across the country, often with just a single modelmaker working alone such as at Taylor Made Models and Finch & Fouracre.

Having allowed both commercial and in-house architectural modelmakers to better capture the organic shapes of twenty-first century architecture, increase the level of detail in models, and save time in making complex components, 3D printers quickly proved themselves as useful companions in the making of architectural models rather than as the potential replacements they had initially been feared to be. Within just twenty years the anxiety surrounding their introduction expressed at the 1996 Hertfordshire conference had faded into history, and alongside the CNC machine and the laser cutter, 3D printers had become just another tool at the modelmaker's disposal. The rapid transition to digital processes that architectural modelmaking underwent in the late-1990s and early-2000s in many ways marked a line in the sand; however, as with the basic tools of the profession having remained largely unchanged for almost a century, the processes of modelmaking were ripe for modernisation. Throughout the twentieth century, architectural modelmaking had become an increasingly complex activity, with every new development bringing about improvements in quality, accuracy, realism, and creativity. The profession itself, once dominated by the ever-present Thorp and a confident and relentless desire for more realistic models, had massively diversified with dozens of companies competing for work while specialising in either realistic marketing or abstract competition models. Nothing was ever taken away, however, and the cost of creating architectural models had outpaced their market value, making the need for more efficient processes more important than ever.

What digital manufacturing technologies such as the laser cutter and the 3D printer offered modelmakers were means of automating their most repetitive and time-consuming tasks. The resulting time savings could then be used to reduce the number of hours required to make a model and lower its underlying costs, or to reinvest that time back into the model to add additional detail, further raising the standards of what could be achieved (Figure 8.13). Reflecting on the impact the introduction of CAD/CAM processes had on the profession, modelmaker Lee Atkins noted that 'when people ask what technology has done to your industry, I kind of feel it has taken a lot of the monotony away.'[60] Adam Burdett at Unit 22 agreed:

> I don't think any skills have disappeared. You still need to cut with a scalpel. They are still needed, but the average day now for a modelmaker that is running a project of any size that has any detail on it is likely to spend on average fifty percent of their time sat in front of a computer.[61]

Figure 8.13 Architectural model made by Unit 22, 2008.

Source: Image courtesy Unit 22.

Former RSHP Head of Modelmaking Mike Fairbrass felt there was a certain inevitability to the adoption of digital manufacturing processes in modelmaking during this period, observing that 'it is what every craft does. . . . They identify the things that take the longest time and make them faster, and get the same or similar result, or sometimes even better,'[62] with Stephen Fooks having made the similar point that within the history of architectural modelmaking, 'when any new change – a new material or process – comes along, it is always about efficiency, about trying to make the same thing within an ever-shrinking cost envelope.'[63]

With the added benefits of CNC machines, laser cutters, and 3D printers, architectural modelmaking rapidly adapted to employ a combination of both digital and traditional hand-making skills. Modelmaker Dan McWilliam at Farrells observed that despite all the technology now found in a modelmaker's workshop, 'It needs to be hand skills and technology coming together. It is not about using one or the other'[64] (Figure 8.14). The basic sentiment that technology was just another tool for a skilled modelmaker to wield was further emphasised by an increasing number of 3D printing specialists approaching the more traditional architectural modelmakers for assistance when asked to produce complex models. Adam Burdett described how it was 'a lovely feeling for a company to say, "We want to be better than our rivals, so can you make this for us?" What, with our prehistoric techniques and processes? Yes, of course we can. And very reassuring that even with the most modern technology, it can still be improved by skilled labour.'[65]

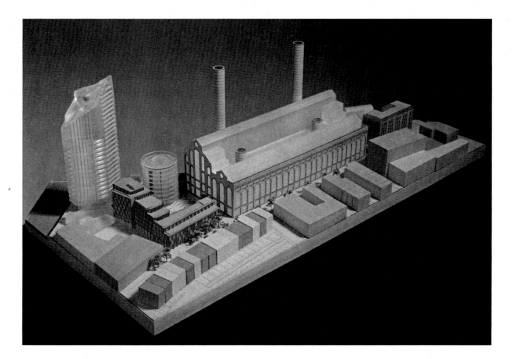

Figure 8.14 Planning model made by Farrells, 2016.

Source: Image courtesy Dan McWilliam.

In 1995, during the peak of anxiety over the introduction of laser cutting and 3D printing, the American modelmaker Richard Tenguerian attempted to calm the debate by arguing that 'tools such as CAD/CAM are at the service of the modelmaker, not the other way round.'[66] For the architectural modelmaker in Britain during the late-1990s and early-2000s, the use of these tools was primarily focused on improving the basic efficiencies of modelmaking, but once established both the laser cutter and the 3D printer began to help realise Ian Mitchell's prediction at the 1996 Hertfordshire conference that such technologies would free the modelmaker's time to be spent on the more creative aspects of modelmaking. Armed with their new digital capabilities, modelmakers entered the twenty-first century confident and ready to push their skills forward and to dedicate their attention to the artistry of architectural modelmaking, reaching the limits of precision and creativity and demonstrating their true mastery of their practice despite the ever-increasing pressures of the competitive and turbulent years ahead.

Notes

1 Brian Holder, 'Introduction,' *The Future of Modelmaking* (Hatfield: University of Hertfordshire, 1996), 2.
2 Angar Oswald, *Architectural Models* (Berlin: DOM, 2008), 9.
3 Alexander Shilling, *Architecture and Modelbuilding* (Basel: Birkhauser, 2018), 196.
4 M. Hauschild and R. Karzel, *Digital Processes* (Munich: Edition DETAIL, 2012), 7.
5 Thomas Fisher, *Communicating Ideas Artfully* (New York: Steelcase Partnership, 1990), 14.
6 Patrick McKeogh, interview with Dorothy Hill, October 3, 2018. https://archmodelsnetwork.home.blog/.
7 Tina Miller, interview with author, April 30, 2018.
8 Ian Mitchell, 'Developments in America,' *The Future of Modelmaking* (Hatfield: University of Hertfordshire, 1996), 1.
9 Ibid, 3.
10 Trevor Crout, 'Scalpel to Computer Control,' *The Future of Modelmaking* (Hatfield: University of Hertfordshire, 1996), 1.
11 Stephen Fooks, interview with author, May 8, 2018; Lee Atkins, interview with author, June 10, 2019; Neil Merryweather, interview with author, October 8, 2019.
12 Fooks, interview.
13 Robert Kirkman, interview with author, April 29, 2019.
14 Atkins, interview.
15 Will Strange, interview with author, December 11, 2017.
16 Alec Saunders, interview with author, March 13, 2018.
17 Fooks, interview.
18 Merryweather, interview.
19 Strange, interview.
20 Mitchell, 'Developments in America,' 4.
21 Fooks, interview
22 Crout, 'Scalpel to Computer Control,' 2.
23 David MacKay, interview with author, January 5, 2018.
24 Saunders, interview
25 Richard Tenguerian, 'Model Making,' *Progressive Architecture*, November, 1995, 42.
26 Kamran Kiani, interview with author, August 5, 2019
27 Akiko Busch, *The Art of the Architectural Model* (New York: Design Press, 1991), 57.
28 Merryweather, interview.
29 J. Rawson, 'Small Beginning: Modelmaking,' *Architects' Journal* 191 (January 17, 1990), 65; Paul Woods, interview with author, September 10, 2019.
30 Fooks, interview.

31 Simon Hamnell, interview with author, November 13, 2018.
32 Ibid.
33 Mike Fairbrass, interview with author, September 13, 2019.
34 Christian Spencer-Davies, interview with author, June 6, 2019.
35 Kirkman, interview.
36 Danton-Rees, interview.
37 Hamnell, interview.
38 Merryweather, interview.
39 Fairbrass, interview.
40 Matthew Driscoll, interview with author, January 22, 2018.
41 Burdett, interview.
42 Merryweather, interview.
43 Fooks, interview.
44 Fairbrass, interview.
45 Bruno Gordon, interview with author, November 14, 2017.
46 John Blythe, interview with author, March 26, 2018.
47 Saunders, interview.
48 Driscoll, interview.
49 Neil Vandersteen, interview with author, March 26, 2018.
50 Fairbrass, interview.
51 Driscoll, interview.
52 Gordon, interview.
53 Brian Rafzlaff, *Digital Craft: 3D Printing for Architectural Design* (London: Lee 3D, 2016), 59.
54 Ibid.
55 Merryweather, Interview
56 Karen Moon, *Modelling Messages* (New York: Monacelli Press, 2005), 12.
57 Fairbrass, interview.
58 Paul Miles, interview with author, March 20, 2018.
59 Merryweather, interview.
60 Atkins, interview.
61 Burdett, interview.
62 Fairbrass, interview.
63 Fooks, interview.
64 Daniel McWilliam, interview with author, February 19, 2018.
65 Burdett, interview.
66 Richard Tenguerian, 'Model Making,' *Progressive Architecture*, November, 1995, 14.

Chapter 9

Creative Ambitions

By the beginning of the twenty-first century architectural modelmaking in Britain had matured into a thriving industry. With the first degree-educated modelmakers graduating from Bachelor of Arts courses in modelmaking at Hertfordshire and Bournemouth, the broad stylistic palette encompassing both realism and abstraction now firmly established, and the efficiency gains brought about by the adoption of digital manufacturing processes having been fully embedded, the profession had been thoroughly modernised. The benefits of the modelmaker's digital toolkit had only been partially realised, however, and during the first decades of the new millennium digital technologies began to be applied in far more creative ways, propelling the quality, artistry, and sophistication of architectural modelmaking to ever-increasing levels. The growing complexity of architectural models, while welcomed by both architects and property developers alike, saw the much-needed efficiency gains that CAD/CAM processes such as the laser cutter had introduced quickly outpaced by ballooning expectations of how those same processes could be put to creative uses.

Still adhering to the inquisitive, adaptable approach established by John Thorp more than a century earlier, modelmakers in the early twenty-first century are today finding themselves in a remarkably similar situation to those who had witnessed the enormous growth in the size and complexity of models during the 1930s, further stimulating the ongoing search for new processes and materials in the hope of rebalancing the efficiencies of architectural modelmaking against its new creative potential. Weathering almost constant economic turmoil, the story of architectural modelmaking in Britain in the twenty-first century so far has been one of unrelenting pressures and rising expectations but also of innovation, creativity, and artistry. In just twenty years the making of architectural models has become more challenging, more technically complex, and more demanding than ever before, and the skills of the modelmaker have continued to expand as the technological expectations of their practice have evolved.

Digital Creativity

With the laser cutter and 3D printer having removed the most time-consuming and repetitive manual processes of basic architectural modelmaking, the first decade of the twenty-first century saw architectural modelmakers begin to experiment with what else their new digital tools and processes could achieve. Leading the way in this new era of both artistic and technical creativity was the second generation of modelmakers

DOI: 10.4324/9781003298007-10

to have been trained in the 'Arup School.' Despite George Rome Innes' retirement from teaching at Rochester, the influence of the Arup Associates' approach to architectural modelmaking had continued to expand throughout the 1990s and into the early-2000s as the Arup philosophy of creative and abstract modelmaking had by this time been firmly embedded into the curricula of the universities and further education colleges that were running modelmaking courses at the time. When Rochester graduate Ben Moss set up the HND in modelmaking at the Bournemouth and Poole College of Art and Design (later Arts University Bournemouth) in 1992, the Arup template was put in place there, while Richard Armiger, through his teaching on the modelmaking HNDs at St Albans College of Art and Design (later becoming part of the University of Hertfordshire), was instrumental in imbedding the Arup approach within that institution. Through his company, Network Modelmakers, Armiger had also by this point become the leading conduit for creative modelmakers to establish themselves in the profession, with many noted future modelmakers passing through his doors. Benefiting from the continued dominance of the Arup School within modelmaking education, a new generation of highly talented and creative modelmakers set up shop, with A Models (founded by Christian Spencer-Davies), Millennium Models (started by Simon Hamnell), and Base Models (led by Matthew Driscoll) quickly becoming known for their highly creative and individualistic approaches to architectural modelmaking, extending the legacy of the Arup workshop and updating it with the application of the modelmaker's twenty-first century digital tools and processes.

Christian Spencer-Davies established A Models having learned his trade working for Richard Armiger after switching from a career as a designer at Terrance Conran's partnership. Having seen the devastating effects of the early-1990s recession on architectural modelmaking first hand, Spencer-Davies was determined to combine both the impressive creativity he had seen at Network Modelmakers with a much more cost-conscious sense of efficiency,[1] and A Models quickly gained a reputation for making the most expressive and creative architectural models available (Figures 9.1), the photographer Andrew Putler having noted that their models were often art objects rather than models in the traditional sense.[2]

Simon Hamnell, an early St Albans graduate who had been taught by Richard Armiger, spent the first decade of his career working at a range of modelmaking workshops that included both Network Modelmakers and Arup itself, and in the late-1990s saw an opportunity to establish his own company following the closure of Arup's in-house modelmaking workshop during a period of cost-cutting at the practice. Arup had only recently expanded its modelmaking capacity with the kitting out of an expensive new workshop in what had formerly been Thames Television's prop-making department on Euston Road in London. Working there as a freelance modelmaker, Hamnell offered to purchase the equipment and to continue to make models for the company on a third-party basis. Moving into shared premises with the designer Ron Arad, for whom he also acted as an in-house modelmaker in lieu of rent, Hamnell found demand for his services skyrocketing and within a short period of time was busy making models for some of the biggest national and international architectural projects of the day[3] (Figure 9.2). Continuing to provide models for Arup, Hamnell's company, Millennium Models, was considered by many to be a direct extension of the Arup modelshop's approach, using not just their machinery but many of their techniques and aesthetics as well.[4]

Figure 9.1 Conceptual model of Will Alsop's OCAD building, made by A Models, 2009.

Source: Image courtesy Christian Spencer-Davies.

Figure 9.2 Model of the V&A Spiral, made by Millennium Models, 1996.

Source: Image courtesy Simon Hamnell.

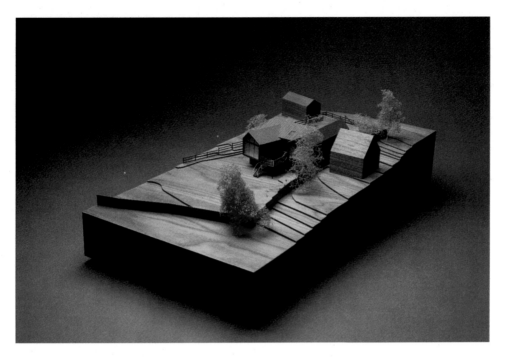

Figure 9.3 Model of Holly Lodge, made by Base Models, 2020.
Source: Image courtesy Base Models.

A few years later, Rochester graduate Matt Driscoll, having worked for both Millennium and Network Modelmakers, set up Base Models during the PFI building boom of the early-2000s, initially renting workshop space from Millennium before finding his own premises and expanding into a twelve-strong team known for making highly creative models for architects such as Zaha Hadid, Foster + Partners, and David Adjaye Associates.[5] As with Millennium, Base favoured working in timber (Figure 9.3), partly due to the personal preference of the company's three directors but also due to the number of competition models they produced, where timber's forced abstraction suited the conceptual and often ambiguous nature of the architecture their models were commissioned to represent.[6]

As they had all been trained in the Arup School through their connections to Rochester, Arup, and Richard Armiger, the trio of Spencer-Davies, Hamnell, and Driscoll all deliberately set out to avoid making the realistic marketing models favoured by developers and, being keen to differentiate themselves from both their competition and each other, continued to develop new styles for architectural models armed with the now standard digital tools of the laser cutter and 3D printer. During the period in which they all started their businesses the demand for more abstract architectural models was booming, primarily for entry into architectural competitions, the trend for which had continued to expand throughout the 1990s. At Millennium Models in particular, Simon Hamnell found that, as with Richard Armiger's models for the 1991 Venice Gateway competition, he was being asked to provide multiple models for the same competitions all for different architectural practices, forcing the need for individuality. Largely favouring timber models in the tradition of the Arup modelshop, Millennium quickly became a highly regarded and successful firm of modelmakers as a result of their eye-catching competition models, and Hamnell found himself catering to a core of three or four architectural practices that were commissioning models on a regular basis.[7] For Hamnell, what set companies like Millennium and A Models apart from their competitors was their people: 'First of all, they knew they would be talking to me, and if they weren't, everyone here could speak the same language, so there was no issue of a them and us scenario. We all understood their needs.'[8] While developers largely knew what they wanted and which modelmakers could deliver the standards of realism they required for marketing models of completed designs, architects, particularly during the early stages of a design for a competition panel, needed much more of a dialogue with a modelmaker to develop the look of the model while the design of the actual building was so ill-defined.

With most competition submissions being more or less unfinished concepts put forward to be refined once the winning contract had been awarded, the models that Millennium and A Models produced naturally tended towards more abstract styles and reduced palettes of materials and colours.[9] Timbers were heavily used, in direct opposition to the plastics-based realism of the marketing model, firmly in the Arup style, but timber models were also much less labour intensive to make and comparatively easy to modify compared to a full-colour Perspex model, reflecting the cost-conscious attitude of those who had seen the effects of the 1990s recession. For Christian Spencer-Davies at A Models the challenge was not to be creative but 'to do so economically.'[10] Materials were often left in their natural state rather than attempting to imitate the full-scale materials of a proposed building, while added hints of colour and texture through the use of etched metals such as phosphor bronze, stainless steel, or nickel silver brought their models alive, the metals being carefully lacquered so not to discolour over time.[11]

Although broadly following the spirit of the Arup School of architectural model-making, the modelmakers at Millennium, A Models, and Base were able to draw from a radically different set of tools than David Armstrong and his team of modelmakers at Arup had access to during the 1960s and 1970s. The first application of digital processes by this new generation of creative modelmakers was in using the laser cutter to precisely cut and engrave timber veneers for building façades and contoured landscapes (Figure 9.4), but it was once the creative potential of laser-cut Perspex was realised that abstract models began to expand from their Arup-inspired timber palette, with modelmakers exploring and developing entirely new visual and material languages.

Having been the dominant material used in realistic models since the 1950s, Perspex had been largely side-lined in favour of timber as the default material in abstract models as a direct result of the Arup influence during the 1980s. The creative use of Perspex had been explored to a limited extent through the work of modelmakers such as Richard Armiger and Ademir Volic and their models for Zaha Hadid during the early-1990s, but it was only when the laser cutter was introduced and its ideal suitability for cutting and engraving Perspex in more creative ways was exploited that new possibilities were opened up for the use of plastics in representing architecture in more abstract styles. Whereas timber models naturally forced abstraction due to their

Figure 9.4 Model of Kings Cross Station, made by Millennium Models, 2008.

Source: Photograph by Andrew Putler. Image courtesy Simon Hamnell.

lack of detail and strong intrinsic material associations, timber also carried a warm, traditional feeling that did not sit well with ultra-modern designs such as Hadid's organic architecture or the futuristic industrial shapes of the high-tech movement. The crispness of laser-etched unpainted Perspex and its light-transmitting properties provided a strong alternative that could be used to create dramatic effects such as the glowing block-like forms of Millennium's 2006 interior model for Marks & Spencer (Figure 9.5).

While the stacking of Perspex to create solid block models was not in itself a new approach, having been used by Thorp as early as the 1950s, the ease of creating such a model with a laser cutter saw this method of model construction become a widely used style during the early-2000s, with the Richard Rogers Partnership (later RSHP) leading the way (Figure 9.6). Mike Fairbrass, then Head of Modelmaking at the practice, recalled that 'we liked to experiment, and the first and obvious thing we did with [lasers] was the stacking of Perspex, which was the easy thing to do.'[12] Such was the success of this approach that the style was quickly emulated; Simon Hamnell at Millennium noting the ubiquity of the stacked Perspex model, remembering that they were 'for a while just stacked Perspex, and then with elevations on, which I think we did first.'[13] The use of laser-cut timber veneers to clad stacked Perspex blocks offered a quick and visually appealing way of representing buildings during early design stages, while for larger-scale and more highly detailed presentation models the combination

Figure 9.5 Perspex interior model made by Millennium Models, 2006.

Source: Image courtesy Simon Hamnell.

Figure 9.6 1:1,000 scale laser cut stacked Perspex model made by RSHP modelshop, circa 2007.

Source: Image courtesy Mike Fairbrass.

of laser-cut timber veneer and Perspex glazing could be used to produce dramatic contrasts. At the Richard Rogers Partnership, the use of unpainted laser-cut fluorescent Perspex became a highly identifiable look for the practice's models (Figures 9.7 and 9.8), the style emerging through the need for an impressive but quick-to-produce visual language for concept models.[14] With a strong diagrammatic feel that captured the high-tech approach to architecture that the practice favoured, the style that the team created 'expressed the intent of a scheme and the excitement, and was a bit like a vibrant hand sketch; it had that kind of energy to it.'[15]

Efficiency and creativity combined with the Rogers style, with the time savings generated by the speed and efficiency of the laser cutter freeing the modelmakers' time to be spent experimenting and developing new creative ways to use both the technology and Perspex together in radical new ways. Working collaboratively, Fairbrass

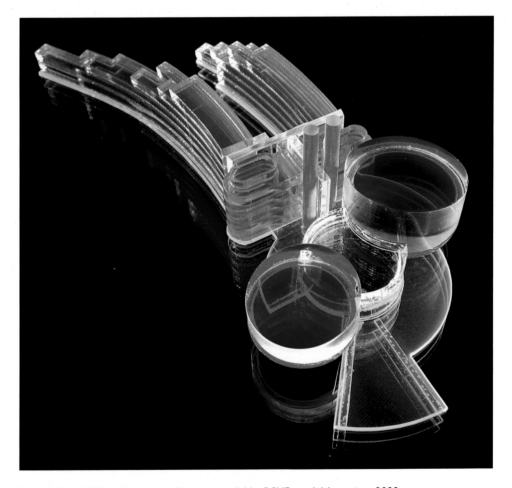

Figure 9.7 1:1,000 scale laser cut Perspex model by RSHP modelshop, circa 2000.

Source: Image courtesy Mike Fairbrass.

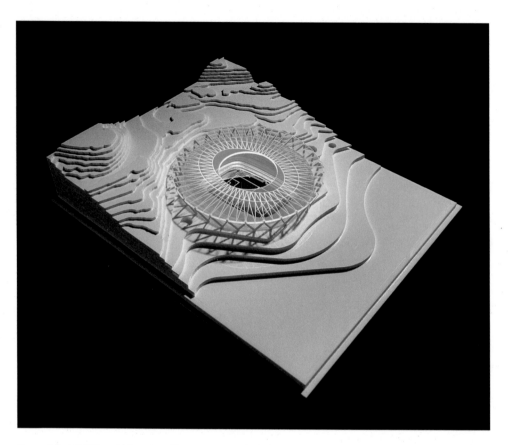

Figure 9.8 1:5,000 scale laser cut Perspex model by RSHP modelshop, circa 2013.

Source: Image courtesy Mike Fairbrass.

at Rogers and Hamnell at Millennium went on to produce several highly creative laser-cut Perspex models for exhibitions, including an entirely transparent model of the Leadenhall building that was lit from below to create a ghostly x-ray appearance (Figure 9.9). For Mike Fairbrass the effect produced using laser-cut Perspex was vital in maintaining the model's relevance: 'The thing you can't do with digital renders very effectively is abstraction. Typically, abstract models have used timber because no one is going to think you are going to make the whole thing out of giant blocks of wood, and so they understand it is an abstraction. The same was with edge glow Perspex, you just got it was an impression, an abstraction.'[16] With the quality of digital renders constantly improving, the creative push of modelmakers such as Fairbrass, Hamnell, and Spencer-Davies helped the architectural model retain its position as a favoured ambassador of the architectural profession, using modern technology to capture the essence of a design in ways that had previously been unthinkable.

At the same time that the laser's artistic potential was being explored by Fairbrass and the second wave of Arup School modelmakers such as Hamnell, architectural

Figure 9.9 Model of the Leadenhall Building, made by Millennium Models, 2004.

Source: Image courtesy Simon Hamnell.

modelmakers at the more-established firms including Pipers, Kandor, Unit 22, and Thorp, and within the growing number of in-house modelmaking workshops at architectural practices such as Foster + Partners, were putting the modelmaker's new digital tools to equally effective use in driving forward the levels of detail and realism in more traditional marketing models (Figure 9.10). One of the most significant changes the laser cutter brought was the ability to increase the amount of detail at any given scale. Whereas models below 1:100 scale had previously generally been treated as simple blocks, the laser allowed for the same detail found on a 1:100 scale model to be achieved at much smaller scales, even at 1:1,000.[17] Simple small-scale housing estate models could now include brick detail and clear windows, previously having been made as solid blocks. Neil Vandersteen at Foster + Partners is clear that the laser cutter directly increased the complexity of architectural models, noting that the technology allowed for 'more details, more animation . . . the model being far more detailed now than it used to be.'[18]

For all the positive benefits the creative application of technology brought to architectural modelmaking during the early-2000s, the increasing levels of precision and

Figure 9.10 Model of Moor House, made by Pipers, 2002.
Source: Image courtesy Pipers Model Makers.

complexity and the inclusion of much finer detail meant that the efficiency gains that digital manufacturing processes had initially brought with them were quickly lost. Modelmaker Neil Merryweather noted that 'if you do something quickly it doesn't take long before people want more of it, and they want it in less time,'[19] and with the profession having been bolstered by an increased demand for such models during a building boom driven by government-instigated PFI contracts for new schools and hospitals, the higher expectations of detail and creativity in architectural models that the modelmaker's digital tools had enabled ultimately came at the wrong time. With most of the efficiency gains of the previous decade now absorbed by the application of digital technologies for creative purposes, the profession was subsequently ill-equipped to weather the biggest collapse in property prices in modern history that unexpectedly took place in 2008.

The Limits of Complexity

The impact of the 2008 financial crisis was far more damaging to the profession than the early-1990s recession had ever been, with most architectural modelmakers left in a desperately precarious position because of the sudden freeze of property development that followed. Worst hit were the more creative modelmakers such as Millennium and A Models, who had made their names providing abstract models for architects to submit to competitions, as few developers or publicly funded organisations were able to even consider financing new projects at the time. 'We were the barometer because the timeline of our work was so fast that we knew pretty much instantly. Our work was so speculative that we knew what was happening months before even most architects did. There was a day when suddenly there were no jobs, no conversations at all, it all just literally stopped,' recalled Christian Spencer-Davies.[20] Limited work continued to trickle through for marketing models of developments nearing completion, as selling them suddenly became all the more urgent, but overall architectural modelmaking in Britain ground to an almost complete standstill. Simon Hamnell at Millennium was employing fourteen modelmakers before the crash, but within three months he had been forced to let all but one go: 'It was brutal, soul destroying. We just went into work and looked at the phone and it didn't ring for months.'[21] The drought in orders lasted for around eight months, placing many companies in dire financial circumstances. Flick Models and the much-admired modelmaker Niamh Billings both closed their doors, while the combination of redundancies and the termination of the large number of freelance contracts many of the larger firms such as Pipers and Kandor relied on meant that over the space of the following twelve months perhaps as many as two hundred architectural modelmakers left the industry in pursuit of work elsewhere.

By the time demand began to return to anywhere near sustainable levels during 2010, most modelmaking companies had exhausted their financial reserves. Thorp, now under the ownership of Atom, was able to save on costs by moving out of their newly built studios in Sunningdale and into Atom's own premises in the village, renting out the space to provide a much-needed alternative income. Competition between modelmakers became intense as the entire industry was fighting for the same few commissions, driving prices downward and placing further pressures on profit margins. Developers became canny to the situation, often playing several modelmakers against one another, knowing that everyone was so desperate for work that they would be willing to accept far lower payments than normal. With the creative application of technology having wiped out the efficiency gains of the 1990s, and the financial crash stripping talent out of the profession and forcing prices downward, many modelmakers found that the pressures of just surviving day to day continued for many years after the economy had supposedly rebounded. The release finally came with the influx of foreign investment into London's property market, but this too, while providing much-needed work, also added to the modelmaker's problems. The intensive competition between companies and a demand for even more technically creative and complex models drove their size and basic costs to ever more excessive levels, placing additional pressures on modelmakers to push their technical and creative boundaries while at the same time searching for new efficiencies to sustain themselves.

During the recovery from the 2008 financial crash London became a highly desirable location for property investment, with billions of pounds of foreign money pouring in from China, Russia, and the Middle East, creating an intense period of competition between the major property developers that in turn instigated a push for more sophisticated marketing models to help drive sales. International property fairs such as MIPIM in Cannes became annual expositions where every major developer wanted showstopping architectural models to impress and overshadow their competitors, while architectural models in marketing suites as the centrepieces of a developer's attempts to woo potential buyers became increasingly important (Figure 9.11).

Figure 9.11 Model of The Waterman, Greenwich, made by 3DD, 2018.

Source: Image courtesy 3DD.

Having been used to sell property in marketing suites and estate agents' windows since the 1930s, the change that occurred in the post-crash residential market in London was that the developers behind these properties were not aiming at local buyers but were instead targeting wealthy foreign investors, intending to sell not just a single apartment to an owner-occupier, but perhaps five or six properties to a single investor. Models for London-based developments began to be commissioned in duplicate, with one to be used in the local marketing suite in the city and another flown around the world to be shown to potential foreign buyers directly (Figure 9.12). Models suddenly had to be not only visually impressive but also constructed to withstand being shipped in flight cases, often in pieces that were designed to fit back together on arrival.[22] The added expense of doing so directly fuelled the emergence of architectural model-makers setting up business in China, India, and the Middle East, all of whom began competing for major marketing model contracts at extremely low prices. In Britain these companies were initially greeted with a degree of scepticism due to the questionable quality of their early work, but as they began to refine their processes and gain experience, Chinese competitors in particular became a major concern for many of the larger British firms. Modelmaker Stephen Fooks recalled being asked to quote for model that he priced at £30,000, but the client ended up paying merely £10,000 for a comparable model from a company in China instead.[23] Chinese modelmaking firms were able to produce models extremely cheaply and quickly; RJ Models in Shenzhen, for example, employed over seven hundred modelmakers in a factory-sized workshop. The efficiencies offered by Chinese modelmakers were therefore extremely attractive propositions for developers seeking to maximise their marketing budgets. Adding further pressure on British modelmakers, these new international competitors served to shrink not only their reach into the global market but also affected demand for British-based investment projects aimed at foreign buyers.

Despite the competition from China, the demand for architectural models in Britain nevertheless returned to growth as the sheer volume of new high-rise developments in London began to outpace any building boom in London's recent history. Projects such as The Shard, 20 Fenchurch Street, The Heron, Pan Peninsula, Newfoundland Quay, and Landmark Pinnacle saw billions of pounds being invested, with the size of these developments again being far beyond what most architectural modelmakers were used to working on. Landmark Pinnacle in Millwall alone was proposed at seventy-five floors with nine hundred apartments at a cost of over £300 million to build. With such substantial sums of money at stake, the property developers behind these projects were highly incentivised to ensure they were fully occupied on completion, resulting in aggressive marketing strategies with significant budgets. By 2015 the developer Berkeley Homes had become the biggest commissioner of architectural models in the country,[24] and competition between the major developers became a crucial driving force behind a demand for grander and more sophisticated architectural models to be displayed in marketing suites. The hold of the property developer over architectural modelmaking that had caused so much tension between modelmakers and architects in the 1970s had returned, only this time the commercial realities of the post-crash market meant few architects were in a position to complain. Alec Saunders at Thorp noted the difference: 'After the crash, all the public building contracts had dried up and suddenly all the cranes in London were building residential developments. The biggest and best architects out there were all designing residential buildings. The thing

Figure 9.12 Model of Neo Bankside, made by 3DD, 2015.

Source: Image courtesy 3DD.

they once hated with a passion was now where the money was.'[25] With architects including Norman Foster, Richard Rogers, Zaha Hadid, and Herzog and de Meuron all putting their names behind major residential towers in London, the ideological concerns of the 1960s and 1970s were long forgotten, and most modelmakers – and architects – found themselves at the mercy of the major property developers in determining whether they had a future.

With many of the developments targeting the high-end luxury market, the models used to sell these properties had to be equally sophisticated as developers were striving to make their own sales pitches better than their competitors', resulting in increasingly high expectations of technological complexity and interaction within the architectural models they commissioned. Suddenly a race was on, with modelmakers clamouring for projects and fuelling a drive for innovative approaches while simultaneously seeking out new efficiencies to make these models profitable. With well-known and award-winning architects on board, property developers also began to expect a greater degree of artistry in the models they commissioned. Whether this was under the influence of the architects involved or simply a canny marketing choice to project an architect's brand through their models is unclear, but the effect was a blurring of the line between the traditional marketing model and the more abstract models that were favoured by modelmakers working in the Arup School (Figure 9.13).

Aside from an increased demand for creativity and abstraction, lighting and interactivity became commonly requested features within architectural models that were destined for use in luxury marketing suites. Whereas digital technologies had previously been used as tools and processes in the making of architectural models, modelmakers suddenly found themselves being asked to integrate digital technologies as features of the models themselves, throwing them into entirely new areas of technical expertise to unlock new and unexplored creative avenues.

The ability to interact with an architectural model in some way had been steadily growing since the early-1990s, with simple keypads allowing potential buyers to select the number of an individual house or apartment and to light it up on the model to see exactly where it was. For developers, the easier someone could envisage themselves living in a specific property the more likely they were to gain a sale, and with advances in touchscreen technology from 2010 onwards, developers began to demand even more sophisticated means of interaction.[26] The use of lighting in architectural models to increase realism and to create a sense of spectacle dates back as early as Ernest Twining's illuminated model of the National Cash Register Factory made in 1924; however, by the start of the new millennium it had already become expected that a model in a marketing suite would include some form of interactive lighting (Figure 9.14). This was particularly challenging to achieve if each light needed to be controlled by a button or keypad. To wire a model in this way each room had to contain an individual bulb with two wires trailing all the way through the building, hidden behind walls and ceilings, to a junction box controlled by a keypad. The amount of wiring involved could extend to several hundred metres, and models often had to be designed to incorporate cooling fans to prevent the bulbs from warping the Perspex. Modelmaker David MacKay remembered an early interactive model he made of a residential development in Knightsbridge that melted due to the heat from the six hundred bulbs inside.[27] Interactive lighting was also extremely costly; for Capital Models to wire a model of an apartment building that contained three hundred homes added £6000 to

Figure 9.13 Presentation model made by Unit 22, 2011.

Source: Photograph by Andrew Putler. Image courtesy Unit 22.

Figure 9.14 Lighted architectural model made by Pipers, 2015.

Source: Image courtesy Pipers Model Makers.

the cost of the model,[28] and for one particular masterplan model Mike Fairbrass at Rogers, Stirk, Harbour, and Partners used over five kilometres of fibreoptic cable to transmit light from fluorescent tubes hidden underneath the baseboard.[29]

The development of LED strips, and particularly programmable LEDs where individual LEDs could be controlled in sequence, proved to be significant timesavers and were a much-needed efficiency driver, as by 2010 the inclusion of lighting in an architectural model had become a standard expectation, and not just for marketing models: 'It got to the point where lighting was just routine. If you were making a model it would have lights in it as a matter of course.'[30] One particularly innovative example of the use of lighting was Millennium Models' 2015 model of RSHP's design for the Antwerp law courts that employed photo-luminescent paper that glowed when a small electrical charge was applied (Figure 9.15), while the Bristol-based modelmaking company Amalgam generated much interest in its model of Foster + Partners entry into the Yongsan masterplan competition in 2009, using 3D-printed and chrome-plated buildings lit through coloured gels from below to create a distinctive neon effect.

Figure 9.15 Model of Antwerp Law Courts, made by Millennium Models, 2015.

Source: Image courtesy Simon Hamnell.

With LEDs having become the standard method of lighting architectural models, the next major development was the introduction of touchscreen interfaces to control them. By selecting a particular property from a menu, the screen could then show interior views while the model lit up to indicate where the specific apartment was located. 3DD took this concept further in making models that physically rotated to orientate the selected apartment to the viewer, one model even rising vertically to show the specific location of an apartment's underground parking space, revealed within a pop-out drawer in the baseboard.[31] High-end marketing models had rapidly become hybrids of physical models and digital media with built-in flatscreens displaying additional information, the architectural model returning to levels of extravagance and complexity not seen since the inter-war years modelmaking boom. At international property shows models began to balloon in size to show proposals for entire cities, costing many hundreds of thousands of pounds each, and almost always incorporating some form of digital animation through built-in LED panels or advanced light projection techniques to provide moving information overlays (Figure 9.16).

The technical knowledge required to make such interactive marketing models was not inconsiderable and provided an additional challenge for modelmakers to adopt new skills that extended considerably beyond what might be recognised as those

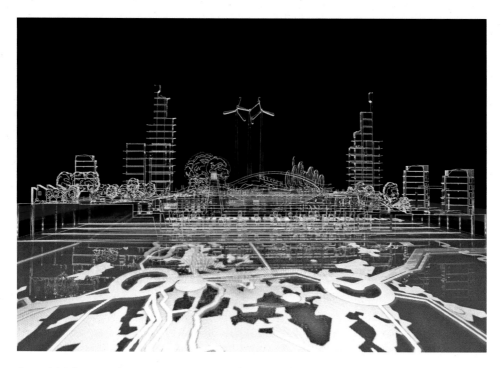

Figure 9.16 Perspex architectural model incorporating an animated LED screen below, made by RSHP modelshop, circa 2008.

Source: Image courtesy Mike Fairbrass.

of traditional architectural modelmaking. Coding and programming, user-interface design, servomotors, and hydraulics became unexpectedly important new areas of expertise for modelmakers to tap into, once again finding creative ways in which to employ new technologies. With property developers eager to push the boundaries of showmanship in their marketing strategies, modelmakers were equally pushed to challenge the boundaries of technical innovation, and the architectural model during the digital age of the early twenty-first century became more technically and creatively sophisticated than it had ever been. As with the inter-war years boom in the twentieth century, however, there was a growing sense that the complexity of architectural models might once again be reaching the limit. In her 2005 study of the architectural model, the architectural historian Karen Moon, in observing that the model had become highly advanced, asked whether it was possible that the model might one day become too complex, 'too clever for its own good?'[32] The sheer technical complexity that marketing models reached in the decade that followed her statement suggests that Moon may indeed have been right, having noticed the early warning signs of what was to come.

The prices of high-end marketing models commissioned after the 2008 financial crash steadily increased as the requirement for more interactive features intensified, with 3DD alone receiving five contracts for models worth over £200,000 each in 2018. Foster + Partners' enormous model of their five-billion-dollar design for the Apple Campus in California was similarly costly, while the extremes to which high-end models reached during this period are perhaps best exemplified by 3DD's model of Foster + Partners' design for the Bloomberg Headquarters in London, commissioned to occupy the foyer of the completed building during its opening ceremony in 2017. Constructed at 1:50 scale, the model was fully detailed internally with every workspace realistically portrayed (Figures 9.17 and 9.18). To illuminate the model bespoke lighting panels were ordered from Perspex directly, each twenty-millimetre-thick sheet cut to the precise shape required, with built-in LEDs around the edges and an etched graduated pattern on their upper surfaces in order to project even light levels across the entire sheet. Floor plates were laser etched and then painted to closely resemble real timber, with over £200,000 of 3D printing sub-contracted to various bureaus to create the internal furnishings and the distinctive bronze panels on the building's exterior. The completed four-metre-wide model was extremely heavy with each of its three sections weighing a quarter of a ton, and so to support its own weight the model had to be designed with solid aluminium columns that provided genuine structural support. Taking twelve weeks to make in a workshop space specially rented for the project, and with over thirty thousand separate components, it was the largest and most expensive model 3DD had ever made.[33]

Figure 9.17 Model of the Bloomberg London Headquarters, made by 3DD, 2017.

Source: Photograph by Luke Hayes. Image courtesy 3DD.

Figure 9.18 Interior of the Bloomberg London Headquarters model, made by 3DD, 2017.

Source: Photograph by Luke Hayes. Image courtesy 3DD.

Architectural Modelmaking in Britain Today

At the time of writing the Bloomberg model stands as one of the most expensive and technically complex architectural models ever made in Britain, indicative of the extreme levels of spectacle and showmanship that have become expected in high-end marketing models. With the efficiency gains that the introduction of CAD/CAM processes brought about during the 1990s now long forgotten as the same technologies have been applied in further expanding the creativity, realism, and complexity of models, so too have the costs involved in making them increased. Today, twenty-first century architectural modelmaking during the digital age has become a highly expensive activity, and the steady increases in detail and sophistication of the past twenty years have eaten into many modelmakers' profits, with expectations having risen above the prices clients are prepared to pay. In today's highly pressurised market the importance of identifying efficiencies in the process of making architectural models continues to be a significant priority, and with a range of advanced digital manufacturing methods at the modelmaker's disposal, choosing the right process for each task has become an important consideration, with modelmakers on the constant lookout for new and more efficient ways of making, such as Foster + Partners' investment in a seven-axis robotic sculpting arm for the practice's modelmaking workshop.

Managing client expectations has also become a growing problem for many modelmakers as they attempt to balance creativity and complexity with cost and practicality. As modelmaker Stephen Fooks has remarked, modelmakers are not making Faberge eggs. 'You might be making something that looks as brilliant as one in the end, but a model is not the same. Those objects are about the hours the craftsperson has put in, while our work is more about hitting a deadline.'[34] Robert Danton-Rees agrees: 'You have to work out what is practical and possible within a certain timescale, and you have to get the balance right between the level of detail a client wants and the budget they have to spend.'[35] External pressures continue to build, with the London property boom that has been a major source of work for many commercial modelmakers in recent years now turning against them; the light industrial sites that are ideally suited for modelmakers to work from having become prime targets for the construction of towering residential skyscrapers. Millennium Models found themselves surrounded by modern development at their site in Islington, Kandor moved to Stratford due to high rental increases, and 3DD similarly moved from Shoreditch to Dartford in Kent to escape encroaching development and rising rents. Christian Spencer-Davies even led a long-running community campaign to prevent A Model's light industrial site in Camden from being replaced by a luxury apartment complex, having previously moved there from Shoreditch for the very same reason only a few years before.

Faced with rising expectations from clients, increased costs and the threat of redevelopment looming over their premises, competition from Chinese modelmakers, and a wildly fluctuating market because of the 2008 financial crash, Brexit, and the COVID-19 pandemic, many commercial modelmakers have exhausted their financial reserves. 'Margins are shrinking,' Stephen Fooks has observed. 'We are pretty much charging what we were fifteen years ago, but all the prices of labour and materials have gone up. You just have to make a model a lot quicker so you can turn over more in the same amount of time.'[36] Millennium Models closed its doors in 2018 with Simon Hamnell retiring and unable to find anyone willing to take over the still-profitable business, while A Models shut down in 2020 shortly before the COVID-19 crisis took hold. At the same time, however, new modelmaking outfits such as Grain, Azur-MGM, and New Venture Models have launched themselves into the marketplace, while Unit 22, Kandor, Pipers, Base Models, Thorp, Capital, Amalgam, and many dozens of others continue to thrive. The outputs of the in-house modelmaking workshops within architectural practices such as RSHP, Feilden Clegg Bradley Studios, Simpson Haugh, Farrells, Make Architects, and countless more have also continued to grow, with Foster + Partners alone employing over fifty modelmakers across its three workshops. Progress has also been made in diversifying the workforce, with women now constituting around thirty to forty percent of the profession, although it is notable that very few directors or owners of commercial architectural modelmaking companies are female. Within in-house modelshops, however, the glass ceiling has been somewhat easier to break through, with many women now occupying senior roles such as workshop managers and head/deputy head of department positions. Architectural modelmaking today is also a global profession, albeit with Britain firmly at its centre. Across Europe and North America the employment of professional modelmakers within in-house architectural practices continues to flourish, although the existence of commercial architectural modelmakers in Europe remains far less common than in Britain, while in China, India, and the Middle East the growth of large-scale commercial modelmaking firms continues apace.

Today's architectural modelmakers are undeniably under pressure, but as this history has revealed, it has so often been during times of adversity and challenge that modelmakers have completed their best work. Whether it was in searching for new materials during the pressures of the inter-war years, pursuing life-or-death levels of realism in secret wartime workshops, facing drastically new forms of architecture that their traditional processes and materials could not replicate, adapting to radical shifts in architecture's relationships with its communicative media, or embracing new technologies that threatened to make both the model and the modelmaker redundant, architectural modelmakers have consistently risen to the challenges they have faced.

Throughout the one hundred and forty years since John Thorp first opened his business in London, creativity, curiosity, and adaptability have remained central to the modelmaker's success. Thorp's approach of applying a generalist attitude to a specialist outcome and drawing from whatever materials and processes were right for the task has guided architectural modelmaking to become much more than a traditional craft specialising in a singular material or technique. A recent study of the most important skills an employer looks for in a modelmaker highlighted 'flexibility and problem solving' as the attributes most in demand.[37] Whether pursuing realism, abstraction, or technical sophistication, architectural modelmaking is inherently a creative act, limited only by the ambitions of modelmakers themselves and the budgets and imaginations of their clients.

Despite the availability of fully digital alternatives, architectural models today remain highly successful and cherished objects, refusing to relinquish their role as the unofficial ambassadors of architectural design.[38] Behind this success, and behind almost every architectural model shared beyond an architectural practice's walls in Britain, stands the architectural modelmaker. Their fundamental role, refined over almost a century and a half, is to communicate an idea, and the skills and abilities wielded by today's modelmakers owe much to the ingenuity and creativity of those who came before them: John and Leslie Thorp; Ernest Twining; Kenneth McCutchon; the V-Section modelmakers such as Margaret Watson, Leslie Yeo, and Nancy Hayes; Nick Quine; David Armstrong; George Rome Innes; Richard Armiger; and hundreds more. Today's architectural modelmakers continue in their tradition, constantly honing both their technical abilities and creative ambitions to bring architecture's dreams into miniature reality, quietly maintaining their position as the true, yet unseen, masters of scale and vision.

Notes

1 Christian Spencer-Davies, interview with author, June 6, 2019.
2 Andrew Putler, interview with author, June 7, 2019.
3 Simon Hamnell, interview with author, November 13, 2018.
4 Roger Hillier, interview with author, April 30, 2018.
5 Matthew Driscoll, interview with author, January 22, 2018.
6 Ibid.
7 Hamnell interview.
8 Ibid.
9 Spencer-Davies, interview.
10 Ibid.
11 Driscoll, interview.
12 Mike Fairbrass, interview with author, September 13, 2019.

13 Hamnell, interview.
14 Fairbrass, interview.
15 Ibid.
16 Ibid.
17 Stephen Fooks, interview with author, May 8, 2018
18 Neil Vandersteen, interview with author, March 26, 2018.
19 Neil Merryweather, interview with author, October 8, 2019.
20 Spencer-Davies, interview.
21 Hamnell, interview.
22 Driscoll, interview.
23 Fooks, interview.
24 Lee Atkins, interview with author, June 10, 2019.
25 Alec Saunders, interview with author, March 13, 2018.
26 Atkins, interview.
27 David MacKay, interview with author, January 5, 2018.
28 Danton-Rees, interview.
29 Fairbrass, interview.
30 Ibid.
31 Atkins, interview.
32 Karen Moon, *Modelling Messages* (New York: Monacelli Press, 2005), 135.
33 Atkins, interview.
34 Fooks, interview.
35 Danton-Rees, interview.
36 Fooks, interview.
37 Will Strange, interview with author, December 11, 2017.
38 Moon, *Modelling Messages*, 129.

Bibliography

Abercrombie, S. 'Creative Playthings.' *Horizon*, July, 1978.

Abrams, Janet. 'Models of their Kind.' *Independent*, August 26, 1988.

Abrams, Leonard. *Our Secret Little War*. Bethesda: International Geographic Information Foundation, 1991.

Adams, J. K. 'Letter to the Editor.' *Architect and Building News*, March 27, 1969.

Alberti, Leon Batista. *On the Art of Building in Ten Books*, trans. J. Leach and R Tavenor. Cambridge: MIT Press, 1988.

'The Architectural Exhibition.' *The Builder*, April 28, 262, 1860.

'Architectural Models.' *The Builder's Journal*, July 4, 1906.

Armstrong, David. 'Model Making at Arups.' *The Arup Journal*, November, 1966.

Asbury, H. 'He Has Built Fame with Cardboard.' *Popular Science Monthly*, June, 1920.

Atkinson, Helen. *The Festival of Britain: A Land and its People*. London: I.B. Taurus, 2012.

Audsley, Berthold. 'Miniatures and their Value in Architectural Practice.' *The Brick Builder*, September, 1914.

Baker, Malcolm. 'Representing Invention, Viewing Models.' In Soraya de Chadarevian and Nick Hopward (eds.) *Models: The Third Dimension of Science*. Stanford: Stanford University Press, 2004, 19–42.

Bayley, Thomas. *The Craft of Model Making (Fifth Revised Edition)*. Leicester: Dryad Press, 1959.

Bayley, Thomas. *The Craft of Model Making*. Leicester: Dryad Press, 1938.

Blake, Peter. *The Master Builders*. New York: Norton and Company, 1976.

Briggs, Martin. 'Architectural Models II.' *The Burlington Magazine for Connoisseurs*, April 1929.

Briggs, Martin. *A Short History of the Building Crafts*. Oxford: OUP, 1925.

Brown, E. A. *Making Models in the Drawing Office*. Richmond: Draughtsman & Allied Technicians' Association, 1971.

Buck, Stan. *Ernest Twining: Model Maker Artist & Engineer*. Ashbourne: Landmark Press, 2004.

Busch, Akiko. *The Art of the Architectural Model*. New York: Design Press, 1991.

Buttolph, Suzanne. 'Great Models.' *The Student Publication of the School of Design North Carolina State University*, vol 27, 1978.

Carolin, Peter. 'Sense, Sensibility and Tower Blocks.' In Elaine Harwood and Allan Powers (eds.). *Housing the Twentieth Century Nation*. London: Twentieth Century Society, 2008, 97–112.

'Charing Cross Bridge.' *The Times*, January 29, 1930.

'Charing Cross.' *The Times*, February 17, 1930.

Chisholm, John. 'Rehearsal for Reality.' *The Architect and Building News*, February 27, 1969.

Collins, P. 'Architectural Modelmaking.' *American Homes and Garden*, vol 12, no 8, 1915.

Croft, C. 'David Rock: "Architecture is the Land of Green Ginger" or "Form Follows Culture."' In Elaine Harwood and Alan Powers (eds.) *The Seventies: A Lost Decade of British Architecture*. London: Twentieth Century Society, 2012, 65–73.

Crout, Trevor. 'Scalpel to Computer Control.' *The Future of Modelmaking*. Hatfield: University of Hertfordshire, 1996.

Davies, Christopher. *Thinking about Architecture*. London: Lawrence King, 2011.

Deriu, Davide. 'The Architectural Model in the Age of its Mechanical Reproducibility.' In *Proceedings of the Second International Conference of the European Architectural History Network, Brussels, 2012*. Brussels: Contactforum, 2012, 166–170.

Downing, Taylor. 'Spying from the Sky.' *History Today*, November, 2011.

Dowson, Phillip. 'Introduction.' In *Arup Modelshop*, brochure, Arup Associates, 1990.

Drexler, Arthur. *The Architecture of the Ecole des Beaux-Arts*. London: Secker and Warburg, 1977.

'Editorial.' *The Builder's Reporter*, September 18, 1906.

Eisenman, Peter. 'Preface.' In Kenneth Frampton and Silvia Kolbowski (eds.). *Idea as Model*. New York: Rizolli, 1981, 1.

Elser, Oliver, and Schmal, Peter (eds). *The Architectural Model: Tool, Fetish, Small Utopia*. Frankfurt: DAM, 2012.

Ettlinger, Leopold. 'The Emergence of the Italian Architect during the Fifteenth Century.' In S. Kostof (ed.) *The Architect: Chapters in the History of the Profession*. New York: OUP, 1977, 108–130.

'Exhibitions.' *British Plastics*, vol 17, no 198, November, 1945.

Fankhanel, Teresa. *The Architectural Models of Theodore Conrad*. London: Bloomsbury, 2021.

'The Fascination of Models.' *The Building News*, March 28, 1924.

Fisher, Thomas. *Communicating Ideas Artfully*. New York: Steelcase Partnership, 1990.

Fletcher, Bannister. 'The Inaugural Address.' *The Architectural Journal*, November 9, 1929.

Forman, A. *How to Make Architectural Models*. London: The Studio, 1946.

Frampton, Kenneth, and Kolbowski, Silvia. *Idea as Model*. New York: Rizolli, 1981.

Gardiner, Juliet. *The Thirties*. London: Harper Collins, 2011.

Gaunt, Adrian. 'The Value of Models.' *The Illustrated Country Review*, November, 1924.

Gerrewey, Christophe van. 'What are Rocks to Men and Mountains? The Architectural Models of OMA/Rem Koolhaas.' In Bas Princen and Krijn Koning (eds). 'Models: The Idea, The Representation, and Theory.' *Oase* 84, 2011, 31–36.

Gibberd, Frederick. *Town Design*. London: The Architectural Press, 1962.

Gillespie, Richard. 'The Rise and Fall of Cork Models Collections in Britain.' *Architectural History*, vol 60, 117–118, 2017.

Girouard, Mark. *Robert Smythson and the Architecture of the Elizabethan Era*. Chicago: University of Michigan, 1966.

Giurgola, Romaldo. 'Modelling.', In Suzanne Buttolph (ed.). 'Great Models.' *The Student Publication of the School of Design North Carolina State University*, vol 27, 67–68, 1978.

Goldberger, P. 'Post-Modernism: An Introduction.' *Architectural Design*, April, 1977.

Goobey, Alastair. *Bricks and Mortals*. London: Century Business, 1992.

Gough, Piers. 'Model Makers.' *Architects' Journal* 177, April 27, 1983.

Graves, Michael. 'Thought Models.' In Suzanne, Buttolph (ed.). 'Great Models.' *The Student Publication of the School of Design North Carolina State University*, vol 27, 43–45, 1978.

Grumbine, LeRoy. 'The Use of Scale Models as an Aid to the Architect.' *The Western Architect*, June, 1925.

Hall, Peter. *Cities of Tomorrow*. Oxford: Blackwell, 2002.

Hallsall, Christine. *Women of Intelligence*. Stroud: The History Press, 2012.

Hartman, Graham. 'Some Observations on the Influences of Architectural Models.' In Suzanne Buttolph (ed.). 'Great Models.' *The Student Publication of the School of Design North Carolina State University*, vol 27, 31–33, 1978.

Harvey, William. *Models of Buildings: How to Make and Use Them*. London: Architectural Press, 1927.

Harwood, Elaine, and Powers, Alan (eds). *The Seventies: A Lost Decade of British Architecture*. London: Twentieth Century Society, 2012.

Hauschild, M., and Karzel, R. *Digital Processes*. Munich: Edition DETAIL, 2012.

Hendrick, Thomas. 'The Achievements of Cockade.' In M. Banham and B. Hillier (eds.). *A Tonic to the Nation*. London: Thames and Hudson, 1976, 163–165.

Hendrick, Thomas. *Model Making as a Career*. London: Percival Marshall, 1952.

Hendrick, Thomas. *The Modern Architectural Model*. London: Architectural Press, 1957.

Hobbs, Edward. *House Modelling for Builders and Estate Agents*. London: The Architectural Press, 1937, vii.

Hobbs, Edward. *Model Maker's Workshop*. London: Percival Marshall, 1934.

Hobbs, Edward. *Modern Handicraft Materials and Methods*. London: Cassell, 1932.

Hobbs, Edward. *Pictorial House Modelling*. London: Crosby Lockwood and Son, 1926.

Holder, Brian. 'Introduction.' *The Future of Modelmaking*. Hatfield: University of Hertfordshire, 1996.

Hoyt, Robert. 'World's Fair Models.' *Pencil Points*, July, 1939.

Hubert, Christian. 'The Ruins of Representation.' In Kenneth Frampton and Silvia Kolbowski (eds). *Idea as Model*. New York: Rizolli, 1981, 17–27.

ICI. *Perspex: The First Fifty Years*. Darwen: Imperial Chemical Industries, 1984.

King, Ross. *Brunelleschi's Dome*. London: Vintage, 2008.

Knights, L. 'A Model to Build On.' *OS Weekly*. September 11, 1980.

Kynaston, David. *Austerity Britain*. London: Bloomsbury, 2008.

Kynaston, David. *Family Britain*. London: Bloomsbury, 2010.

Lange, A. 'This Year's Model.' *Journal of Design History*, vol 19, no 2, 2006.

Lansdown, Helen. *Digital Modelmaking*. Marlborough: Crowood Press, 2019.

Lee & Hunt Ltd. *Reliable Machine Tools by the Best Makers*. Nottingham: Lee & Hunt Ltd, 1934.

Leslie, Fiona. 'Inside Out: Changing Attitudes Towards Architectural Models in the Museums at South Kensington.' *Architectural History*, vol 47, 159–200, 2004.

'The London Drawing & Tracing Office.' *The Builder*, November 27, 1897.

'A London Plastics Exhibition.' *British Plastics*, vol 18, no 210, November, 1946.

MacEwan, M. *Crisis in Architecture*. London: RIBA Enterprises, 1974.

Manzini, Ezio. *The Material of Invention*. London: The Design Council, 1986.

Marr, Andrew. *A History of Modern Britain*. London: Macmillan, 2007.

Marriott, Oliver. *The Property Boom*. London: Abingdon Publishing, 1989.

McCutchon, Kenneth. 'Architectural Models.' *Architects' Journal* 84, October 17, 1936.

Meikle, Jefferey. *American Plastic*. New Jersey: Rutgers University Press, 1997.

Mindrup, Matthew. *The Architectural Model: Histories of the Miniature and the Prototype*. Cambridge: MIT Press, 2019.

Mitchell, Ian. 'Developments in America.' *The Future of Modelmaking*. Hatfield: University of Hertfordshire, 1996.

'Model.' *The Builder's Dictionary Vol II*. London: Bettesworth and Hitch and Austen, 1734.

'Models and Moulding.' *British Plastics*, vol 19, no 222, November, 1947.

Moon, Karen. *Modelling Messages*. New York: Monacelli Press, 2005.

Morris, Mark. *Models: Architecture and the Miniature*. Chichester: Wiley-Academy, 2006.

Murray, Robert. 'Models and Scotch.' *Pencil Points*, July, 1939.

Neilson, Maria. 'Form Follows Culture: Architectural Models in London 1970–1990.' MA diss., Royal College of Art, 2013.

'New Building for the Royal Academy.' *Mechanics Magazine*, April 12, 1828.

Newman J., and Newman, L. *Plastics for the Craftsman*. London: George Allen & Unwin, 1972.

'Notice.' *The London Gazette*, April 13, 1827.

Nunn, J. 'Models and their Making.' *The Builder*, June 26, 1942.

Oswald, Angar. *Architectural Models*. Berlin: DOM, 2008.

Parker, E. 'The Model for Architectural Representation.' *Architectural Forum*, April 30, 1919.

Partridge, John. 'Roehampton Housing.' In Elaine Harwood and Allan Powers (eds). *Housing the Twentieth Century Nation*. London: Twentieth Century Society, 2008, 113–120.

Partridge's Models. *Art of the Model Maker*. London: Partridge's Models, 1949.

Pearson, Ian. 'Allied Military Model Making during World War II.' *Cartography and Geographic Information Science*, vol 29, no 3, 227–241, 2002.

Perry, H. 'A More Heat-Resistant Acrylate Material.' *British Plastics*, October, 1943.

Pfaendler, Ray. 'Architectural Models.' *The Architectural Review*, July, 1966.

Physick John, and Darby, Michael. *Marble Halls*. London: V&A, 1973.

Pommer, Richard. 'The Idea of "Idea as Model".' In Kenneth Frampton and Silvia Kolbowski (eds.). *Idea as Model*. New York: Rizolli, 1981, 3.

Porter, Tom, and Neale, John. *Architectural Supermodels*. London: Architectural Press, 2000.

Powers, Alan. *Britain: Modern Architectures in History*. London: Reaktion, 2007.

Pugh, Martin. *We Danced All Night*. London: Vintage, 2009.

Rafzlaff, Brian. *Digital Craft: 3D Printing for Architectural Design*. London: Lee 3D, 2016.

Rawson, J. 'Small Beginning: Modelmaking.' *Architects' Journal* 191, January 17, 1990.

Reid, Kenneth. 'Architectural Models.' *Pencil Points*, July, 1939.

Scott, Peter. *The Making of the Modern British Home*. Oxford: OUP, 2013.

Scuri, P. 'Skyscraper Business.' *Domus* 660, April, 1985.

Shilling, Alexander. *Architecture and Modelbuilding*. Basel: Birkhauser, 2018.

Silver, N., and Boys, J. *Why is British Architecture so Lousy?* London: Newman, 1980.

'The Small World of Malcolm Allan.' *Beetle Bulletin*, 39 (1976), 6.

Soutar, A. 'Made in Court.' *The Strand Magazine*, May, 1910.

Sparke, Penny. *The Plastics Age*. London: V&A, 1990.

Starkey, Bradley. 'Models, Architecture, Levitation: Design-Based Research into Post-Secular Architecture.' *The Journal of Architecture*, vol 11, no 3, 323–328, 2006.

Stavric, Milena, Sidanin, Predrag and Tepavcevic, Bojan. *Architectural Scale Models in the Digital Age*. Vienna: Springer, 2013.

Stewart, Graham. *Bang! A History of Britain in the 1980s*. London: Atlantic Books, 2013.

Summerson, John. *Architecture in Britain 1530 to 1830*. London: Penguin, 1954.

Sutton, V. 'Making Architectural Models. *Model Maker*, July, 1952.

Taylor, John. *Model Building for Architects and Engineers*. New York: McGraw Hill, 1971.

Taylor, Norman. *Architectural Modelling and Visual Planning*. London: Cassell, 1959.

Tenguerian, Richard. 'Model Making.' *Progressive Architecture*, November, 1995.

Thorp, John. 'How to Make Models of Buildings.' *The Builder's Journal*, January 9, 1901.

Thorp, John. *Models of Buildings, Estates, Works, etc. for Exhibitions or Law Cases*. London: London Drawing & Tracing Office, 1913.

Threadgill, Richard. 'Modelmaking.' *Architects' Journal* 186, July 1, 1987.

Turner, Barry. *Beacon for Change*. London: Aurum, 2011.

'Two Interesting Models.' *The Builder's Journal*, February 21, 1900.

Valeriani, Simona. 'Three-Dimensional Models as "In-Between Objects" – the Creation of Knowledge in Early Modern Architectural Practice.' *History of Technology*, vol 31, 26–46, 2012.

Wahlberg, H. *1950s Plastic Design*. Atglen: Shiffer, 1999.

Weaver, L. *Exhibitions and the Arts of Display*. London: Country Life, 1925.

Wells, Matthew. 'Relations and Reflections to the Eye and Understanding: Architectural Models and the Rebuilding of the Royal Exchange, 1839–44.' *Architectural History*, vol 60, 1–23, 2017.

Wickham, P. *Modelled Architecture*. London: Percival Marshall, 1948.

Wilton-Ely, John. 'The Architectural Model 1: English Baroque.' *Apollo Magazine*, 250–251, October 1968.

Wilton-Ely, John. 'The Architectural Models of Sir John Soane: A Catalogue.' *Architectural History*, vol 12, 5–38, 81–101, October, 1969.

Yarsley, V., and Couzens, E. *Plastics*. London: Pelican, 1941.

Index

Note: Page numbers in *italics* indicates figures on the corresponding page.